A Practitioner's Guide to Public Archaeology

A Practitioner's Guide to Public Archaeology

Intentional Programming for Effective Outreach

Edited by

Elizabeth C. Reetz and Stephanie T. Sperling

ROWMAN & LITTLEFIELD
Lanham • Boulder • New York • London

Published by Rowman & Littlefield
An imprint of The Rowman & Littlefield Publishing Group, Inc.
4501 Forbes Boulevard, Suite 200, Lanham, Maryland 20706
www.rowman.com

86-90 Paul Street, London EC2A 4NE

British Library Cataloguing in Publication Information Available

Library of Congress Cataloging-in-Publication Data Available

Library of Congress Control Number: 2024941412

ISBN 978-1-5381-8081-5 (cloth)
ISBN 978-1-5381-8082-2 (paperback)
ISBN 978-1-5381-8083-9 (electronic)

Contents

Contents

Acknowledgments

The editors cannot express enough gratitude for all of the book contributors. It isn't easy to balance extra projects, and our contributors are appreciated for generously sharing their time and knowledge. Their expertise is invaluable, and everyone learned so much.

Stephanie would like to express a heartfelt appreciation to her family for generously providing the space and support needed to help create this book.

Elizabeth is extremely grateful to the University of Iowa Office of the State Archaeologist for their ongoing encouragement and financial support of this project. Many thanks also to Jeanne Moe, Gwynn Henderson, John Doershuk, and Cherie Haury-Artz for their insights and guidance.

And to those who are working hard to professionalize archaeology education and institutionalize public outreach programs—you *are* making a difference.

Foreword

For YEARS, my friend, Elizabeth Reetz, and I lamented the lack of a guide that explained how to do public archaeology. We dreamed of a resource that offered not only the basic step-by-step of it, but also discussed its variations, nuances, and subtleties. With such a book in hand, we were *confident* folks new to the discipline would stop reinventing the wheel and making the same mistakes we made over the course of decades of trial and error. Instead, they could spend their time expanding and deepening their practice with a solid grounding in the fundamentals.

Now, thanks to Reetz and her partner in this endeavor, Stephanie Sperling, our dream has come true—a *real* practitioner's guide! They have assembled a broad array of authors who share their knowledge and experience concerning every aspect of public archaeology: from conceptualization to assessment. This book will help guide the next generation of archaeologists in best practice for years to come. Anyone interested in pursuing public archaeology activities of *any sort* will find authentic help here. *YOU* will find help here!

My purpose in writing this foreword, however, is not to discuss the practical topics covered in this very useful book. The authors have done an excellent job of that.

Instead, I ask you to pause for a minute and consider the *opposite* of practical.

"So what?" "Why does this matter?"

Careful readers will find, tucked into this book's many suggestions and case studies, what I consider "middle range" answers—explanations or justifications—to the "So what?" of public archaeology. To enhance site protection and inspire stewardship. To learn about archaeology and heritage. To help teachers realize mandated educational goals. To inspire appreciation of cultural diversity.

Early in my public archaeology career, two colleagues from very different contexts challenged me to think beyond those middle range answers. Back then, I offered some of those same explanations. They pressed me. "Why does *that* matter?" I fumed. I fussed. What on EARTH did they *want* from me?"

One colleague explained: Teachers don't care about your sites, your data, your research. They have educational standards to meet and students to teach. What's in it for them? Indeed! Another colleague chided me: Without assessment, do you even KNOW what folks are learning? Yikes!

As I considered their responses, it occurred to me that my answers *were* pretty self-serving. And then I understood why they had pressed me: they were challenging me to think more deeply. They were asking me to look for more profound and significant purposes. They wanted to know, "Why does this matter on an *existential* scale?"

Years before their challenges, I had realized that straight-up archaeology had become no longer enough for me. Of course, I still loved the personal intellectual challenges, the discoveries, the social world of archaeology. Oh, the passion with which we debated over pitchers (and pitchers) of beer, sharing the thrill of new insights and aha moments! But I felt increasingly selfish. We were talking about these fascinating ideas and wonderful discoveries only among ourselves. There had to be a deeper purpose to archaeology. That realization had drawn me, in the early 1990s, to "archaeology education" in the first place.

Huh. So, what *did* drive me so passionately to share with non-archaeologists what I knew about the archaeological process and archaeological discoveries? Why *was* it so important to me that "regular" people understood?

Over time (and it has taken time), I have discovered some answers. I could not have articulated them back then, because I had never really thought about archaeology in that way before.

"So what?" "Why does this matter?"

Archaeology matters because it offers a view into the past, into the deep past, like no other discipline. The archaeological record holds stories of peoples and cultures long gone. It is, sometimes, the only record. Archaeological sites are documents, and archaeologists have been trained to read those documents.

Objects are powerful. They inspire. They hold stories. They challenge us to question the ways we think humans have always been.

But objects are only part of it. The stories they tell are the most meaningful when we consider objects in context, immersed in the places where historic events happened. We can touch the past through objects and historical places. And in doing so, we can see our own place in history.

Archaeology matters because it can serve as a vehicle to understanding and appreciating diverse ways to be human. Archaeology reveals how people have negotiated their world, with all their differences and strangenesses. In the twenty-first century, when tolerance and understanding seem to be in such short supply, understanding all the different ways to be successfully human is critical.

Archaeology shows us the ebb and flow of cultures and beliefs, political systems and religions, and the role changing climate plays in culture change. It reveals the uncertainty that is the human condition, and the incredible resilience and creativity that people have applied to meet the challenges they faced. Archaeology can be a vehicle for social justice, connecting descendants with the objects and sites of their ancestors, and together, archaeologists can help them tell their stories and reclaim their past.

So, before you head off in search of the "How do I . . ." I ask you to take a minute and think about how you would answer, "*Why* do I?" What drives your passion? What goals have you set? Not the learning goals you will set for your audiences, but *your* goals. What's *your* deeper purpose?

Why is public archaeology important to *you*?

I have found that my answers are clarifying what drives my passion. My answers sustain me through challenges, and they point me toward projects and collaborations.

Many public archaeology practitioners have not lost sight of the excitement that first set them on a course toward archaeology. They want to share the wonder they discovered studying the patterns of objects people left behind and the stories those patterns hold. Indeed, I would submit that public archaeologists are storytellers, and they feel passionately that it is their responsibility to share with others, stories about what archaeologists do, or how archaeologists do what they do, or what archaeologists have learned. We owe it to our diverse publics AND we owe it to those long-ago peoples who cannot speak for themselves to do our very best to share those stories; and to reflect, assess, and improve.

Public archaeology is diverse. I have found it empowering, humbling, and at times, profound. In sharing with the public, I have learned so much.

So, here's to you, dear reader—to discovering your own answers to the "So what?" of public archaeology and why it matters to you. And, in that discovery, to finding personal fulfillment.

A. Gwynn Henderson
Education Director, Kentucky Archaeological Survey
February 2024

Preface

> The practice of educating the public is considered a necessity to sustain the discipline of archaeology.[1]

Archaeology, the study of the ancient and recent human past through material remains, is inherently interesting and exciting to children and adults alike. Many archaeologists say that engaging with the public is a cornerstone of the profession and one of the most important factors that will inspire a stewardship ethic and an appreciation for cultural diversity and the past. Others stress that in order to sustain archaeology as an academic area of study (not to mention a career-making line of work), we must have ample public funding and support. Thus, archaeologists approach outreach in a variety of ways, often participating in programs and events like public lectures, classroom visits, field trips, and fairs. But are we effective in our efforts?

Public outreach requires investments in time, staff, and funding, all of which are often scarce or under-supported. Sometimes outreach is deprioritized or cut when timelines and budgets are stretched or project priorities shift. This may leave us feeling ill-prepared and stressed during an event and simply happy just to get through it. Other times, we dive in enthusiastically, but sometimes blindly. Are we considering all the elements necessary to make these programs effective and impactful? Did we connect with the audience and provide accessible opportunities for all learners? Are participants walking away with greater awareness, knowledge, or skills? Were there forgotten logistics that were only obvious in hindsight?

The goal of this book is to help address these questions and eliminate some of the guesswork for many who, simply put, do not have the support needed to create intentional and effective programming. Whether you have done public outreach for years or are a student curious about working with the public, we hope this will make it all a little less daunting.

In *A Practitioner's Guide to Public Archaeology: Intentional Programming for Effective Outreach*, more than three dozen public archaeology and heritage education professionals contributed instructions and advice based on our own successes, failures, and lessons learned. The authors serve as active volunteers and leaders in educational initiatives for the Society for American Archaeology, Society for Historical Archaeology, Archaeological Institute of America, Society of Black Archaeologists, Project Archaeology, and Institute for Heritage Education, among many others. We represent county, state, and federal agencies, academic institutions, museums, nonprofits, and private businesses across the United States and Ireland, and we hope that the breadth of our skills and experiences connect with archaeologists and those doing outreach in multiple settings. While this book is not representative of the global field of public archaeology, we hope that the content within may be built upon and expanded in future works that align with programs across the world.

NOTE

1. Kate Ellenberger and Lorna-Jane Richardson, "Reflecting on Evaluation in Public Archaeology," *AP: Online Journal in Public Archaeology* 8 (2018), http://dx.doi.org/10.23914/ap.v8i1.141.

Introduction

Elizabeth C. Reetz and Stephanie T. Sperling

Archaeologists affiliated with museums, parks, academic institutions, government agencies, commercial businesses, societies, and other heritage organizations conduct a variety of public programs. However, we too rarely communicate about the approaches, successes, and challenges involved with planning and implementation. To our detriment, and a primary reason for creating this book, archaeologists interested in outreach receive little to no academic training or professional development to build needed skills. Many of us learn by trial and error and are sometimes unaware that others are undergoing similar challenges. We do not carefully consider how to connect with different audiences, design programs and resources with an accessibility mindset, or conduct assessments to determine if we're making positive impacts. Compounding these issues, the COVID-19 pandemic rapidly changed the way we think about and do outreach. Digital lectures, webinars, and hybrid options are now integrated into the public archaeology tool kit, highlighting new needs and concerns regarding resources, feasibility, and capacity, as well as methodology, privacy, safety, and accessibility. In short, we are required to become jacks-of-all-trades, but we don't know what we don't know!

WHAT IS PUBLIC ARCHAEOLOGY?

Public archaeology is a long-standing and growing field of study and practice in both academia and compliance. Not easy to define, public archaeology is, according to Gabriel Moshenska, a tangle of overlapping definitions and interpretations, many of them the result of different national, organizational, and educational traditions.[1] McDavid and Brock describe it (but do not define it), as the arena in which archaeologists and multiple publics enact existing ethical assumptions and (as laws and ideas shift) experiment with new ways of working together.[2] In this book, we generalize public archaeology as the communication of archaeological concepts to various audiences through some form of program or event. Likewise, this book uses other names, with no fixed definitions, that archaeologists use for projects that involve the public, such as "archaeology education," "community archaeology," "outreach," "interpretation," and "engagement."

There are some excellent volumes on public archaeology, but in comparison to other archaeological topics, the library is very small. This handbook is inspired by recent manuscripts that focus on public archaeology case studies, concepts, and theory, as well as foundational literature that many use and reference.[3] In particular, *The Archaeology Education Handbook: Sharing the Past with the Kids*, published in 2000, is still a relevant must-have for anyone working extensively with K–12 youth. Books on public programming methods and strategy exist for professions like museum education[4] and outdoor education,[5] which have many parallels and some applicability to public archaeology. But there has never been a step-by-step "how-to" guide written for archaeologists who create programs for multiple publics. We intend for this book to act as an instructional, concise guide that explains key components of in-person or digital programs from start to finish. For brevity, we do not cover the creation of written outreach such as K–12 curricula, exhibitions, interpretive media, or social media, even though they are a large component of education and outreach in this field. However, there are parallels and overlap with the planning and development stages of such materials, and we touch upon this where applicable.

Public Archaeology as Programmatic Practice

In the United States, the Antiquities Act of 1906 impelled the importance of public education and the accessibility of archaeological information in governmental efforts to protect public lands.[6] The first documented efforts in archaeological education occurred nearly half a century later in the 1950s.[7] In the 1960s and 70s, the passage of major federal legislation to protect and preserve cultural resources, primarily the National Historic Preservation Act (NHPA) of 1966, incorporated public and private interests in archaeology with governmental interests and propelled the need for public outreach. In the late 1980s, scattered efforts arose to implement educational programs and projects across the nation, including the Public Archaeology Working Group at the National Park Service. In 1988, the passage of amendments to the Archaeological Resources Protection Act (ARPA) gave federal land managing agencies their marching orders.[8] Several enduring programs including Project Archaeology and Passport in Time grew out of the 1988 amendments and increased national interest in public education. The 1989 "Save the Past for the Future Conference" in Taos, New Mexico, kicked off major conversations about education and the dire need to effectively connect with the public due to looting and vandalism. It also prompted the formation of the Public Education Committee of the Society for American Archaeology.

New organizations like The Heritage Education Network (THEN); the Institute for Heritage Education; Florida, Oklahoma, and Utah Public Archaeology Networks; and a wide variety of governmental agencies, academic institutions, nonprofits, and societies now support dedicated outreach programs and other efforts. There are countless professionals who have been working for decades to advance the field of public archaeology. Often overlooked, they continue to innovate programming and conduct and publish research with a goal to institutionalize this profession.

PROFESSIONALIZING PUBLIC ARCHAEOLOGY

Regardless of the achievements noted above, those with expertise in connecting with the public are rarely considered specialists in the same way that archaeologists regard, for example, a field director or lithics analyst. There is a necessity for increased acknowledgment, sufficient program funding, and salaries commensurate with the specialized skill set needed for effective outreach. Those with these skills are uniquely positioned to bridge the gap between the discipline and the public, advocate for historic preservation, and stress the importance of cultural resource management as a viable profession, but a lack of support mutes these messages. It is imperative for our field to demonstrate the value of public outreach. The fact that this specialization is growing and people are working hard to institutionalize archaeological and heritage education is exciting. But there still are not enough public archaeologists to combat looting and vandalism and inspire the next generation of cultural stewards. Every archaeologist, regardless of career level, specialization, expertise, or primary job responsibilities should participate in public outreach, either directly through programming or simply by supporting it whenever you can!

WHO SHOULD USE THIS GUIDE?

This book is for cultural or natural resources professionals, academics, and those who want to improve public education and outreach skills, whether you are just beginning a course of study or are decades into a career. Many of you conduct public outreach as opportunities arise, but it is not the primary focus of your job. You may have learned about public archaeology in college and participate in a few events through work or archaeological society volunteerism but were not taught the key components of creating and delivering public programming from the perspective of outreach professionals. The guidance provided here will hopefully inspire a creative mitigation project, assist you with planning an archaeology month event, help you give a more impactful presentation in your child's classroom, or even encourage you to institutionalize education and outreach at your firm or agency.

Some of you are employed as full-time outreach professionals for agencies, museums, parks, and historical societies, and may have background credentials in education and interpretation. More likely, you shifted over to this type of position from one that was focused heavily on fieldwork or analysis and are learning program development and communication techniques off the cuff or through occasional professional conference sessions. Because we typically work in silos and rarely network with peers to workshop our skills, this handbook strives to provide standardization to our approaches and eliminate some of the guesswork that consumes our scarce resources.

If you are an undergraduate or graduate student working to become an archaeology professional, this serves as a practical guide that you can add to your "tool kit" while starting your career. Academic staff and faculty who teach courses on general archaeology and public archaeology can integrate this book into coursework so students can immediately put the concepts covered into practice and create an impactful program based on advice from professionals. Public outreach training and experience are great on résumés!

Finally, for informal educators who work at museums, nature centers, or parks and would like to integrate archaeology into your programming, this book provides perspectives from professional public archaeologists to add to your knowledge base.

ABOUT THIS BOOK

A Practitioner's Guide to Public Archaeology is organized into four primary sections structured to walk you from the first stages of planning to the final stage of assessment. Throughout the book, we include textboxes that exemplify successes and challenges with various logistics and program types. The handbook concludes with appendices to help you create a library of ready-to-go planning files for present and future programs.

Section I: Preparation and Planning for Effective Outreach Programs

Chapter 1 introduces pedagogical approaches to contextualize teaching and learning and help you strategize educational best practices to integrate into your programs. Chapter 2 discusses the various audiences we may encounter during public programs, and chapter 3 provides a much-needed perspective about accommodating people with diverse needs and abilities. We get into the nuances of planning in chapter 4 with a primer on creating an intentional project plan to anchor your program. Chapter 5 provides guidance to identify resources and collaborative partnerships necessary to carry out or improve your efforts. Finally, chapter 6 details important logistics regarding permissions, privacy, marketing, and budgeting.

Section II: Implementing Public Archaeology Programs and Events

Chapters 7 through 9 describe the most common categories and types of outreach, including all-ages opportunities, such as lectures, virtual programs, table events like fairs or festivals, site tours, outdoor recreation opportunities, and public dig and lab days; K–12 activities inside and outside of the classroom; and community-based, lifelong learning initiatives like site stewardship programs. You will discover ideas and techniques and learn about common challenges.

Inevitably, something may go wrong during your program. Chapter 10 covers how to deal with unexpected challenges and reflects on public outreach before, during, and after the COVID-19 pandemic. As an example of this, chapter 11 provides an in-depth case study from an Irish company that modified and innovated numerous programs throughout the pandemic to connect with and engage communities across Ireland and beyond.

Section III: Understanding and Communicating Impact and Success

Chapter 12 explains assessment and evaluation as it applies to archaeology programming and provides guidance on how to measure your impact. In chapter 13, you will learn the basics of creating a research design and professionally publishing your work to help build the research base that is so greatly needed in this field.

Section IV: Putting It All Together

Chapter 14 reviews what you have learned, poses a list of important questions to consider during your intentional preparation and planning, and encourages a mindset for continuous learning and improvement. Several appendices provide worksheets and tools that will help you craft your own detailed work plan.

SUMMARY

The work of public archaeologists is challenging, but also deeply rewarding. When faced with questions or challenges, this guide can serve as a practical reference to help you find relevant content and implement best practices that align with your needs. Consider how this information can be adapted to your situation and explore the additional resources listed in each chapter. But above all, infuse joy and enthusiasm into the planning and execution of your public archaeology programs. Your passion and curiosity for uncovering the past can be infectious!

NOTES

1. Gabriel Moshenska, ed. *Key Concepts in Public Archaeology* (London: UCL Press, 2017), 3, doi:10.14324/111.9781911576419.
2. Carol McDavid and Terry Brock, "The Differing Forms of Public Archaeology: Where We Have Been, Where We Are Now, and Thoughts for the Future," in *Ethics and Archaeological Praxis* (New York: Springer, 2015), 159, https://doi.org/10.1007/978-1-4939-1646-7_11.
3. John H. Jameson, Jr., ed. *Presenting Archaeology to the Public: Digging for Truths* (Walnut Creek, CA: AltaMira Press, 1997); Karolyn Smardz and Shelley J. Smith, eds. *The Archaeology Education Handbook: Sharing the Past with Kids* (Walnut Creek, CA: AltaMira Press, 2000); John H. Jameson and Sherene Baugher, eds., *Past Meets Present: Archaeologists Partnering with Museum Curators, Teachers, and Community Groups* (New York: Springer-Verlag, 2007); Skeates et al., eds. *The Oxford Handbook of Public Archaeology* (Oxford University Press, 2012); Eleanor M. King, ed., "Special Issue: Designing and Assessing Public Education Programs in Archaeology," *Advances in Archaeological Practice* 4, no. 4 (2016); Moshenska, *Key Concepts*; Katherine M. Erdman, ed. *Public Engagement and Education: Developing a Fostering Stewardship for an Archaeological Future* (New York: Berghahn Books, 2019); Susan J. Bender and Phyllis Mauch Messenger, eds. *History and Approaches to Heritage Studies* (Gainesville: University of Florida Press, 2019); Susan J. Bender and Phyllis Mauch Messenger, eds. *Pedagogy and Practice in Heritage Studies* (Gainesville: University of Florida Press, 2019); Camille Westmont, ed. *Critical Public Archaeology: Confronting Social Challenges in the 21st Century* (New York: Berghahn Books, 2022).

4. Katie Stringer, *Programming for People with Special Needs: A Guide for Museums and Historic Sites* (Lanham, MD: Rowman & Littlefield, 2014); Tara Young, ed. *Creating Meaningful Museum Experiences for K-12 Audiences: How to Connect with Teachers and Engage Students* (Lanham, MD: Rowman & Littlefield, 2021).
5. Ken Gilbertson et al., *Outdoor Education Methods and Strategies*, 2nd ed. (Champaign, IL: Human Kinetics); Julie A. Ernst et al., *Evaluating Your Environmental Education Programs: A Workbook for Practitioners* (Washington, DC: North American Association for Environmental Education, 2009).
6. Smardz and Smith.
7. Francis P. McManamon, "Public Education: A Part of Archaeological Professionalism," in *The Archaeology Education Handbook: Sharing the Past with Kids* (Walnut Creek, CA: AltaMira Press, 2000), 17; Carol J. Ellick, "A Cultural History of Archaeological Education," *Advances in Archaeological Practice* 4, no. 4 (2016), 426.
8. Archaeological Resources Protection Act of 1979, Pub. L. No. 100-555, §14; 119 Stat. 499 and Pub. L. No. 100-588, §1(c)) §1(d), 102 Stat. 2983 (1988).

Section I

Preparation and Planning for Effective Public Archaeology Programs

1

Pedagogy and Educational Best Practices

Nichole A. Tramel and Jeanne M. Moe

Public outreach inherently involves a teacher-learner dynamic. Whether you are communicating a simple archaeological concept to passers-by at an archaeology fair or highlighting new research at a scholarly lecture, an awareness of how people learn and how to effectively teach them can greatly impact the translation of your message. And if you're not adequately getting your message across, what is the point of public outreach?

Before you begin to strategize an event or choose a target audience, it is essential to become familiar with teaching and learning dynamics. The people we interact with at public programs and events have a vast range of knowledge, skills, curiosity, and awareness, and there is no one-size-fits-all approach to teaching them. However, a basic understanding of pedagogy and educational strategies is an important starting point.

Pedagogy refers to the method and practice of teaching, especially a traditional subject or a theo-retical concept.[1] This chapter highlights select pedagogies and educational terms that are particularly relevant for archaeologists who are planning and delivering public programs. We also introduce the basics of cognitive psychology, the theory of constructivism in education, and best practices that pub-lic archaeologists should understand to align their programs and events with their established goals and outcomes. Whether your audience is formal or nonformal, your job is to serve them with the best quality educational experience possible.

FORMAL, NONFORMAL, AND INFORMAL EDUCATION

The terms "informal," "nonformal," and "free-choice" have been used inconsistently for decades, especially between disciplines, which problematically devalues some types of learning and education relative to others.[2] Some practitioners conflate informal and nonformal learning, but we maintain that it is useful to differentiate them when considering how to best orchestrate learning encounters in nonformal environments. Some scholars identify free-choice learning (lifelong, self-motivated, and self-directed) as informal education, while others present free-choice learning as being a crucial part of, but not necessarily synonymous with, informal learning.[3] Because museum education, science education, and interpretation research shape the terrain of archaeology education, we look to these fields to inform some of the defining features of these terms:

- Formal: Usually refers to traditional classroom education such as K–12 and higher education.
- Nonformal: Refers to discrete educational events that occur outside of formal classrooms.
- Informal: Refers to ongoing education which occurs throughout life, both incidentally and via self-directed pursuits, through interactions, reading, television, hobbies, and travel.

Archaeologists who do public outreach should be prepared to present in both formal and nonformal settings. Teachers and educational organizations frequently approach archaeologists to assist with resources and presentations in formal settings. For instance, an instructor may invite an archaeologist to visit a classroom or offer a lesson that ties into a specific unit and meets a curricular objective. Similarly, a college, university, or municipal parks and recreation department may ask an archaeologist to develop continuing education courses for lifelong learners.

If an archaeologist is leading a program that was opted into by a student or parent, not a teacher, it is most likely nonformal programming situated in a setting like a site, park, library, or museum. These provide an almost unlimited number of opportunities for archaeologists, including open houses; site, facility, or recreational tours; summer or school break camps; archaeology and history fairs; family days at museums and sites; and public lectures (see chapters 7 and 8).

Regardless of learning venue, archaeology is an excellent tool for teaching scientific and historical inquiry, cultural understanding at a deep conceptional level, and citizenship.[4] Without the restrictions of a formal education system, archaeologists have more freedom to incorporate strategies that have been shown to be effective but are difficult to implement within the constraints of formal education systems, such as free-choice learning. Despite the latitude this relative freedom affords, nonformal educators only have their learners' attention for a limited time. Unlike students in a classroom, learners in nonformal education settings choose to be there because of the expectation that the experience itself will be intrinsically valuable. They decide the nature and degree of participation. Provocative subject matter and innovative engagement opportunities help nonformal educators attract and hold attention.

PEDAGOGY AND BEST PRACTICES RELEVANT TO ARCHAEOLOGY OUTREACH

People learn through "imitation, instruction, conversation, self-reflection, and exploration" in all (informal, nonformal, and formal) learning settings.[5] Pedagogy can also refer to "something that teachers do, but don't generally talk about," as well as the theory, method, and practice of teaching and the act and assessment of learning.[6] Ultimately, pedagogy draws from many disciplines (education, psychology, neuroscience, social sciences, etc.) to study and integrate the "computational, social and neural" components of "how people learn" with the explicit objective of improving learning.[7]

Cognition and Constructivism

Cognition is "the mental action or process of acquiring knowledge and understanding through thought, experience, and the senses."[8] In 1969, cognitive psychologist David Ausubel famously said, "the most important factor influencing the meaningful learning of any new idea is the state of the individual's existing cognitive structure at the time of learning."[9] The goal of instruction is to allow learners to integrate new knowledge with existing knowledge for longer retention and the ability to apply it and transfer it to other contexts. Constructivism as a theory of knowledge asserts two main principles: (1) knowledge is not passively received but actively built up by the cognizing (thinking) subject (learner); and (2) the function of thinking is adaptive and serves the organization of the experiential world, not the discovery of reality.[10]

Whether working in a formal or nonformal setting, learners are not empty vessels that can be filled with information transmitted from instructors. While educators can—and should—carefully construct content to emphasize a few main takeaways, learners have their own ideas, beliefs, and values that affect if and how information is noticed, received, integrated, and understood. The best instruction includes reflection and the opportunity for instantaneous correction or affirmation to prevent misunderstanding.

Bloom's Taxonomy

Bloom's Taxonomy is a theoretical framework for learning that is grounded in educational psychology and based on a constructivist approach to learning.[11] This framework identifies three domains of learning: cognitive (knowledge), affective (attitudes), and psychomotor (skills-based). It includes levels of learning that ascend in complexity; these are described with action verbs that are used to formulate measurable learning outcomes (see appendix F). Basically, mastery of fundamentals must be achieved to optimize learning as complexity increases, which aligns with the general order of how learners process information. In essence:

- Before one can understand a concept, they must remember it.
- To apply a concept, one must first understand it.
- To evaluate a process, one must have analyzed it.
- To create an accurate conclusion, one must have completed a thorough evaluation.[12]

It is important to be aware of the amount of time you will spend with your participants when formulating instructional methods and learning outcomes for both formal and nonformal programs. For most public archaeology events like information and activity booths, lectures, site tours, or single classroom visits, you can typically expect participants to achieve lower levels of learning, such as obtaining new knowledge, gaining a general awareness, or becoming familiar with a basic skill. Participants in longer, more intensive programs like summer camps, field schools, and certification programs could eventually reach the highest levels of learning. Your learners may not start at the lowest level, but introducing complex concepts without knowing if they have mastered lower-level fundamentals will inhibit the process of learning.

The Learning Cycle

Following the constructivist approach, public programs should be designed using a learning cycle.[13] The learning cycle is important for acquisition of new knowledge and concepts, and it helps students understand where they are in the learning process. Project Archaeology, a national archaeology education program first launched in the early 1990s, uses a learning cycle in its curricular materials (figure 1.1). The instructor checks in with students to see what they already know and prepares them to learn more before introducing new concepts and content. Students then reflect to understand what they learned and how it connects to other knowledge before they perform an assessment to demonstrate their mastery of the enduring understanding (i.e., the big idea that learners should remember well into the future).[14] In some Project Archaeology lessons, the assessment is part of instruction and comes before students reflect on new knowledge.

Ongoing assessment throughout the learning cycle is critical in revealing and addressing misconceptions. Research shows that misconceptions can impede learning, are difficult to change, and must be identified and dispelled before a more accurate understanding can be acquired.[15] For example, archaeologists commonly encounter the conflation of archaeology and paleontology. A survey conducted in 2023 showed 47 percent of Americans who responded think that archaeologists study dinosaurs.[16] Create multiple ways to address common misconceptions during your programs and build procedures to dispel them before introducing new content.

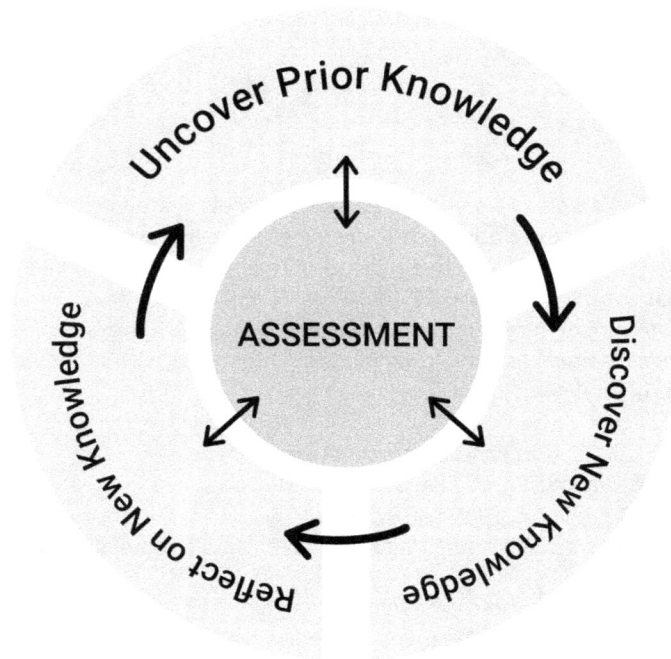

Figure 1.1. The Project Archaeology Learning Cycle. *Courtesy of Elizabeth Pruitt, Adapted with permission from* Project Archaeology: Investigating Shelter

Thematic Learning

Teachers across the United States are often required to teach specific content at each grade level and using theme-based units can be very helpful.[17] For example, teachers in third and fourth grades usually teach about state history, and in the fifth and sixth grades, they advance to US and world history. Some productive themes in archaeology are subsistence, shelter, migration, community organization, artistic expression, and human ecology. As these themes are familiar to diverse groups of people, they can help create a connection between abstract archaeological concepts and everyday, contemporary life.

"Garbology" is a common theme for archaeology outreach. The concept of trash is familiar to even the youngest students. By interpreting themes of human activities, art, shelter, subsistence, or other aspects of life and culture using modern trash, students make a connection with the essence of archaeological science. They do not have to know exactly what an unfamiliar artifact like debitage is or how it was created to understand that archaeologists study objects left behind by past peoples and can interpret activities and patterns based on context.

The National Park Service's interpretation resource guide for archaeologists advises how to thoughtfully select themes for programs.[18] It provides a succinct interpretive formula: "(Knowledge of the Resource + Knowledge of the Audience) x Appropriate Techniques = Interpretive Opportunities" and offers a seven-step process that promotes connecting artifacts (tangible cultural heritage elements) with universal concepts. The guide encourages the use of multiple illustrative examples (e.g., stories, activities, images) that evoke both intellectual and emotional reactions in learners. Everyone can relate to universal concepts, but they will create meaning in their own unique ways. Archaeologists may want to use universal concepts from the associated grade level(s) to add additional layers of relevance.

Nichole A. Tramel and Jeanne M. Moe

Relevance

Personalized learning centers participants' unique abilities and perspectives, an inherently respectful practice that acknowledges the intelligence, beliefs, values, motivations, and insight of each participant and makes the subject at hand more relevant to the learner. Relevance, or "personal meaningfulness," stimulates an emotional response that primes the brain for learning, promotes connections between existing and new information and retention, and influences if and how participants apply what they learned.[19]

Scholars caution against underestimating the powerful role of emotion in education. After enumerating the many ways that emotion impacts learning, McTighe and Willis conclude simply that cognition happens because of emotion.[20] Educators should use novel, surprising, thought-provoking and/or emotionally captivating "hooks" to grab learners' attention, prompt an emotional response, and thus prepare learners to engage with the content.[21]

Multiple Intelligences

Learners must construct their own knowledge. But note, not everyone learns in the same way. The best public programs are multimodal and vary the way the information is presented to include different multisensory formats (auditory, visual, kinesthetic) that allow for various ways to access, connect with, and retain content.[22]

In response to the reliance on IQ tests to determine innate intelligence in children, Howard Gardner identified seven types of intelligence (and later added an eighth) he developed into the Theory of Multiple Intelligences.[23] He thought that IQ tests relied on only two types of intelligence (logico-mathematical and linguistic) and did not measure others. While Gardner never intended his theory to apply directly to curriculum and instruction, it caught fire and has dominated much of American education for nearly forty years, even though it has never been confirmed with empirical data.[24] However, it still provides insight into varying instructional methods for audiences to access new knowledge through different avenues.[25] Table 1.1 provides examples for using this theory in archaeological instruction.

Not every public program or instructional event can address all of these, but using as many as possible can help more participants connect with the content and fulfill your educational goals.[26]

Table 1.1. Archaeological Education Activity Examples that Align with Gardner's Multiple Intelligences

Intelligence	Activities
Verbal-Linguistic	Reading oral histories, writing scientific reports, group discussions
Mathematical-Logical	Conducting scientific and historical inquiry, representing data in graphs or charts
Visual-Spatial	Exploring archaeological and ethnographic maps, drawing maps or artifacts
Bodily-Kinesthetic	Mending artifacts, excavating levels, placing artifacts in context on a map
Interpersonal	Working with partners or in small groups
Intrapersonal	Reflecting on new knowledge, conducting a self-evaluation
Musical	Writing or performing a song to interpret archaeological data
Naturalistic	Considering geography and environment as it relates to archaeological inquiry and content

Inquiry-Based Learning, Object-Based Learning, and Place-Based Learning

As archaeology is the study of past peoples through material culture and human-environment interactions, pedagogies that focus on inquiry, objects, and place are a natural fit for teaching it. Object- and inquiry-based activities can be integrated into multiple formats, and these theories are grounded in evidence-driven pedagogical practices that have been shown to increase satisfaction and retention.[27] Research on place-based education demonstrates that it fosters increased comprehension, retention, and motivation to learn; promotes self-confidence, critical thinking, self-motivation, and socialization skills; and improves environmental stewardship.[28]

These pedagogical approaches are central to Project Archaeology. Although its curricular resources are primarily targeted at formal educators, many lessons can be used in nonformal settings. For example, Project Archaeology educators adapted their "Every Picture Tells a Story" lesson into "Artifact Analysis" and "Reading a Building," activities to use anywhere someone encounters a tangible element of cultural heritage. Other museums and heritage institutions have similar versions based upon John Hennigar Shuh's popular 1983 article "Teaching Yourself How to Teach with Objects."[29] These activities are versatile, scalable, and accessible and lead learners through systematic and reflective step-by-step observation and inference processes to study unfamiliar artifacts, buildings, or landscapes.

Figure 1.2. A middle school student in an archaeology day camp shares her observations and inferences about a museum object with her fellow students. *Courtesy of University of Iowa Office of the State Archaeologist*

Combining object- and inquiry-based learning has applications beyond artifact analysis exercises. Project Archaeology educators use the same prompts and questions contained in "Artifact Analysis" and "Reading a Building" at field sites and museums to guide learners through various activities. Some of these have included interpreting artifact assemblages at archaeological sites, comparing material assemblages from different cultures, sorting artifacts from fossils, and dressing up as archaeologists and explaining the significance of each prop.[30]

Through such object- and inquiry-based learning, learners can use their background knowledge, observations, and inferences to create and test hypotheses about an object's function, as well as the object's form, content, and context.[31] Learners can also formulate their own questions and ask them in multiple modes like oral or written descriptions and visual arts, which makes object-based learning uniquely accessible to all ages and abilities. Although observations of cultural heritage are often visual, archaeologists can lead learners in observing artifacts through touch, sound, smell, and taste. Object-based learning does not require reading or rich background knowledge on a topic; if learners are able to utilize one or more senses, they can participate.

Place-based education is highly applicable to public archaeology. This type of learning and teaching is situated in spatial or physical localities that are given meaning by human experiences; it is cross-disciplinary and intercultural, informed and contextualized by natural, cultural, and socio-economic attributes.[32] It is conscious of, and intentionally leverages both students' and instructors' sense of place, enabling them to find personally relevant meanings and develop attachments to the places they study.[33] Archaeologists may want to incorporate place-based learning to offer ways for participants to address a community need (e.g., active, hands-on programs for excavation and/or interpretation volunteers, site monitoring, and service learning).

Textbox 1.1. Placed-Based Education in an Indigenous Setting: Miskwaabikang (Red Cliff, Wisconsin)

Heather Walder, Marvin DeFoe, and John L. Creese

In Indigenous communities across Turtle Island (North America), educators initiating archaeological outreach can benefit from applying place-based pedagogical strategies. Since 2018, the Red Cliff Band of Lake Superior Chippewa's Tribal Historic Preservation Office (THPO) and academic archaeologists have co-created Geté Anishinaabe Izhichigéwin Community Archaeology Project (GAICAP) in Miskwaabikang, the Red Cliff Indian Reservation in northern Wisconsin. Together, we have been investigating site occupation histories and local narratives while integrating community engagement throughout our archaeological practice. Such efforts productively de-center archaeological investigations; artifacts are only one small part of what makes a place meaningful. The stories and spirits unique to individual places shape Indigenous understandings of history, and archaeology may add to this knowledge.

Educational events have included formal classroom outreach, youth and Elder outreach in both laboratory and field settings, a foodways and technology workshop, public lectures, and paraprofessional/Tribal Monitor training. Adult volunteer Tribal Monitor training blends formal classroom teaching with hands-on field experience in survey and excavation. This weeklong informal certification program run through the Red Cliff THPO has coordinated with GAICAP's archaeological field school for three seasons, training Tribal members from Red Cliff, nearby Mashkiziibing (Bad River), and other Nations around Wisconsin. We have encouraged youth involvement from around the region, including a summer 2023 three-day

Figure 1.3. As part of a site tour, Walder highlights a "natural amphitheater" space used in early 20th century tourism events; guests and staff access the area using canoes. *Courtesy of M. Kaeske, 1854 Treaty Authority*

visit from the 1854 Treaty Authority Education/Outreach division seasonal staff members. These Ojibwe college students with no prior experience with archaeology learned informally alongside field school participants.

Identifying and protecting historic places in the community utilizes archaeological fieldwork, but also oral history and storytelling; these ways of knowing the past are integral to Ojibwe culture, and we incorporate Indigenous language whenever possible. An Ojibwe phrase is relevant here: *gaawin anishaa* or "nothing without a purpose." Educational events must articulate intentionally with other initiatives and goals, and our work in Miskwaabikang finds common cause with broader projects of land reclamation, cultural programming, and language revitalization. This work is challenging: some survey areas are relatively remote with limited infrastructure (e.g., parking, road access, bathrooms), requiring additional logistics to serve as place-based educational environments. The THPO maintains a small fleet of canoes for various outreach activities; paddling our guests to project locations is a common part of GAICAP outreach. This extra effort is not without a purpose: telling stories using archaeology benefits learners by immersing them in the places where historic events happened.

In various forms, GAICAP has applied both formal, K–12 classroom-based educational outreach in collaboration with the School District of Bayfield and informal all-ages events held in both laboratory and fieldwork settings in Miskwaabikang. Community members may walk in an ancestor's footprints when encountering an ancient object. Participants have reflected on the emotional weight of finding or handling objects such as an ancient copper tool or lithic debitage recovered *in situ* from a village site. When conducting these educational events, as an academic archaeologist and settler-scholar, I (Walder) am acutely aware of my outsider status in these spaces. As a non-Indigenous educator, I am trusted to provide a culturally appropriate and meaningful educational experience for Tribal youth. This weighty responsibility requires specific consideration of the harms that archaeology, as a discipline with a history of colonial practices, has caused in Indigenous communities.

Nichole A. Tramel and Jeanne M. Moe

For archaeologists considering ways to develop partnerships with First Nation and Indigenous heritage experts, we suggest a place-based framework for education and outreach as a good starting point. Community engagement in such settings is both an ethical imperative and a practice that strengthens archaeological interpretations of key locations. Take time to listen to Elders and resident knowledge-holders who are willing to share their insights and local understandings. You can respectfully offer archaeology as one pathway of investigation while recognizing the significance of Native Nations' oral histories, traditional cultural and ecological knowledge, and non-Western ways of knowing the past. Find out what places on the landscape are especially meaningful, listen to community questions and concerns about those places, and develop programs that intentionally engage people in those spaces. Culturally informed, place-based pedagogy has the potential to reach learners who might not otherwise engage with archaeology in formal educational settings, opening doors to more diversity in our discipline.

Authorial note: Heather Walder (University of Wisconsin-La Crosse) co-directs GAICAP with John Creese (North Dakota State University) in partnership with Red Cliff Tribal Historic Preservation Officer, Marvin DeFoe. This textbox synthesizes ongoing discussions among these project leaders.

PLANNING AND UNDERSTANDING BY DESIGN

Any successful project must begin with good planning (see chapter 4). *Understanding by Design* provides an excellent starting point for developing both classroom-ready lessons and successful public archaeology programs.[34] The Understanding by Design model (UbD) has been around for twenty-five years and is solidly based on learning research. While the typical approach to curriculum design is anchored in how to teach the content or activities, UbD begins with learning goals in mind. In many ways, it resembles a good research design for archaeological inquiry.[35] It works in both formal and nonformal venues and provides opportunities to relate learning to previous experiences and knowledge to make new information both accessible and memorable. Similarly, reflection and self-evaluation in UbD help learners integrate new knowledge into existing cognitive structures.

Sometimes UbD is called "backward design" because the curriculum designer begins with identifying the end results that they hope to achieve through the learning experience. These are broad concepts or "big ideas" that learners should remember well into the future, referred to in UbD as "enduring understandings." Students uncover (or construct) these enduring understandings through a series of essential questions. Next, the designer determines what constitutes evidence of understanding and designs assessments accordingly. Finally, the designer decides what knowledge and skills the student will need to uncover the enduring understanding, and then plans learning activities accordingly. This model provides a rigorous process for ensuring that all elements of curriculum design are included, and the resulting whole helps learners achieve the desired results. The actual development process is not necessarily linear but rather iterative.

Beginning in 2002, a team of educators and archaeologists developed *Project Archaeology: Investigating Shelter* using UbD and authentic archaeological data to support the inquiry process.[36] *Investigating Shelter* and all other Project Archaeology curricular materials are based on four overarching enduring understandings:

1. Understanding the past is essential for understanding the present and shaping the future.
2. Learning about cultures, past and present, is essential for living in a pluralistic society and world.
3. Archaeology is a systematic way to learn about the past.
4. Stewardship of archaeological sites and artifacts is everyone's responsibility.

To date, Project Archaeology curriculum guides based on UbD have been distributed to more than 6,000 educators. All rely on the four overarching enduring understandings, which are tweaked to accommodate authentic archaeological data and specific themes for inquiry such as shelter, subsistence, migration, and artistic expression. Formative assessment of the materials show that students were able to achieve the enduring understandings following classroom instruction.[37]

Although UbD is primarily used when developing curricula, the framework can be applied as a planning template for any format of outreach program (see appendix G). As in formal education, backward design is useful in nonformal program planning to promote transmission of essential messages that align with goals and outcomes. Nonformal educators should also assess learners' receipt and understanding of messages.

TEACHING ARCHAEOLOGY

While only about 3 percent of an average person's time is spent in formal education, it is important for forming the cognitive structures upon which we "hang" new knowledge throughout our lives. If archaeology is not included in school curriculum, it will probably never be considered as an important way of understanding the world or the past, but rather as an interesting but esoteric pursuit of "discovery" by elites.[38] Integrating public archaeology outreach with formal education and providing nonformal opportunities to reach young learners will help to establish a foundation for understanding the past, but only if we do it effectively.

This chapter provided a basic overview of a few of the pedagogies and teaching methodologies that archaeologists can apply while doing public outreach. The nuances of teaching and learning go far beyond what we can cover here. Use this overview and resources to plan and deliver effective programs in both formal and nonformal learning environments. Understanding how people learn and how to effectively teach them will provide a strong foundation for impactful public archaeology programming. However, this is just the beginning. Keep these pedagogies in mind as you learn to plan with intention and get to know your audience in the upcoming chapters. These elements of program planning are intrinsically related, and each can serve as a starting point. For example, you might have a good idea of who your audience is, and thus can choose an appropriate pedagogical approach. Or your program may have a specific purpose that drives your goals, so you use instructional approaches that will best help you meet those outcomes. Don't be afraid to think outside the box!

NOTES

1. *The Oxford College Dictionary*, 2nd ed., s.v. "Pedagogy," 2007, Oxford University Press.
2. Kathryn A. Stofer, "Informal, Non(-)formal, or Free-choice Education and Learning? Toward a Common Terminology for Agriscience and Ag-STEM Educators," *Journal of Human Sciences and Extension* 3, no. 1 (2015): 9, https://doi.org/10.54718/KAEH8579.
3. William F. McComas, "Informal (Free Choice) Science Learning," in *The Language of Science Education*, ed. William F. McComas (Rotterdam: Sense Publishers, 2014); https://doi.org/10.1007/978-94-6209-497-0_48; Lynn Dierking, "Lessons without Limit: How Free-Choice Learning is Transforming Science and Technology Education," *História Ciências Saúde-Manguinhos* 12, no. S1 (2005): 145–60, https://doi.org/10.1590/S0104-59702005000400008.
4. Jeanne M. Moe, "Archaeology Education for Children: Assessing Effective Learning," *Advances in Archaeological Practice* 4, no. 4 (2016), 441–53.
5. Mike Sharples, *Practical Pedagogy: 40 New Ways to Teach and Learn* (New York: Routledge, 2019), 3.
6. Sharples, *Practical Pedagogy*; Christothea Herodotou, Mike Sharples, Mark Gaved, Agnes Kukulska-Hulme, Bart Rienties, Eileen Scanlon, and Denise Whitelock, "Innovative Pedagogies of the Future: An Evidence-Based Selection," *Frontiers in Education* 4, article 113 (2019), https://doi.org/10.3389/feduc.2019.00113; Sharples, *Practical Pedagogy*.

Nichole A. Tramel and Jeanne M. Moe

7. Sharples, *Practical Pedagogy*, 3–4.
8. *The Oxford College Dictionary*, s.v. "Cognition."
9. David P. Ausuel and Floyd G. Robinson, *School Learning: An Introduction to Educational Psychology* (New York: Holt, Rinehart and Winston, 1969), 143.
10. Ernst von Glaserfeld, "Constructivism in Education," in *International Encyclopedia of Education*, ed. T. Husen and T.N. Postlethwaite (Oxford/New York: Pergamon Press, 1989), 162.
11. Benjamin S. Bloom, *Taxonomy of Educational Objectives: The Classification of Educational Goals. Handbook 1: Cognitive Domain* (New York: McKay, 1956); Lorin W. Anderson and David R. Krathwohl, eds. *A Taxonomy for Learning, Teaching, and Assessing: A Revision of Bloom's Taxonomy of Educational Objectives* (New York: Longman, 2001).
12. Jessica Shabatura, "Using Bloom's Taxonomy to Write Effective Learning Outcomes," University of Arkansas: Tips, updated July 26, 2022, https://tips.uark.edu/using-blooms-taxonomy/.
13. Josephine G. and Martin G. Brooks, *The Case for Constructivist Classrooms* (Alexandria, VA: Association for Supervision and Curriculum Design, 1993); Edmund A. Marek and Ann M.L. Cavallo, *The Learning Cycle: Elementary School Science and Beyond*, rev. ed. (Portsmouth, NH: Heinemann, 1997).
14. Cali A. Letts and Jeanne M. Moe, *Project Archaeology: Investigating Shelter*, rev ed. (1998; repr., Bozeman: Montana State University, 2012).
15. John D. Bransford, Ann L. Brown, and Rodney R. Cocking, eds., *How People Learn: Brain, Mind, Experience, and School* (Washington, DC: National Academy Press, 2000).
16. "New Poll Finds Continued Support for Archaeology in the US," Society for American Archaeology, updated June 29, 2023, https://www.saa.org/education-outreach/public-outreach/public-perceptions-studies.
17. Lynn H. Erickson, *Stirring the Head, Heart, and Soul: Refining Curriculum and Instruction*, 2nd ed. (Thousand Oaks, CA: Corwin Press, 2001).
18. Teresa A. Moyer, Heather Hembrey, and Barbara J. Little, "Interpretation for Archeologists: A Guide to Increasing Knowledge, Skills, and Abilities," Archeology Program, National Park Service, updated March 12, 2018, https://home1.nps.gov/Archeology/IforA/index.htm.
19. Sara Bernard, "Science Shows Making Lessons Relevant Really Matters: Personal Relevance is as Vital to the Learning Brain as it is to the Person Learning," George Lucas Education Foundation, Edutopia, updated December 1, 2010, https://www.edutopia.org/neuroscience-brain-based-learning-relevance-improves-engagement; Stacy J. Priniski, Cameron A. Hecht, and Judith M. Harackiewicz, "Making Learning Personally Meaningful: A New Framework for Relevance Research," *The Journal of Experimental Education* 86, no. 1 (2018), 11–29; https://doi.org/10.1080/00220973.2017.1380589; Mary Helen Immordino-Yang and Antonio Damasio, "We Feel, Therefore We Learn: The Relevance of Affective and Social Neuroscience to Education," *Mind, Brain, and Education* 1, no. 1 (2007), 3–10, https://doi.org/10.1111/j.1751-228X.2007.00004.x.
20. Jay McTighe and Judy Willis, *Upgrade Your Teaching: Understanding by Design Meets Neuroscience* (Alexandria: Association for Supervision and Curriculum Development, 2019), 139.
21. McTighe and Willis.
22. Amanda Morin, "What is Multisensory Instruction?" *Understood*, accessed October 28, 2023, https://www.understood.org/en/articles/multisensory-instruction-what-you-need-to-know .
23. Howard E. Gardner, *Frames of Mind: The Theory of Multiple Intelligences*, rev ed. (1983; repr., New York: Basic Books, 2011).
24. "Multiple Intelligences: What Does the Research Say?" George Lucas Education Foundation, Edutopia, updated July 20, 2016, https://www.edutopia.org/multiple-intelligences-research; Luc Rousseau, "Neuromyths and Multiple Intelligences (MI) Theory: A Comment on Gardner," *Frontiers in Psychology* 12, no. 12 (2021), https://doi.org/10.3389/fpsyg.2021.720706; Youki Terada, "Multiple Intelligences Theory: Widely Used, Yes Misunderstood," George Lucas Education Foundation, Edutopia, updated July 20, 2018, https://www.edutopia.org/article/multiple-intelligences-theory-widely-used-yet-misunderstood.
25. Rousseau, "Neuromyths and Multiple Intelligences."
26. Scott B. Christie, "The Brain: Utilizing Multi-Sensory Approaches for Individual Learning Styles," *Education* 121, no. 2 (2000); Edutopia, "Multiple Intelligences."

27. Glenys McGowan, Gerhard Hoffstaedter, and Jennifer Creese, "Object Based Learning in the Social Sciences: Three Approaches to Haptic Knowledge Making," *Teaching Anthropology* 11, no. 2 (2022), 97–107; John Hennigar Shuh, "Teaching Yourself to Teach with Objects," *Journal of Education* 7, no. 4 (1982), 8–15.

28. Paul R. Sheppard, Brad A. Donaldson, and Gary Huckleberry, "Quantitative Assessment of a Field-based Course on Integrative Geology, Ecology, and Cultural History," *International Research in Geographical and Environmental Education* 19, no. 4 (2010), 295–313; David Sobel, *Place-based Education: Connecting Classrooms & Communities* (Great Barrington, MA: The Orion Society, 2004).

29. Vicki Dale, Nathalie Tasler, and Lola Sánchez-Jáuregui, "Object-Based Learning: Active Learning Through Enquiry," in *100 Ideas for Active Learning*, ed. Tab Betts and Paolo Oprandi (Sussex: University of Sussex, 2022), https://doi.org/10.20919/OPXR1032/69.

30. Rebekah Schields, Nichole Tramel, and Erika Malo, "Archaeology Fairs and Measuring Informal Learning" (PowerPoint presentation, 82nd Annual Meeting of the Society for American Archaeology, Vancouver, British Columbia, March 30, 2017).

31. "Object-Based Learning," Fort Lewis College Center of Southwest Studies, accessed November 4, 2023, https://swcenter.fortlewis.edu/learn/object-based-learning.

32. Steven Semken, "Place-based Teaching and Learning," in *Encyclopedia of the Sciences of Learning*, ed. Norbert M. Seel (New York: Springer, 2012), 2641–42.

33. Steven Semken and Carol Butler Freeman, "Sense of Place in the Practice and Assessment of Place-based Science Teaching," *Science Education* 92, no. 6 (2008), 1042–57.

34. Grant Wiggins and Jay McTighe, *Understanding by Design*, 2nd ed. (Alexandria: Association for Supervision and Curriculum Development, 2005).

35. Jeanne M. Moe, "Conceptual Understanding of Science through Archaeological Inquiry," (EdD diss., Montana State University, 2011); Jeanne M. Moe, "Best Practices in Archaeology Education: Successes, Shortcomings, and the Future," in *Public Engagement and Education: Developing and Fostering Stewardship for an Archaeological Future*, ed. Katherine P. Erdman (New York: Berghahn Books, 2019), 215–36.

36. Letts and Moe, *Project Archaeology*, 7.

37. Michael Brody, Jeanne M. Moe, Joelle Clark, and Crystal B. Alegria, "Archaeology as Culturally Relevant Science Education: The Poplar Forest Slave Cabin," in *Public Participation in Archaeology*, ed. Suzie Thomas and Joanne Lea (Woodbridge, UK: The Boydell Press, 2014), 89–104; Moe, "Archaeology Education for Children;" Moe, "Archaeology in Schools."

38. Eleanor M. King et al., "A Conversation on Heritage, Archaeology, and Education in the United States," *The Heritage Education Journal* 1, no. 1 (2022), https://theheritageeducationnetwork.org/the-heritage-education-journal.

RECOMMENDED RESOURCES

Wagner, Laura, and Cecile McKee. *Language Science for Everyone*. Cambridge University Press, 2023.

Wiggins, Grant, and Jay McTighe. *Understanding by Design*. 2nd expanded ed. Alexandria, VA: Association for Supervision and Curriculum Development, 2005.

2

Understanding and Connecting with Audiences

Rebecca L. Simon

Many of us had to take a mandatory public speaking course in college where the instructor stressed the importance of knowing your audience before the engagement. Little did we realize then that these lessons would stay with us throughout our careers.

As professional public archaeologists, this concept is imperative. People who attend or participate in our programs are unique in their interests and abilities, and their backgrounds, motivations, and expectations will impact their experience. There are no guarantees that what works for one audience will work with another, or even the same audience in a different context. However, the more we understand our participants, the better we can structure our programs and events to meet a spectrum of needs and expectations.

Public archaeology programs come in many formats; thus, audiences are just as varied. While we cannot cover every participant attribute in this chapter, we will provide an overview of who commonly attends our programs, some variables that may affect their experience, and advice on how to improve our ability to understand and connect with people.

DEFINING OUR AUDIENCE

Terms such as "community," "stakeholders," "participant," and "students" are typically used interchangeably with "audience" in the context of public archaeology. In many cases, there is no problem with such flexibility of terminology, but there are situations when these terms take on very different meanings. For example, there are often fundamental differences between a community member who would like to learn more about local archaeology and a stakeholder who will be financially or socially affected by your activities. "Participant" more often refers to an active audience (excavating, surveying, piecing together pottery, finding the items in an exhibit scavenger hunt), and "student" refers more to a passive audience (listening to the lecture or reading a book/article/blog).

This chapter broadly refers to an "audience" as the person or persons who are intended to receive and engage with a message, presentation, or program. Whenever possible, your lecture, training, tour, classroom visit, etc., should consider several attributes of the people who attend. To communicate most effectively, try to understand the characteristics, preferences, and expectations of the audience as you develop the program. Tailor your messages to suit the needs and interests of the people who show up, and you will enhance the likelihood of successful communication and engagement. Occasionally, your "audience" will be collaborators and stakeholders. In these cases, you will need to convey information to foster meaningful connections and achieve shared goals.

COMMON PUBLIC ARCHAEOLOGY AUDIENCES

There is a common misconception that the public archaeology audience is simply anyone who is not an archaeologist. However, people who attend our programs are diverse, nuanced, and occasionally archaeologists themselves! The audience composition should influence the scale and depth of our public initiatives and be considered early in the planning process. If our anticipated audience can be succinctly defined, we can better meet their expectations, present more targeted information, and teach specific skills on a learning level aligned with their abilities. For longer-term programs that focus on community engagement, see chapter 9 for more insights.

Children

Archaeology is not commonly included in educational curricula. The programs we provide to schools and youth groups or the family-friendly events children might attend with their parents are often the only outlets for kids to learn about archaeology. Introducing youth to archaeology is possibly one of the most influential ways we can inspire future generations of preservationists and cultural stewards.[1] Depending on your own background and personality, you either enjoy working with children or try to avoid it at all costs. Outreach with children might intimidate you because of previous experiences that were stressful or unsuccessful, and it is possible these experiences were influenced by a disconnect between your content and delivery and their abilities or ways of learning.

Piaget's theory of cognitive development implies that instructional methods and content need to be consistent with how students develop cognitively, as children cannot "learn" if they cannot understand what they are being asked to learn.[2] At about age eleven to twelve, around sixth grade, children begin to move from concrete thought to formal abstract thought with skills in deductive reasoning. Archaeology as a concept is inherently abstract, which forces learners to process associations between tangible and intangible concepts. With younger grades, use concrete examples to connect the past with the present so that children can relate to something tangible in their own lives, such as family, shelter, or food, and with older grades, complement some of your abstract concepts with concrete ones to strengthen connections.

Understanding some basic pedagogical approaches like multiple learning styles and constructivism (see chapter 1) can help us more effectively connect with children. Teachers or youth group leaders are also resources who can answer questions about their students and provide some necessary insights to help you adapt your program (see chapter 8). Additionally, maintaining a greater staff-to-participant ratio when doing hands-on or group activities will allow you to allocate attention to individuals who work or learn at different paces.

Older Adults

Older adults, who may be retired, often pursue social and educational opportunities that align with their passions, interests, and free time. A scan of the audience at most public archaeology events, particularly lectures, will often show a high percentage of older adults in attendance, especially if the public program is held during typical work hours. Many have held on to dreams throughout their lives of working as an archaeologist and are deeply interested in your subject matter.

Compared to other participant groups, older adults generally have a higher number of individuals with visual or auditory impairments and mobility or cognitive considerations. Be conscientious about your program or event location, background distractions, technological support, speaking volume, tone, and cadence. Clarity of audiovisual materials can improve participant engagement, comprehension, and accessibility (see appendix B).

Descendant Communities and Indigenous Peoples

In a field that strives to understand people in the past, it should go without saying that understanding and connecting with descendant and Indigenous communities is standard for public archaeology. These audiences may be presenting with us or partners in collaboration. No matter the case, not everyone has the same needs, opinions, expectations, or taboos. Grouping and generalizing these individuals when doing public outreach is too often the case and results in disingenuous messaging. Remember, they are living people; do not freeze them in the past when referring to them in presentations and lessons.

Approach collaborations with humility, respect, and a genuine willingness to listen and learn from their experiences and perspectives. The best way to understand these audiences is to interact with them and build relationships. Ask questions. Share a meal. Bring a gift. Do not expect a descendant or Indigenous person to be interested in or capable of speaking for their entire community. Invite them to attend your programs as learners and participants, without expectations. Working with descendant communities can contribute to the preservation of cultural heritage and is crucial for maintaining the richness of human history and diversity.

Stakeholders and Interested Parties

Often, public archaeology programs are developed with support from administrators, contractors, developers, agencies, property owners, and community partners. This might include funding, resources, or partnerships. In compliance work, archaeologists commonly use the terms "stakeholder," "constituent," and "interested party." These terms are not simply legalese for "general public" and not all government agencies use them in the same way.

Stakeholders and interested parties often have monetary and/or political investments and motivations, but may also have emotional, cultural, and ethical investments. They might attend or participate in your programs to learn and build skills or emphasize their involvement. They also may attend to see firsthand the impacts of their investments, which may influence their willingness to support future initiatives. Interacting with stakeholders during a public event provides a more informal and hopefully less stressful opportunity for you to communicate your passion and commitment to public archaeology and advocate for continued support.

MEET YOUR AUDIENCE WHERE THEY ARE

Each unique public program or event requires a different combination of approaches to connect with your audience based on their background. Your program goals and outcomes should provide guidance on which audience you aim to reach, whether general or targeted, and what methods and techniques you will use to connect with them. Seek to understand someone else to learn about yourself and become a more effective practitioner. Be aware of your own attitudes and assumptions about demographics, socioeconomic status, and physical and mental abilities, and how any preconceptions might impact your own expectations for your participants.

Demographics

Basic demographic data that includes age, gender, race, ethnicity, and geography are the building blocks of understanding an audience. Economics, politics, education, ideology, language, and identity also play a large role in how people approach and process experiences. When planning and implementing public programs, consider and account for the sociocultural attributes of your audience. Considering these elements will provide you with valuable insights to improve your programs and increase success. Take time to learn about greeting taboos, common misconceptions and stereotypes, language barriers or nuances, appropriate attire, sacred acts, and other practices. This will show your care and consideration for your audience. However, to be very clear, understanding the audience does not guarantee avoiding uncomfortable situations.

Accessibility

Make an effort to provide accessible and inclusive opportunities (see chapter 3). People at our programs and events will likely have a range of cultural or language backgrounds, learning abilities, mobility capabilities, physical limitations, and tactile sensitivities. Too often, recognizing and facilitating opportunities for those with different physical and cognitive capabilities is seen as simply a matter of compliance or a one-off scenario, if it is thought of at all. Consider these attributes as opportunities for a different type of connection instead of disabilities. If working with neurodivergent audiences (people with brain development different from the norm for whatever reason, medical or otherwise), prepare interactive programming to navigate a story in a slightly circular fashion.[3] Acknowledge that our audiences have varying needs; a "one-size-fits-all" approach is not always feasible.

Preconceptions

You may have to field antagonistic questions or comments during your program. Often, these are influenced by political ideologies, stereotypes (particularly about Indigenous people), or popular media that promotes pseudoarchaeology. Some people might distrust you or perceive you as a gatekeeper or "ivory tower elitist," potentially because of your education, place of employment, or scientific beliefs.

Attempting to correct or realign someone's question or comment is often tense in a public setting. Approaching from a perspective of, "this is how I understand, based on the research I've done . . ." rather than becoming combative or the "authority" may help to defuse a situation and open avenues for constructive communication. However, there is no guarantee how conversations will go, regardless of the approach. Sometimes you may just have to continue with your presentation or politely thank the person for engaging and walk away. In certain situations, you may be pressed to express political or ideological opinions. Archaeology is inherently political, and many professionals are representing an agency. In those situations, care should be taken to avoid personal opinions being construed for the positions of your organization.

PRACTICAL TACTICS TO CONNECT WITH YOUR AUDIENCE

Multiple factors will affect how well you connect with your audience. Your aptitude for understanding your audience will ultimately result from a combination of professional skills, common sense, and respectful interactions. Improving these skills will help you to better plan, adapt, and choose appropriate instructional techniques. Be knowledgeable about pedagogical frameworks that are useful in public archaeology programming (see chapter 1). In the end, shifting your outreach from a mindset of "what is being taught" to "what is being learned" and recognizing the similarities and differences within your audience will provide opportunities to build relationships, understanding, and trust.

Figure 2.1. Unearthing Our Past logo.
Courtesy of Unearthing Our Past Consulting, LLC

Textbox 2.1. Embracing Discomfort

Mia L. Carey

One of the earliest pieces of advice my mentor gave me when I began facilitating inclusion and equity conversations (you may call them trainings) in 2017, was that I needed to learn to meet people where they were, not where I wanted them to be. It has long been a guiding principle among diversity, equity, and inclusion (DEI) practitioners, but it presents different challenges depending on the audience you are working with and the topic you are discussing. It is intended to consider that audiences will have a range of understanding and may be at different points in their experience with or knowledge of DEI topics, but it can fall short when "where people are" varies drastically within a given space.

My primary audience, typically, is other archaeologists, museum professionals, and public historians. Most of the conversations I facilitate are about race and racism, white supremacy, and how we as individuals, regardless of our racial or ethnic identity, intentionally or unintentionally, support these systems of prejudice, discrimination, and oppression. These are topics that, understandably, can be extremely polarizing and are often met with varying forms of resistance. More importantly, these topics reveal the range of stages that individuals are in with developing their own racial identity and in their anti-racism journeys. One of my greatest challenges in developing and facilitating conversations about controversial topics has been navigating where to meet people. There is a fine line between making people "comfortable" and making them uncomfortable. My role as a facilitator is to help my audience strengthen their mindsets, encourage individual behavioral changes, and encourage independent growth and accountability.

Here are three lessons I have learned along the way that I think can be universally applied to many types of public programming:

1. *Always set the tone.* I start every conversation the same way: establishing conversational agreements or guidelines that outline how we are going to have a productive conversation; discussing the expectations that the audience should have of the conversation and what I expect from them; discussing how they should engage with me and with others, though usually, this is for virtual audiences; and finally having them participate in a community builder. These steps may seem tedious, but they help me foster a brave space in which we can navigate discomfort and conflict without derailing the conversation or encouraging resistance.

2. *Always level set.* Before I develop each conversation, I consult with my clients to get insight into what type of environment I am walking into. This can include background information about problems that have arisen or about team dynamics. I do this to get

a better understanding of where people are and where I can potentially meet them. Regardless of how much prep work I do, there are always instances where it is not enough. This is where level setting comes in. I always go over basic definitions and concepts and then build on them. This way, people who are more comfortable with challenging topics are still gaining new knowledge, and I am not encouraging resistance with those who are not.

3. *Take time to process and reflect.* I end each conversation by asking my audience to reflect on what they have learned and how they are feeling. It gives them a chance to process their emotions and it gives me an idea of how close I have come to meeting them where they are. Setting the tone at the beginning of the conversation makes people more comfortable, leading to increased openness and a willingness to ask questions they may have hesitated to ask before.

The following four practical tactics aim to enhance communication and engagement in public archaeology programs with a goal of being inclusive and respectful:[4]

1. *Be clear and direct.* In most cases this means to use simple, plain language. This does not mean "dumb it down." Just keep in mind that your participants are not going to have a thesaurus or jargon translator. If an unfamiliar word must be used, define, or explain it. Using deliberate language also allows participants (both active and passive) to see a measure of commitment and respect to the research, context, and people that make up the program or project.
2. *Tell a story.* Many public archaeology audiences will be most accustomed to the Western construct of a story—beginning, middle, end. For those programs, organizing the big takeaways, relevant facts, and interesting details into a story will minimize confusion and allow you to stay succinct. There are important times when this approach may not be as appropriate. For example, some Indigenous knowledge contexts and perspectives are not linear, and these audiences may not relate to a strictly linear story.
3. *Center the audience.* Making the audience a part of the story fosters the idea that they should care and that the information being shared, learned, or discovered is important. Connect your content to their place and their history. You may have some of this knowledge prior to your program or event, but you can also assess your audience by asking questions to learn what they already know or what is important to them. This can take as little as a few minutes upfront during your program.
4. *Be flexible and humble.* Public archaeology always involves people, and people are dynamic. No matter the amount of preparation, rarely does everything go perfectly. There will be times when your audience is different from what you expected. Perhaps the audience demographics are a mystery until everyone enters the room. There will be other times when the audience responds in the exact opposite manner than you expected. What to do in these moments? Flexibility and humility are some of the most important traits a public archaeologist can have. You will need to adapt. Offer yourself continual opportunities to observe and work with the public, develop an array of outreach and communication skills, and cultivate a sense of humor during more stressful situations.

Even if at the outset the audience appears to be the same from program to program, other factors will impact how smoothly any given program will go. A classroom rotation might include one enthusiastic group that jumps at the chance to participate, but the next rotation is full of quiet kids. Parents might bring along their preschoolers to a library program geared toward teenagers. Non-English-speaking families might come across your information or activity table at a fair. Being

Rebecca L. Simon

Textbox 2.2. Words Matter

A. Gwynn Henderson and Linda S. Levstik

> *"Sticks and stones may break my bones, but words will never hurt me."*

This classic child's taunt is not altogether true. Words *can* hurt people. And as public archaeology practitioners, we need to be mindful of the words we use and how we use them: in the educational materials, worksheets, and slides we prepare, and in the presentations we give. We also must consider how our various audiences are hearing and processing our words. Our educational effectiveness suffers if we do not. A process of mindful reflection, however, encourages us to continually improve our practice, and we can grow into more effective communicators and educators.

Our intention is not to freeze you into inaction or make you worry about every word you say. But as we assessed public archaeology programs to improve their effectiveness,[1] we discovered how the words we use can set up speed bumps to deep conceptual understanding, often carrying subtexts that unintentionally promote misconceptions and stereotypes.

Two Words That Confuse . . . and One That Doesn't

"Story." Simple enough. Everyone knows what this word means, right? Not exactly. After returning to their classrooms from a daylong archaeological field program, we asked fifth-grade students to write a story about their experience or an artifact they had found.[2] We got stories, alright. Marvelous stories. *Fantastical* creative stories. We were surprised and deeply disappointed. Where had we gone wrong?

As we worked through our assessment, we realized that the students had heard "creative writing." We had neglected to mention the assignment's most critical element: their story had to be *evidence-based*. Like all good archaeological research, we wanted the students to use evidence to tell "stories" about the people who had once lived at the site. The lesson: be very clear and make sure students know if you are seeking fiction or evidence-based nonfiction.

"Puzzle." The work of archaeologists is often described as "putting together pieces of a puzzle to tell stories about the past." Though tinged with reality, this metaphor generates confusion. An archaeological site is indeed a puzzle, but it is rarely complete—or even a single puzzle. At stratified sites, for example, multiple puzzles are layered and intrude into one another. Differential preservation and the destruction of archaeological sites through looting or by natural causes add to the problem.

Carefully explain to your audience that archaeologists are like puzzle whizzes who put pieces together to better see a more complete picture. But the complete picture is rare or impossible. And yet . . . by gathering information from a variety of sources, archaeologists can catch a glimpse of that larger image.

"Detective." We found this word is a good one to use, considering detectives use evidence to put together as complete a picture of what happened as possible. Archaeologists share this curiosity for uncovering the past. As a result, a detective metaphor is particularly germane to inquiry-based instruction. It requires posing a question that sets your audience on a quest for answers.

Words That Disrespect

Over time, we have become uncomfortable with words that we once used routinely. We suggest that anyone working to dispel stereotypes and misconceptions about long-ago peoples avoid words such as the three below, whose subtexts erase or dehumanize groups of people.

"Prehistoric." We rarely explain that this word actually refers to the history of pre-*literate* societies. Without adding that qualification, we consign all peoples who lived before written documents developed as *pre*-historic peoples: having no history. That is simply not true. It is an ongoing challenge to replace "prehistoric," but we prefer "deep history" because that offers a broad and relatively neutral cultural label.

"Slave." A slave is a commodity, bought and sold and enumerated in wills—objectified and dehumanized. *Enslaved people*, however, were stripped of their freedom by powerful *enslavers*, but they are clearly human. Furthermore, the word "enslaver" clarifies the power dynamic at play.

"Pioneer." A pioneer is the first person or group of people to settle in a place, to accomplish a particular feat or task, or do something new with common things. Indigenous peoples are North America's only pioneers, in the first sense of the word. Europeans who settled in North America were colonists or settlers, but they were not pioneers. They were not the first people to settle the Western Hemisphere.

Figure 2.2. As part of their monthlong archaeology unit, fifth graders spent a day excavating alongside archaeologists. *Courtesy of the Kentucky Archaeological Survey*

Mixing Contexts, Mixing Words

Context is everything in archaeology. Mixing artifacts from different contexts leads to confusion. In public archaeology programming, context is everything, too. So, when we use the words of description/observation in the context of inference/interpretation, confusion and objectification of long-ago peoples' lives can occur.

Consider this example. Archaeological sites are places where past human activities left behind patterns of artifacts. When describing/observing a place from a purely archaeological perspective, terms like "site" or "artifact" are perfectly legitimate to use. In *this* context.

But archaeological sites *also* are places where people once lived and worked and played and died. Through inference/interpretation based on archaeological evidence, sites become houses or camps or towns or cemeteries. In the telling, an artifact becomes a knife or weapon or jar or necklace. And so, we should use terms like these in *this* context.

When you carefully consider word choices, you close the distance between your audience and the people about whom we are talking. By matching our words to the context, we emphasize peoples' humanity, agency, and intelligence. Archaeologists study sites and artifacts to learn about how long-ago people lived and to understand the diversity of the human experience. The words we use must reflect that purpose.

Notes

1. A. Gwynn Henderson and Linda S. Levstik, "Reading Objects: Children Interpreting Material Culture," *Advances in Archaeological Practice* 4, no. 4 (2016), 503–16, https://doi.org/10.7183 /2326-3768.4.4.503; Linda S. Levstik, A. Gwynn Henderson, and Jennifer S. Schlarb, "Digging for Clues: An Archaeological Exploration of Historical Cognition," in *Understanding History: Recent Research in History Education*, eds. Rosalyn Ashby, Peter Gordon, and Peter Lee, vol. 4, *International Review of History Education* (London: RoutledgeFalmer, 2005), 37–53.
2. A. Gwynn Henderson and Linda S. Levstik, "What DO Children Learn When They Go on a Fieldtrip to Henry Clay's Estate?" *Forum Journal of the National Trust for Historic Preservation* 19, no. 1 (2004), 39–47.

aware of multiple learning modalities (auditory, visual, physical) and incorporating any combination thereof into the way you deliver content or demonstrate skills will provide more ways for your audience to participate.

DO YOUR HOMEWORK

The success of your program depends on you understanding your audience. Practical steps for establishing connections and navigating potential group dynamics occur in the preparation phase, during the event, and in your post-event reflection.

Before the Program

Whether your prospective audience is predetermined or unknown, here are some simple actions to take during program planning to better understand the attendees.

1. *Research.* Programs for fourth graders are different from those for college students and equally different from those for retirees looking to follow their passions. In any case, it is wise to research demographics, your location, expected audience, and any parameters that might impact your audience's experience or your content delivery (e.g., limited to an indoor space, aligning to an

educational standard). Archaeologists are first and foremost researchers, so this should be obvious and straightforward.

2. *Talk to program partners.* When your participation is planned, organized, or requested by a collaborator such as a teacher, colleague, or community program coordinator, that person is your frontline source. Ask them questions about audience demographics, prior knowledge and experiences, as well as expectations.

3. *Talk to your registrants.* If your audience is largely pre-determined through advanced registration, take the opportunity to add some questions about prior knowledge or expectations during the event registration process. For example, an open-ended "What are you hoping to learn?" can prompt responses that allow you to structure or adapt your content to better align with audience expectations. You may not have the flexibility to plan a program entirely around their responses, but you can make a point to address these topics throughout your lecture or demonstration. You could even consider developing a needs assessment for long-term, regular, or recurring programs.

4. *Talk to colleagues and past audiences.* New practitioners must remember the decades-long history of archaeologists doing public outreach programs. You can learn what worked and what did not by communicating with colleagues. Additionally, some audiences have been attending programs for years and they can provide insider information to audience expectations and historical context. They can advise you on what to consider in every circumstance, from the "brand-new program" to the "revitalization of the gold standard." The practitioners and audiences that came before might have strong connections and opinions. Respectfully integrating their ideas while being honest about your direction or intentions can be a careful dance, but it is an important step in understanding the audience and avoiding roadblocks.

5. *Take notes.* As you research, conduct pre-assessments, and communicate with partners, registrants, and colleagues, document what you learn. Keep this information in a file along with your scope, budgets, program plan, etc. This information will help you frame your current program and provide a reference for future programs. See appendix A for a template to document this information.

During the Program

Continue your preparation and homework throughout the program. Start by asking introductory questions or doing icebreakers when you do not know your audience or if they are ever-changing. Love them or hate them, the right icebreaker can help to quickly understand and assess a group of people. Make sure your questions and topics are generic enough for diverse audiences, as well as meaningful for you as program organizer. Don't forget to participate so that your audience learns more about you!

Whether your participants are a captive audience learning an excavation skill or they are coming and going during an archaeology fair, pay attention to them. Do their facial cues demonstrate understanding or engagement? Are people checking watches, phones, or staring into space? Do questions ask for more clarification or demonstrate understanding and take the conversation deeper? Outreach is about engagement, so ask audience questions, have a conversation, and be obvious when adjusting if that can create connection. The more time you take to understand and assess during your event, the more your skills align with audience needs.

After the Program

So how do we know that we are successful in understanding and connecting with the audience? Assessments help us understand programmatic success and impact (see chapter 12) and are critical to the future of public archaeology. Before a report with matrices and graphs quantitatively measuring engagement and educational value, measure success by your interactions. Your audience will say, "Thank you," "I learned so much," or "I really appreciated it when . . ." regardless of how many broken taboos or uncomfortable moments occurred, if you truly connected. You will also get "other" comments if you don't. Keep in mind this is an ongoing process, and one of the most meaningful aspects of public archaeology is your own growth.

NOTES

1. Elizabeth C. Reetz, Cherie Haury-Artz, and Jay A. Gorsh, "Strengthening a Place-Based Curriculum through the Integration of Archaeology and Environmental Education," in *Public Engagement and Education: Developing and Fostering Stewardship for an Archaeological Future*, ed. Katherine P. Erdman (New York: Berghahn Books, 2019), 74–108.
2. David C. Engleson and Dennis H. Yockers, *A Guide to Curriculum Planning in Environmental Education* (Madison: Wisconsin Department of Public Instruction, 1994).
3. "Neurodivergent," Cleveland Clinic, updated June 2, 2022, https://my.clevelandclinic.org/health/symptoms/23154-neurodivergent.
4. (Adapted from) Stephanie Gibson, "NEPA Document Tips and Tricks," (Presentation at the Colorado Department of Transportation Environmental Planning Branch Face to Face meeting, Golden, CO, October 25, 2023).

3

Advancing Inclusivity in Archaeology

Amelia S. Dall

> Nothing about us without *all* of us.

We all know the saying "Nothing about us without us," first invoked by the South African disability rights movement in the 1990s. But does this quote ring true for all disabled individuals? Unfortunately, no, as d/Deaf people are often excluded from this conversation. Hence the emphasis on the word "all" in the quote.

EQUITY PRACTICES IN ARCHAEOLOGY

Ensuring accessibility for all disabled people (i.e., those who were born disabled and those who were disabled later in life) is crucial for promoting equity, with profound impacts for our profession. Likewise, we must foster multicultural sensitivity and diversity within the field of archaeology and at our public programs. In order to enhance our understanding of equitable practices and create an action plan, we need a foundational understanding of relevant concepts and terminology.

In our field, *inclusivity* ensures that people with diverse needs, such as those of us who are individuals with disabilities, are able to participate in and benefit from archaeological research, educational programming, and archaeological site tours. Providing accessible *education and outreach* enables us to reach a wider audience and encourage greater engagement with the discipline. This increases learning, raises awareness, and preserves archaeological knowledge for the future. There are *legal and moral obligations* that we must abide by. Various laws and regulations (i.e., Americans with Disabilities Act [ADA]) mandate accessibility in public spaces, which include archaeological sites, museums, and related institutions. Compliance is required and essential to avoid possible legal consequences and negative public reviews. And finally, there are *ethical considerations*. Archaeology involves the study and interpretation of past human societies. Making the field accessible demonstrates respect for the diverse perspectives and contributions of those who are affected by archaeological research. Table 3.1 introduces additional terms and concepts that we must be familiar with to continue to improve our equitable practices.

Table 3.1. Accessibility Terms and Concepts for Archaeologists Planning Public Programs

Key Terms	Concepts
Universal Design	• Creating products, environments, and experiences used by all people without the need for adaption or specialized designs • Designing sites, tours, and exhibits to be accessible for all users without the need for specialized designs
Physical Accessibility	• Increasing ease for people with mobility challenges to access archaeological sites (e.g., ramps, pathways, and facilities)
Digital Accessibility	• Making archaeological information, databases, and online resources accessible for disabled people • Using accessible techniques (e.g., alternative text for images, proper markup, and designing websites compatible with screen readers)
Inclusive Education	• Making archaeological knowledge and curricula accessible and engaging for students of all abilities • Adapting teaching methods, materials, and assessments
Sensory Accessibility	• Designing archaeological information, exhibits, sites, lectures/presentations, and tours to ensure they are inclusive to people with diverse sensory abilities • Providing availability of sign language, cued sign, or protactile interpreters for those who are deaf and hard of hearing, cued, or deafblind and accessible audio descriptions for those who are oral (i.e., they do not know sign language) • Including tactile materials for blind and/or deafblind people
Cultural Sensitivity	• Ensuring accessibility efforts do not compromise the cultural and historical significance of archaeological sites or artifacts • Striking a balance between accessibility and preservation methods
Visitor Experience	• Enhancing the quality of the experience through accessible features (e.g., guided tours with sign language interpreters and multisensory exhibits)
Collaborative Efforts and Programs	• Working with experts in accessibility and relevant organizations to ensure projects, sites, tours, etc., are as accessible as possible • Validating the lived experiences of disabled people (i.e., understanding the difference between those who were born disabled and those who were disabled later in life) • Establishing permanent opportunities to develop collaborative work
Interdisciplinary Approaches	• Acknowledging accessibility feedback requires collaboration from professionals in other disciplines such as architecture, design, assistive technology, etc.
Compliance	• Adhering to legal requirements and guidelines • Ensuring archaeological activities are in line with national/international standards

UNDERSTANDING THE IMPORTANCE OF ACCESSIBILITY IN ARCHAEOLOGY

Accessibility can be seen as a double-sided coin: two facets, each with its own set of considerations and implications. On one side, there is inclusivity and its numerous benefits. On the other side are the challenges and the scrutinies.

The "Head" of the Coin

The proverbial head of the coin symbolizes accessibility. Ensuring accessibility in public archaeology has many positive impacts that include:

- *Reaching wider audiences* that include individuals with disabilities, elderly adults, families with young children, and people from various cultural backgrounds. Ensuring accessibility also allows a wider range of people to appreciate and learn about different cultures and heritage, leading to greater cultural awareness and preservation.
- *Increased learning and engagement.* Features like audio descriptions of artifacts, tactile exhibits, braille translations of information panels, and sign language interpretations can make archaeological content more engaging and informative.
- *Economic and community benefits.* Accessible archaeological sites and resources can attract a larger number of visitors, including tourists. This, in turn, can boost the local economy and generate greater revenue for conservation, preservation, and research efforts. Boosting accessibility at public archaeology programs and sites also encourages community involvement and participation. It empowers people to take an active role in learning about archaeology and preserving and promoting local cultural heritage.
- *Social responsibility.* Promoting accessibility in archaeology demonstrates a commitment to social responsibility and equity. It breaks down barriers and fosters a more inclusive, equitable, and just society, promoting the rights and dignity of individuals with disabilities.
- *A stronger professional community.* Within the archaeological profession, ensuring that people with diverse needs and abilities can fully participate in and benefit from archaeological research and experiences fosters a sense of inclusivity and diversity.

Efficient Outcomes

There are multiple ways to foster accessibility for our audiences, whether they are attending an event, participating in field or lab work, or simply perusing informal educational resources. While this book primarily focuses on person-to-person archaeological outreach programs, the effective strategies outlined here can apply to other forms of education and interpretation. Regardless of the program type or interpretive medium, our goal should be efficient outcomes, ensuring that individuals with special needs can achieve the same results as those without, thereby optimizing access for everyone. Examples of efficient outcomes that public archaeologists should strive to meet are:

1. *Tactile displays.* These allow visitors, including those with visual and sensory impairments, to touch and feel replicas of artifacts. Such hands-on opportunities enhance understanding and engagement of the cultural heritage shared.
2. *Accessible pathways.* Wheelchair ramps and other related accommodation needs make it possible for individuals with mobility challenges to explore archaeological sites and experience the historical and cultural significance of these places.
3. *Sign language interpretation.* Providing sign language interpreters during guided tours, lectures, presentations, and webinars, ensures d/Deaf and hard of hearing individuals can access the

shared information. There are hundreds of different sign languages used around the world. Common in the United States and bordering countries are American Sign Language (ASL), Lengua de Senas Mexicana (LSM), and Langue des signes du Québec (LSQ).

4. *Audio descriptions.* Including audio descriptions for exhibits, artifacts, and all other related subjects provides additional context for visitors with visual impairments. Often, these descriptions can be accessed through smartphone apps, audio guides, or QR codes. When presenting in person, ask all presenters and demonstrators to verbally describe any images in slides, artifacts or tools, or features and landscapes as they reference them.

5. *Multisensory experiences.* Incorporating sounds, visuals, scents, and tactile materials into archaeological exhibits, tabletop displays, and hands-on activities provides a more immersive experience for all visitors.

6. *Accessible websites and mobile applications.*[1] Organizations, parks, and tours offering accessible websites and mobile apps allow people with disabilities to access research findings, virtual tours, and educational materials.

7. *Collaboration.* Working with disabled people to develop accessible programs, exhibitions, and educational materials can lead to more meaningful and informed archaeological experiences.

8. *Inclusive interpretive programs.* Offer interpretive programs that are designed to accommodate visitors or viewers with specific needs, whether an in-person or virtual program or prerecorded videos. For example, have readily available sign language interpreters for guided tours.

Figure 3.1. 3D-printed replicas accompany photographs and descriptions of artifacts to add a tactile element to the information booth display. *Courtesy of Bernard K. Means*

The "Tail" of the Coin

In any outreach, there are various challenges and considerations to address. Hurdles and obstacles may arise as you strive to make archaeological resources accessible to all. Such issues include:

- *Budget constraints.* Providing accessibility features (i.e., wheelchair ramps, tactile exhibits, sign language interpreters) can be a costly investment, particularly for archaeological outreach programs that face financial constraints.
- *Resource limitations.* Navigating the diverse needs of individuals with different types of disabilities can be intricate and demanding. Crafting solutions for accessibility involves customization for specific requirements, a process that can be time-consuming and may demand additional expertise—such as hiring a qualified professional.
- *Preservation conflicts.* In certain cases, efforts to make archaeological sites fully accessible by installing ramps or altering structures may compromise or conflict with the preservation of their historical and cultural integrity.

Inefficient Outcomes

These challenges should be acknowledged and addressed through careful planning, collaborative efforts, and a commitment to finding balanced solutions that respect the historical significance of cultural heritage while ensuring accessibility for all. Despite our best efforts, we will likely face inefficient outcomes, but it is better to recognize them than ignore them. Examples of inefficient outcomes faced in public archaeology include:

1. *Resource limitations.* Due to budget constraints, some organizations may not be able to provide basic accessibility features, thus limiting access of individuals with disabilities to archaeological sites and exhibits.
2. *Conflicting preservation goals.* Altering archaeological sites to make them accessible, such as adding ramps or railings, may compromise the historical accuracy and authenticity of the site, leading to potential conflicts between accessibility and preservation goals.
3. *Limited accommodations.* Archaeological sites, museums, and other institutions may offer limited accommodations for specific disabilities, such as wheelchair accessibility, but may overlook the needs of people with sensory impairments or cognitive disabilities.
4. *Accessibility gaps.* Incomplete or inconsistent accessibility features can create gaps in the visitor experience, as some areas or exhibits may be accessible while others are not, leading to frustration and negative experiences.
5. *Maintenance challenges.* Maintaining accessibility features can be an ongoing challenge due to possible deterioration and sustaining updates, which may strain financial resources if already limited.
6. *Potential cultural sensitivity issues.* There may be instances where accommodations conflict with the cultural and historical sensitivity of a site or a tour, and decisions in those cases can be ethically and culturally challenging.

Connecting the Two Sides of the Coin

The two sides of the coin are interconnected and inseparable. One cannot fully understand accessibility without considering both aspects. Addressing the challenges and considerations of the "tails" side of the coin is essential to realize the benefits and inclusivity on the "heads" side. Creative solutions and collaboration between various stakeholders can help overcome obstacles and maximize potential benefits of accessibility. Recognizing that, like any coin, accessibility may require trade-offs and compromises.

However, always encourage a balanced approach with the aim to magnify inclusivity while preserving the integrity of archaeological activities and cultural heritage. Flipping the "accessibility coin" reveals different multifaceted perspectives and priorities depending on which side one is examining.

Historically, archaeological outreach programs and research projects are often less accessible due to a lack of awareness and concern for the needs of disabled people. Access barriers are far more common, and limited efforts are made to accommodate diverse audiences. The historical context of accessibility in archaeology has seen significant changes and milestones over the years, reflecting an evolving understanding of the importance of inclusivity.[2] This remains a dynamic and ongoing process. Advocacy, research, and practical efforts continue to advance the field toward greater accessibility influenced by changing social and legal contexts.

SUCCESSFUL ACCESSIBILITY EXAMPLES

Collaborative research projects must involve partnerships between able-bodied archaeologists, disabled archaeologists, and professional experts in accessibility who work together to develop tools, technologies, techniques, and strategies to enhance the accessibility of research, tours, in-person and digital programs, and events. Archaeological organizations across the globe are continuing to innovate and refine their efforts, all while facing challenges and obstacles. If you have an accessibility concern, need, or idea and don't know how to plan for or implement it, do not be afraid to reach out for advice!

One of the best ways to grow and improve our efforts in accessibility is to look to others for examples, advice, and inspiration. The following examples are models for other museums, archaeology-related institutions, and organizations looking to implement accessibility initiatives and equity practices. These examples demonstrate that accessibility in archaeology is achievable.

- Mesa Verde National Park in Colorado (USA) has made significant strides, including the construction of accessible pathways and ramps at key archaeological sites, making ancient cliff dwellings and historical structures reachable for visitors with mobility challenges. The park also offers a variety of interpretive programs, including sign language interpreters (upon request) and tactile exhibits to cater to visitors with sensory disabilities.[3]
- The Stonehenge site in England has implemented accessibility features such as improved pathways and accessible facilities in the visitor center. The new visitor center also provides exhibits with audio description guides, as well as online virtual tours for those who cannot physically visit the site.[4]
- A well-preserved Neolithic village in Scotland, Skara Brae, is a model for accessible archaeological sites. The site managers have created wooden walkways and viewing platforms to ensure visitors with mobility challenges can explore the site. Audio guides with detailed descriptions and tactile exhibits are also available to enhance the experience for those with visual or sensory disabilities.[5]
- Museo de la Ciudad in Ecuador has implemented accessible practices by providing tactile models of archaeological artifacts and incorporating braille labels. They also offer guided tours for visitors who are blind and provide interpreters in Ecuadorian Sign Language.[6]
- The Archaeology Department at the Burke Museum in Seattle, Washington (USA), recently completed a grant-based Blind and Low Vision Project. This was led by a University of Washington student who collaborated with two high school students, all of whom were blind or low vision, to create audio guides and tactile "Archaeology Accessibility Kits" for the Burke's "Our Material World" exhibit. Audio content includes physical descriptions of the space, audio versions of the gallery text, and additional narrations provided by some of the Indigenous members of the Burke staff.[7] The students also produced gallery maps available in large print or tactile formats and placed markers on the floor that can be detected with a cane. The kits include touchable guides for visitors who are blind or have other sensory or learning difficulties.

Figure 3.2. Archaeology in the Community logo
Courtesy of Archaeology in the Community

Textbox 3.1. A Commitment to Inclusion and Accessibility

Alexandra Jones and Mia L. Carey

This chapter opened with the quote, "Nothing about us without us." What better example than a program conducted by Archaeology in the Community (AITC), a DC-based 501(c)(3) nonprofit organization that facilitates and promotes the study and public understanding of archaeological heritage through various hands-on learning programs, professional development opportunities, and community events? Each year, AITC offers two free archaeology workshops, thanks to generous donations and fundraising efforts, to children ages seven through eleven. These workshops are one of the organization's most impactful educational programs because they present students with creative opportunities to infuse archaeology into their understanding of the environment. Between 2015 and 2021, nearly 1,000 students have been exposed to archaeology through these workshops. The students represent a wide array of backgrounds, including children in the foster care system and those with auditory, cognitive, learning, neurological, speech, or visual disabilities. In 2022, AITC was presented with a new opportunity to expand its reach to children and children of parents who are d/Deaf and/or hard of hearing—thus taking a significant step in promoting inclusion and accessibility in archaeology.

After receiving interest from families and community members in 2022, AITC promptly secured funding to purchase six electronic tablets to facilitate learning, enabling the enrollment of ten students whose primary language was American Sign Language (ASL) in the spring session. Among these students were three who were d/Deaf and seven who were the children of d/Deaf parents.

In the spring session of 2023, AITC hosted the first known archaeology workshop solely dedicated to d/Deaf and/or hard-of-hearing students through a partnership with Gallaudet University. This pioneering program was led by Amelia Dall, a d/Deaf ASL-user archaeologist, and Dr. Jones. In addition to having Dall lead the program, AITC hired an undergraduate student from Gallaudet University, who is also pursuing a career in archaeology, to serve as an assistant teacher. This decision was not merely about employment; it provided a valuable professional development opportunity for the student and allowed her to become a part of a supportive community of archaeologists where she felt a sense of belonging.

In addition to offering the ASL workshop, Dr. Jones insisted that AITC staff take ASL classes to ensure effective communication and collaboration with the d/Deaf community. As an organization, AITC remains committed to ongoing learning about disability and ableism. In October 2023, AITC's staff and board participated in the Society for Historical Archaeology's Gender and Minority Affairs Committee pre-conference workshop, "The Curb Cut Effect: Why Addressing Disability and Ableism Benefits Everyone," led by Dr. Mia Carey (Unearthing Our Past Consulting, LLC).

AITC's commitment to inclusion and accessibility should be an invitation for other archaeologists, public historians, and museum professionals to think about how to include people with disabilities and make their programming accessible to all.

Additionally, several archaeological organizations have taken steps to ensure digital accessibility through creating online resources that adhere to web accessibility standards. For example, the Archaeological Institute of America includes an ASL interpreter in their virtual lectures, which are available on YouTube.[8] In the UK, the Enabled Archaeology Foundation, an organization that focuses on exhibiting the skills and activities of disabled archaeologists, offers bespoke online training courses and provides resources and advice for inclusive excavations.[9]

IMPLEMENTING ACCESSIBILITY PRACTICES

We must engage in meaningful dialogue, share best practices, and collaborate with experts in accessibility to ensure our public archaeology programs and events are truly inclusive. Initiate conversations about accessibility within your own archaeological circles. Encourage your colleagues to embrace the principles of universal design (see table 3.1) and promote accessibility as a shared responsibility. Support organizations dedicated to accessibility in archaeology, and those actively participating in or organizing conferences, workshops, or training sessions focusing on these crucial issues.

Within your own organization or course of study, you can undertake some practical actions to promote a widespread discussion of accessibility:

- Host conferences or workshops dedicated to improving accessibility in archaeology, with an understanding of the differences of all disabled people.
- Establish an internal committee or working group to address accessibility issues.
- Develop and disseminate guidelines and best practices for accessibility in archaeological research, lectures, events, in-person/virtual webinars, and so on.
- Find or provide funding for research and publications that focus on accessibility topics within archaeology.

Accessibility considerations can vary greatly among public programs due to format or location. Either you, your collaborating partners, or your host will organize and implement steps to make the program or event more accessible, but no matter the situation, you need to communicate, confirm, and double-check who will carry out each task. Don't assume that planning partners will automatically know or remember to inform you of participant needs. We provide a list of accessibility considerations for the planning and implementation phases of your public program in appendix A.

THE NEED FOR ACCESSIBILITY IN ARCHAEOLOGY IS CRUCIAL

It is important to have an understanding and willingness for accessibility in archaeology. It is not a matter of convenience but a fundamental aspect of preserving cultural heritage, promoting inclusivity and equity, and respecting the rights of individuals with disabilities. There are challenges and potential conflicts associated with accessibility, such as resource constraints, financial difficulties, and concerns about preserving the historical integrity of archaeological sites. These obstacles should not deter efforts but serve as opportunities for creative solutions.

A commitment toward improving accessibility in archaeology aligns with broader ethical and social responsibilities, and it stresses the importance of respecting the dignity and rights of all individuals. It is necessary to comply with existing accessibility laws and regulations; adherence to those standards is not only a legal obligation but a moral and ethical imperative. Emerging trends, such as virtual accessibility initiatives and integration of innovative assistive technologies, are opening up an entirely new future of accessibility methods. We must be the agents of change by advocating for inclusive research, accessible sites, and equitable educational opportunities. It is time for archaeologists, institutions, and policymakers to actively champion the cause of accessibility and ensure it is a top priority in our work.

The future of archaeology holds such incredible promise as we strive to make the field more accessible and inclusive. With every step we take toward accessibility, we inch closer to a future where all individuals, regardless of their abilities, can participate in the rich tapestry of archaeological and heritage preservation. By embracing the challenges and complexities of this endeavor, we position ourselves to lead the way in creating a discipline truly representing the diversity of human history and culture. With innovation, collaboration, and a shared commitment to accessibility, we can reframe the archaeological landscape to reflect the values of inclusivity, equity, and cultural appreciation.

NOTES

1. "Guidance on Web Accessibility and the ADA," ADA.gov US Department of Justice Civil Rights Division, last updated March 18, 2022, https://www.ada.gov/resources/web-guidance/.
2. "Accessing Archaeology: A Conversation on Equity and Ethics," Natural History for Scientists, May 10, 2022, YouTube video, 1:33:48, https://www.youtube.com/watch?v=G2B—jL7KtY.
3. National Park Service, "Accessibility," Mesa Verde National Park Colorado, last updated July 10, 2023, https://www.nps.gov/meve/planyourvisit/accessibility.htm; "Deaf/Hearing Loss," last updated November 28, 2023, https://www.nps.gov/meve/planyourvisit/hearing.htm.
4. "Disabled Access and Accessibility at Stonehenge," StonehengeVisit.co.uk, https://stonehengevisit.co.uk/accessibility.
5. Historic Environment Scotland, "Skara Brae," *Access*, https://www.historicenvironment.scot/visit-a-place/places/skara-brae/access/.
6. "City Museum of Quite (Museo de la Ciudad)," Viator, https://www.viator.com/Quito-attractions/City-Museum-of-Quito-Museo-de-la-Ciudad/overview/d735-a24080.
7. "Archaeology Gallery Accessibility Tools," Burke Museum, https://www.burkemuseum.org/visit/accessibility/archaeology-gallery-accessibility-tools.
8. Archaeology Institute of America, "ArchaeologyTV," https://www.youtube.com/user/archaeologytv.
9. Enabled Archaeology Foundation," Enabled Archaeology Foundation, https://enabledarchaeology.com/.

RECOMMENDED RESOURCES

National Association for the Deaf. "Advocacy Letters." https://www.nad.org/resources/advocacy-letters/.
New England ADA Center. "ADA Checklist for Existing Facilities." https://www.adachecklist.org/.
Stringer, Katie. *Programming for People with Special Needs: A Guide for Museums and Historic Sites*. Lanham, MD: Rowman & Littlefield, 2014.
UNICEF Global. "Accessibility Toolkit." https://accessibilitytoolkit.unicef.org/.

4

Creating an Intentional Strategy

Angela M. Labrador, Randi Korn, and Rebecca Dean

IT ALL STARTS WITH A PLAN

As the old saying goes, "Failing to plan is planning to fail." We all want our public programs to be successful and benefit our audiences and stakeholders. While jumping in and "just doing the work" is enticing, taking the time to carefully plan projects is key. Yet, this foundational step has received little attention. Project planning translates the goals of public archaeology into actionable steps and provides a roadmap for achieving and measuring success.

In this chapter, we delve into the core concepts of project planning, beginning with an introduction to intentional practice philosophy as it applies to public archaeology programs. We outline a practical method for analyzing problems, generating solutions, and crafting related project plans; as well as how to define measurable success. Whether you're a seasoned public archaeologist or new to the field, this chapter equips you with helpful planning tools for programmatic success.

INTENTIONAL PLANNING IN PUBLIC ARCHAEOLOGY PROGRAMS

Intentionality, as a concept, is deeply meaningful. Though a philosophical perception from long ago, it is experiencing a renaissance, because those who work with the public recognize its value when pursuing important educational work. This chapter is about planning—a very pragmatic action, and intentionality emerges from philosophy—a heady discipline, so clarifying the concept and its connection to program planning is important.

Intentionality comes from Medieval Latin *intentio,* which means "ideas or representations of things formed by the mind,"[1] and *intentio* derives from the verb *intendere*, which means "being directed toward some goal or thing."[2] The phrases "ideas formed by the mind" and "being directed toward some goal" are concepts *and* actions familiar to program planners. Additionally, Franz Brentano, whom most philosophers credit with revitalizing intentionality in 1874, notes that "one cannot believe, wish, or hope without believing or wishing something,"[3] suggesting that a deeply felt concept will lead to action. To further connect those concepts to planning work, programmers might articulate the essence of their program, including their hopes for what audiences might experience, and then use those articulations to *direct* decisions and actions *toward* that *goal or thing*. While the original concept of *intentio* focuses on the power of the mind to pursue a goal, programmers use that power to determine which actions to take to achieve their intent—as indicated by the ideas that originated in their minds.

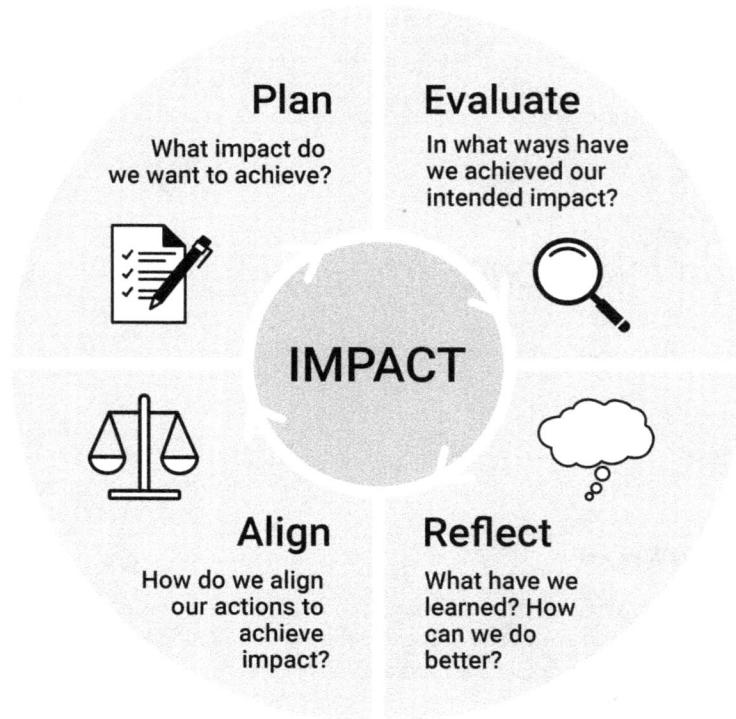

Figure 4.1. Cycle of Intentional Practice. *Courtesy of Elizabeth Pruitt, adapted with permission from Randi Korn (2018)*

The Cycle of Intentional Practice (see figure 4.1) is a diagram you can use to support intentional planning work from conceptualization to actualization. It includes four intentional actions—Plan, Evaluate, Reflect, and Align—situated around the engine that drives all work—the impact you want to achieve. Although the cycle does not explicitly show practitioners' actions, that work is inherent and assumed in the cycle. As a practitioner, you do not need reminding of your daily work because you internalize it; however, sometimes one needs reminding of the *why* behind their work,[4] so Intentional Practice prioritizes purpose. The cycle's design, a circle with four equally important quadrants, invites programmers to start in any quadrant; however, if you ask, "What impact do we want to achieve?" starting with the Plan quadrant makes sense.

Plan

Yogi Berra is credited with the saying "If you don't know where you are going, you'll end up someplace else." Clarifying a destination can suggest which actions you could take to ensure you get there. The Plan quadrant gives programmers a chance to articulate desired impacts. After you envision your intention, you can create strategies to pursue purposeful work. Doing this kind of planning work—creating a vision for the end result (impact) at the outset aligns with Stephen Covey's concept, "Begin [planning] with the end in mind."[5] Such work includes participating in exercises to develop an Impact Statement that becomes part of an Impact Framework. An Impact Statement is one sentence that describes the result of a program (or organization) on audiences. An Impact Framework, a concise document and essential tool for Intentional Planning, provides a guidepost for all planning decisions, resource management, and accountability.

Angela M. Labrador, Randi Korn, and Rebecca Dean

Evaluate

Moving clockwise, the next quadrant is Evaluate. Readying oneself for evaluation includes knowing the target audiences (see chapter 2) and specifically what you want to achieve among them. Consider questions about metrics of success. There is tension between *traditional* metrics of success, which are often focused on how many, and *meaningful* metrics of success, which Intentional Practice associates with making a positive difference in someone's life.[6] The question in the quadrant, "In what ways have we achieved our intended impact?" is about quality, not quantity. This is the quadrant where staff learn to reframe success qualitatively, which will be some of the most important Intentional Practice work programmers will do.

Shifting a mindset from quantity to quality means that reviewing work based solely on numbers—whether it is how many programs were produced or how many attended a program—is moot. More important is determining how the unique qualities of the program positively affected audiences. After shifting one's mindset, evaluation can happen in earnest.[7] Importantly, Intentional Practice views evaluation as a tool for *learning* rather than for judgment, so if an evaluation reveals that the work did not produce desired outcomes, all will ask what they can do better next time.[8]

Reflect

The Reflect quadrant supports evaluation because it prioritizes learning and improvement (the essence of Intentional Practice), asking "What did we learn? How can we do better?" Reflective practitioners think deeply about their work and question how it supports the impact they want to achieve.[9] Staff can study and discuss evaluation data to understand a program's successes and shortcomings, and in the absence of data, staff can reflect on their practices and discuss which ones align with maximizing impact or which ones may inadvertently work against achieving impact. Reflection discussions are most effective and insightful when professionals gather in small interdepartmental groups to respectfully discuss data and practices, take responsibility, and listen to understand—not judge or defend a position. Learning unfolds when all relinquish their ego-driven defenses and erase pre-conceived notions—whether about people or ideas.

Align

The need for alignment can occur frequently during intentional planning. In fact, one can reflect and align whenever necessary throughout planning because the quadrants are neither mutually exclusive nor used in a particular order. Sometimes staff will want to evaluate a long-standing program until they realize they should first align it with the new Impact Framework. Similarly, deep reflection may prompt staff to ask, "How do we readjust our actions to strengthen alignment with our new impact statement?" In both cases, what unfolds next is difficult because of how people might react to changing the *what* and *how* of their work.

When people love what they do, change turns personal. One way to approach this challenge is to remember the two essences of Intentional Practice: 1) the agreed-upon aspiration of the program as noted in the Impact Framework; and 2) everyone's professional learning that has already resulted from their Intentional Practice work. Delving deep into alignment will test everyone's readiness for selfless work; and those who consciously choose to change are prioritizing the public and organizational improvement over their own personal interests.

Part of Intentional Practice is about knowing who you are—as a professional, and also as an organization. Clarifying what the collective organization wants to achieve, and embracing the distinct qualities of your work to move forward together in one singular voice requires living on the Cycle of Intentional Practice.

ADDRESSING PROBLEMS TO ACHIEVE IMPACTS

Intentional planning revolves around impacts at the programmatic and organizational levels. Defining your project's intended impact is a critical opportunity to imagine a new future and the beneficial outcomes your project can deliver—and to whom. This requires moving beyond the nebulous missions of "public outreach" or "public education" as well as the catchall concept, "the public." It's time to think concretely. This section will guide you through analyzing problems and identifying the impacts your project can achieve. Even if you don't have complete control over your program's format or purpose, you can still follow these steps, as the process will direct your planning and provide key information that potential funders require.

Approaching the Problem

An excellent first step toward defining a project's intended impact is to start with the issues that your project addresses. If your project is the solution, what is the problem?

Many public archaeology programs have been informed by a "deficit model" when identifying problems. This model presumes that the public lacks an understanding of archaeology, contributing to a lack of public and political support for the discipline.[10] At one extreme, this model tends toward solutions that favor didactic education, reinforcing the authority of professional archaeologists for the intended benefit of the discipline itself.[11] However, a more moderate approach can result in educational programs that benefit the discipline and its participants. For instance, projects that shift from teaching *about* archaeology to teaching *through* archaeology can meet other educational objectives, such as building critical thinking skills and applying scientific or mathematical principles.[12]

Critics of the deficit model argue that stakeholders' needs should take precedence over the discipline's. Such projects may focus on economic, environmental, or social problems in which public archaeology is one means to achieve such objectives.[13] This is why eliciting stakeholders' needs is essential when planning (see chapter 5). At the same time, remember that such projects may also indirectly address archaeological problems: a potential win-win for archaeologists and other stakeholders.

Analyzing Problems, Crafting Solutions

Like archaeological sites, problems are layered; the key is to analyze the problems before defining solutions. The "problem tree" is a graphical tool project planners use to aid this process (figure 4.2). The tree trunk represents the central problem, roots indicate the causes of the problem, and leaves illustrate the effects of the problem. Developing a problem tree is best done as a collaborative brainstorming session with the project team and a diverse set of stakeholders.[14] The ideas generated during the session are typically recorded on individual index cards, but an online mind-mapping tool can be used if the team meets virtually. Once the completed tree depicts the relationships between your focal problem's cause and effects, you can transform the problem tree into a "solution tree" (see figure 4.2). Refer to appendix G for a step-by-step guide to creating problem and solution trees.

Deconstructing Impact and Designing the Plan

Most public archaeology projects have a central impact statement and multiple potential outcomes. If you complete the problem and solution tree exercise described above, you will have identified the problem, solutions, and potential strategy. Then, you can translate these elements into a more traditional project plan to guide future activities, including fundraising. At its most basic level, a project plan identifies the who, what, when, where, and why of a project's implementation. What are we doing? Who will be doing what, when? How will we do it? Where will it be done? How much will it cost? Why

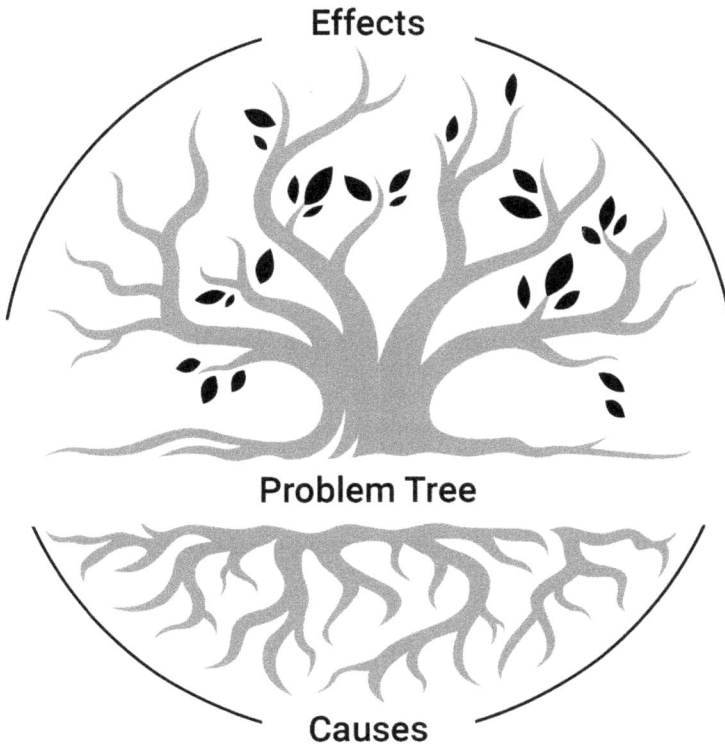

Figure 4.2. A "problem tree" and "solution tree"
Courtesy of Elizabeth Pruitt

Table 4.1. Common Project Plan Components Defined

Term	Definition
Impact	Also referred to as a goal. The overall long-term result that your project is meant to achieve on the public. It answers the questions: Why are we doing this? Who will benefit? An impact statement helps set your priorities, supports decision-making, and guides your direction. It can be intangible and non-measurable.
Outcome	Also referred to as a result or an objective. The anticipated achievement(s) of your project on the public. It should be observable, measurable, feasible, and stated as a desired end state.
Output	Also referred to as a deliverable. The tangible products or services that your project will deliver as a result of the activities. These should be clearly specified and verifiable. All outputs should logically contribute to achieving the project's outcomes.
Activity	Also referred to as a task. The work that the project team will carry out. Each activity should deliver stated outputs and demonstrate how the project will be completed. Each activity should identify the person responsible for its completion and a time estimate.
Indicator	Also referred to as a performance measure. The building block(s) for assessing the success of your project. An indicator defines the specific measurement and means of verification that will be used to monitor and evaluate progress.

are we doing this, and who will benefit? You will address these questions in the following components of your plan: impacts, outcomes, outputs, indicators, and activities. Definitions and synonyms of these terms as used in this book are provided (table 4.1) and derived from current results-based management frameworks,[15] but note that different sectors and funders may use these terms differently.

Once again, project planning is best done collaboratively. Even if one staff member carries out the project, the plan benefits from many eyes. Review your project plan with others in your organization and key stakeholders. Be open to suggestions and expect things to change. You know what they say about the best-laid plans!

To begin a project plan, revisit your solution tree and identify your intended impacts, outcomes, and outputs. Framing these in discrete, measurable terms is good practice. In other words, how will you know when you've succeeded in achieving this impact? How will you know when you've completed this outcome? Answers to these questions are often clarified as "indicators" in project-planning parlance.

Once you have a list of impacts and their corresponding outcomes and outputs, consider the sequence of activities that will produce these outputs and outcomes, sometimes called a work breakdown structure. For each outcome and output, ask:

- What activities must be done?
- Who should complete each activity?
- How long will each activity take?
- What resources or supplies are required for each activity?
- How much will each activity cost in terms of labor and resources?

Identify dependencies in your list of activities to arrange their order: which activities rely on others to be completed first? Which can commence synchronously? If your project has critical deadlines, identify and mark them as "milestones." Then, review the estimated time for all activities leading to that milestone: will you be able to achieve that deadline? Revise and repeat until your schedule is complete and feasible. Follow a similar process for reviewing resources and costs.

Another program planning tool is a logic model (see appendix H). Typically used in programmatic evaluation, logic models are useful for creating and organizing a project plan. You can choose a graphic

Angela M. Labrador, Randi Korn, and Rebecca Dean

illustration or text outline to document your program purpose or needs statement, assumptions, required resources, outputs, outcomes, and impacts. Logic models are not meant to replace a detailed project plan or evaluation plan; they are a succinct way to link your resources to your activities, and then to your anticipated results, and ultimately to impact.

Crafting a detailed work schedule helps square lofty ambitions with reality. You may have to revise the scope of your outputs and outcomes to meet time and monetary constraints, but by the end of the process, you will have a complete list of activities with a timeline that will inform your budget.

CLARIFYING SUCCESS AND IDENTIFYING RISKS

Further Defining Impacts and Outcomes

A program's description of success should be determined while defining its impacts and should flow directly from the intentional planning and problem and solution tree exercises discussed above. Each impact can have multiple outcomes that serve as benchmarks or indicators toward that goal. A learning outcome, sometimes referred to as an objective, is a statement that clearly describes what a participant is expected to know, do, or achieve as a result of an experience. Chapter 1 briefly introduces Bloom's Taxonomy as a framework for creating outcomes using action verbs aligned with cognitive, affective, and psycho-motor domains of learning. Although there are numerous methods for creating learning outcomes, we provide an overview of SMARTE (Specific, Measurable, Attainable, Relevant, Time-Bound, and Equity-Minded), an approach that has been rigorously used for decades.[16] See appendix F for additional information and a guide to writing goals and outcomes.

If an outcome is *specific*, then it clearly defines the expected result. For example, an outcome for a speaker series on local archaeology could be, "audiences will learn that archaeologists use multiple excavation and survey methods," rather than the vaguer "audiences will learn about methods." Similarly, a staff-focused outcome could be, "host at least three lecturers on local archaeology during fall 2024," rather than "host a speaker series." If the outcome is *measurable* and *time-bound*, then some indicators for success are already built into it. In these examples, one knows that the outcomes were successfully met if staff hosted at least three lectures on local archaeology by the end of autumn and audiences demonstrated awareness of multiple archaeological methods.

Creating *attainable* and *equity-minded* outcomes requires experience on the part of the program director to know (a) what is possible to accomplish in the time remaining and (b) what barriers or challenges lead to inequality in the specific context. Setting unattainable outcomes will set you up for failure, while ignoring equity issues is particularly pernicious given the colonial history of archaeology. All programs must assess equity and inclusion (see chapter 3), particularly in relation to descendant communities. For example, research who is participating in the project compared to the demographics of community members and who feels comfortable and welcomed (or not) in the program environment (see chapter 2). If the program director lacks this knowledge, then it is past time to involve community partners in the planning process (see chapter 5).[17]

Finally, outcomes are *relevant* if they align with achieving impact and the program's overall mission. For example, hosting three lectures on local history is only a relevant output if it supports the impact, such as "community members increase their knowledge of local history" or "community members have increased access to local historical and archaeological research." If the program's outcome was, instead, "elementary students learn basic excavation techniques," then a lecture series would be an irrelevant output, regardless of how "SMARTE" it was.

Outputs can be used to define traditional or "meaningful" metrics of success, as defined earlier in this chapter. Traditional metrics of success, such as attendance, fundraising dollars, or volunteer hours, are easy to measure, even after the program. Meaningful metrics, such as audience engagement outcomes—increased knowledge or a community's sense of belonging—are not necessarily difficult or cumbersome to assess. Still, those aspirations need to be embedded in the program from the beginning, and therefore, the outcomes need to be defined from the beginning.

Defining success in terms of outcomes often identifies the steps needed to get there, just as it is often easier to solve a maze by starting at the end and going backward. Understanding by Design (or backward design), introduced in chapter 1, is an example of an educational framework for determining what needs to be in place for a program to "go right." The process begins with defining success, a big takeaway, or an enduring understanding. It continues with determining the activities needed to produce each output and achieve each outcome, and a specific determination of who will do them and when.[18] For example, if a desired outcome of your archaeology lecture series is that the public will have an increased awareness of local history, then every activity—from recruiting lecturers to creating publicity to assessment—needs to be laid out in detail and align with that outcome. The plans should include a timeline (frequently updated as needed), an indication of who is responsible for carrying out each task, and a list of necessary resources and activities; otherwise, critical steps might be missed.

Managing Risk

While careful, backward planning maximizes the chances of success, but no plan survives contact with reality. Fundamentally, plans must be living documents, continuously updated as circumstances change. Weather, pandemics, accidents, political or legal issues, and other upsetting factors cannot always be predicted.

In such an environment of uncertainty, it may not seem practical to develop highly detailed SMARTE outcomes with associated success metrics, a task timeline, and a list of individuals responsible for each task. But it is! The SMARTE approach makes it easier to achieve quick pivots in the face of disaster. Early identification of project assumptions can indicate areas to monitor. Ongoing assessments help identify emergent fracture points, and frequent reference to detailed plans makes it clear when outcomes are no longer feasible and need to be changed.

Better practices suggest that directors identify the most frequent problems that will affect their program, such as weather emergencies, low participation, or changes in venue. Write contingency plans for these specific challenges and prioritize the health and safety of staff and participants. This is where clearly defined impacts and SMARTE outcomes shine: they help identify the most critical components of a program and determine what can be sacrificed to reach the desired outcomes in less-than-perfect circumstances.

MANAGING THE PLAN AND NEXT STEPS

After you draft the plan, your work will shift to managing the project plan to stay on course and achieve its outcomes. Project management is a robust field of practice with many tools, best practices, and professional development opportunities. The same principles that guided your planning should guide your management: expect change, maintain flexibility, be mindful of risks, monitor progress toward outputs and outcomes, communicate and collaborate with your project team and stakeholders, and remain intentional.[19] It's easy to envision a project as a linear path, but remember the Cycle of Intentional Practice: project planning and managing are reflexive processes.

NOTES

1. Tim Crane, "Intentionality," in the *Oxford Companion to Philosophy New Edition*, 2nd ed., ed. Ted Honderich (Oxford: Oxford University Press, 2005), 438.
2. Pierre Jacob, "Intentionality," *The Stanford Encyclopedia of Philosophy Archive,* accessed June 13, 2023, https://plato.stanford.edu/archives/spr2023/entries/intentionality/.

3. Crane, "Intentionality," 438.
4. Simon Sinek, *Start with Why: How Great Leaders Inspire Everyone to Take Action* (New York: Penguin Group, 2009).
5. Stephen Covey, *The 7 Habits of Highly Effective People*, rev. ed. (1989; repr., New York: Free Press, 2004).
6. Randi Korn, "Creating Public Value through Intentional Practice," in *Museums and Public Value: Creating Sustainable Futures*, ed. Carol Ann Scott (London: Routledge, 2013), 31–43.
7. Doug Worts, "Measuring Museum Meaning: A Critical Assessment Framework," *Journal of Museum Education* 31, no. 1 (2006), 41–48; Barbara Soren, "Museum Experiences that Change Visitors," *Museum Management and Curatorship* 24, no. 3 (2009), 233–51.
8. Randi Korn, "The Case for Holistic Intentionality," *Curator: The Museum Journal* 50, no. 2 (2007), 255–64.
9. Donald A. Schön, *The Reflective Practitioner: How Professionals Think in Action* (New York: Basic Books, 1983); Joy Amulya, "What is Reflective Practice?" The Center for Reflective Community Practice at MIT, accessed June 13, 2023, www.itslifejimbutnotasweknowit.org.uk/files/whatisreflectivepractice.pdf.
10. Nick Merriman, ed., "Introduction: Diversity and Dissonance in Public Archaeology," in *Public Archaeology* (London: Routledge, 2004), 5–6.
11. Merriman, *Public Archaeology*.
12. Angela M. Labrador, "Integrating ICH and Education: A Review of Converging Theories and Methods," *International Journal of Intangible Heritage* 17 (2022), 18–36; Merriman, *Public Archaeology*.
13. Merriman, *Public Archaeology*.
14. European Integration Office, *Guide to The Logical Framework Approach: A Key Tool for Project Cycle Management* (Belgrade, 2011); NORAD, *The Logical Framework Approach (LFA): Handbook for Objectives-oriented Planning*, 4th ed. (Oslo: Norwegian Agency for Development Cooperation, Norwegian Agency for International Development, 1999).
15. UNESCO, *Results-Based Management (RBM) Approach as Applied at UNESCO: Guiding Principles* (Paris: UNESCO, 2022).
16. George T. Doran, "There's a S.M.A.R.T. Way to Write Management's Goals and Objectives," *Management Review* 70 (1981), 35–36.
17. Sonya Atalay, *Community-Based Archaeology: Research with, by, and for Indigenous and Local Communities* (University of California Press, 2012), 89–127; DivyaSamuga_Gyaanam+Bheda, "The Assessment Activist: A Revolutionary Call to Action," in *Reframing Assessment to Center Equity*, eds. Gavin W. Henning, Gianina R. Baker, Natasha A. Jankowski, Anne E. Lundquist, and Erick Montenegro (New York: Routledge, 2022); Linda Tuhiwai Smith, *Decolonizing Methodologies: Research and Indigenous Peoples*, 3rd ed. (London: Zed, 2021), 145–61.
18. L. Dee Fink, *Creating Significant Learning Experiences* (San Francisco: Jossey-Bass, 2003).
19. Project Management Institute, *The Standard for Project Management and A Guide to the Project Management Body of Knowledge (PMBOK® Guide)*, 7th ed. (Newtown Square, PA: Project Management Institute, Inc., 2021).

RECOMMENDED RESOURCES

Dionisio, Cynthia Snyder. *A Project Manager's Book of Templates*. Hoboken, NJ: John Wiley & Sons, 2023.
Korn, Randi. *Intentional Planning for Museums: A Guide for Maximizing Impact*. Lanham, MD: Rowman & Littlefield. 2018.
Project Management Institute. *The Standard for Project Management and A Guide to the Project Management Body of Knowledge (PMBOK® Guide)*, 7th ed. Newtown Square, PA: Project Management Institute, Inc., 2021.

5

Identifying and Procuring Collaborators and Resources

Bonnie Pitblado and Alexandra Jones

This chapter begins with the premise that you, the reader, have a sense for the sort of program, event, or initiative you wish to develop, and that you are reading these words because you seek guidance for bringing your idea to life. If that is the case, or if you simply want a sense for what it will take to launch a new undertaking, you are in the right place. We chapter authors, Bonnie Pitblado and Alexandra Jones, represent organizations and programs that we built from scratch through creative collaborations and with scant resources. Combined, we have many years of expertise building programs and learning from our successes and failures along the way.

Bonnie joined the University of Oklahoma (OU) as the Robert E. and Virginia Bell Professor of Anthropological Archaeology in 2012 and founded the Oklahoma Public Archaeology Network (OKPAN) in 2016 with two of her graduate students. OKPAN offers a wide array of community-engaged public programming. For a decade prior to OU, Bonnie directed the Utah State University (USU) Museum of Anthropology and was an associate professor of anthropology. Bonnie began her museum directorship with a zero-dollar budget and with a single, part-time undergraduate student staffer. Both the museum and OKPAN are now stably resourced and adequately staffed to provide a variety of public archaeology programming. Bonnie has a long track record of succeeding (and failing!) to launch new programs, events, exhibits, initiatives, partnerships, and other offerings for public audiences, doing so on shoestring budgets cobbled together from diverse sources.

Alexandra is the executive director for Archaeology in the Community (AITC), an archaeology education organization she founded in 2009. As an archaeology educator for more than sixteen years, Alexandra focuses on making archaeological knowledge accessible to all. She also directed field schools for junior high and high school students while working for the PBS television show, *Time Team America*. Alexandra started AITC with personal funds and a few volunteers, growing the organization and acquiring partnerships with numerous organizations and museums. AITC has expanded to fund and sustain diverse programs throughout the United States and its territories, as well as internationally.

We start with some broad-scale thoughts about the importance of building a strong foundation for any new offering, whether a discrete event or more elaborate long-term program. We then share ideas for (a) identifying and (b) procuring the collaborators and non-human resources necessary to make your vision a reality. We also provide hypothetical examples (strongly rooted in our own experiences) of how our ideas can work.

Figure 5.1. Dr. Jones teaching about archaeology at a high school in Belize. *Courtesy of Archaeology in the Community*

BUILDING A STRONG FOUNDATION FOR YOUR PROGRAM

The single most important step you can take when the kernel of an idea for a public program reveals itself is to remind yourself not to go it alone. Partnerships are your best friend, and they are the key to stretching your resources, human and otherwise. Public archaeology, as stressed throughout this guide, should be conducted in engagement with the communities it serves. Therefore, your first and most important partnerships will be with members of the communities that constitute your target audiences. Later, we will discuss how to identify and cultivate these partnerships.

In addition to forging partnerships early and often, we also encourage you to avoid reinventing any wheels. With over fifty years of formal public educational outreach behind the discipline of archaeology, you and your partners will be hard-pressed to think of a concept that has not been tried before. Whether a simple guest lecture, classroom visit, or "archaeology day," there are models out there that you can follow and organizers who would be happy to share them. Examples of many such projects can be found in section II of this book. Public archaeologists are a collegial bunch who want to share their successes and help you avoid their failures. For that matter, do not restrict yourself to the archaeological community. Anyone who has willingly engaged in outreach events cares about sharing what they know with others—including you.

We have mentioned "failure" a few times, because any successful public archaeologist also has a litany of past "failures" (defined as an outcome other than what they had in mind when they started). Precisely because the best public archaeology involves multiple partners engaging as equals to co-create something new, no single partner can entirely control the outcome of the process. But that is okay. In fact, if you are in it for the long haul, the process is more important than the outcome. So your guest lecture was poorly attended. It happens. But the relationship you built with your partner(s) can be leveraged in the future, and the next time around, you will figure out together how to pack the

Bonnie Pitblado and Alexandra Jones

Textbox 5.1. A Journey of Collaboration and Discovery in Maryland Indigenous History

Rico Newman

People know little to nothing about Indigenous history in this country. In my experience, modern Americans either think things started here around 1600, or they get "an Indian in their head" and see no difference between an Aztec or a Lakota or a Piscataway. This image can be hard to shift, but so much of Native life has vanished.

I am a member of the Choptico Band of the Piscataway community, and I didn't seek archaeology—it walked up on me. I became affiliated with the Maryland Commission on Indian Affairs in the late 1980s, and we hosted archaeology speakers who wanted our opinions about what to do with human remains that were in the possession of the Maryland Historical Trust. This subject is very personal to me, and my first reaction was not positive. I don't know where my ancestors are buried past my grandparents and it's only through oral history that we even know they existed. I demonized archaeologists, but our speakers were very calm and deliberate. I'm glad they came because it opened up an entirely new way of thinking about our history.

The Maryland Historical Trust provided us an inventory of the human remains in their possession, and this was the first time we knew these details. We formed a collaborative committee and after many years and many setbacks, we reinterred several individuals. This process moved the pendulum from focusing on just the opinions of the archaeology community to considering Tribal voices. At the same time, I was invited to many excavations and labs to see how archaeologists document without preconceptions. This impressed me.

Every opportunity I got, I became more engaged and hands-on. It was the thrill of my life to discover where a hunter buried a cache of blades along the Patapsco River but never returned to collect them. During another incredible moment, I was invited to see human remains unearthed by a farmer along the Potomac River. Archaeologists asked for my opinion of what to do with the remains of a woman, an infant, and a dog who were buried with grave goods and in a particular fashion and direction. I asked that these remains stay *in situ*, and it is my understanding that they remain there today.

Archaeologists want to know details about how my people were buried, but unless you collaborate with us, how will you know about our traditions? You only know what a burial bundle means if you bring us into the process. That said, I still have to rely on archaeologists to communicate their interpretations, and they don't always follow up. How else will I learn what they have discovered? I can't go to a library to find out!

Seek opportunities for a meeting of the minds to involve more Tribal people. You will get better attendance if you ask the community what they want to know about their history. Discuss what they want to hear, rather than what you want to tell them. Also consider ways to engage our youth. I had a conversation with a gardening group recently, as we agreed that when a kid plants something and watches it grow, we reinforce the relationship with the earth and spark an interest. Developing a curiosity about our history is the same thing. Use artifacts to talk about how our people used the soil and the river and the land. You can't get every Tribal kid involved, but hands-on archaeology education will catch a few who want to discover the meaning in our cultural material. Gotta keep swinging at it! If you don't swing, you won't hit anything.

house and send your audience home enriched. Be mindful and sensitive when developing partnerships with Indigenous or descendent communities. Building connections with groups who may be deeply invested in your findings can be a time-intensive effort. Although the journey to successful partnerships may be challenging, the rewards are substantial and worthwhile.

The concept of "leveraging" is important in public archaeology. We encourage you to not do too much too quickly. Rather, build programs and programming incrementally, using small successes to leverage increasingly larger ones. As you build and grow, mindfully spend periods of time in relative stasis, working to perfect what you are already doing, rather than racing to the next great program. Chapter 12 of this book discusses assessment. Read it and then collect and use your own assessment data to improve what you are already doing before moving onto something else.

Finally, before we drill down on identifying and procuring partners and tangible resources, we suggest that you prepare yourself to seek out "yes" people and conduct evasive measures when confronted with "no" people. "Yes" people believe that most anything is possible; you need only figure out together *how* to accomplish your goal. "No" people are those who either cannot or choose not to divert from the status quo. "No" people are not bad people; they just are not the folks who will help you accomplish what you want to do. Do not fight them; instead, smile and seek out a "yes" person instead.

IDENTIFYING COLLABORATORS AND RESOURCES

With the preceding foundational principles in mind, let us move on to the nitty-gritty of identifying the human and non-human resources you will need to bring your public program to fruition. Most undertakings will require three elements: people to plan, market, execute, and assess it; physical space to prepare and host it; and funding, supplies, and equipment to carry it from inception to execution to assessment. The more thoroughly and concretely you plan, the more smoothly your program will unfold.

As mentioned, your most important collaborators are members of the communities you aim to serve with your undertaking. The sooner you identify these core partners, the better. That said, there is necessarily a chicken-and-egg dynamic at play in the earliest stages of any community-engaged public archaeology pursuit. You need to have *some* idea of what you want to do, toward what end, and with whom, or you will find it hard to start conversations with prospective partners. However, if your vision is too concrete, you will limit the degree to which you and your future partners can co-create something fresh and of maximum use to your audience.

Our best advice for starting this process is to think not in terms of activities, but in terms of your programmatic goals (see chapter 4). For example, rather than asking yourself who to sponsor as a guest lecturer, ask instead who you want to reach and what you want them to learn. Perhaps you have observed that high school students who visit your small museum have no idea that one can make a living as an archaeologist. Consider how you could change that and who could help you do so effectively. Remember that you do not need to have all the answers; that is what core partners are for.

In this case, you might convene a working group consisting of teenagers and their parents (your audience), high school teachers (those trained to teach your audience), professional archaeologists (those practicing what you think needs preaching), and intellectuals with organic links to the archaeological record (the people we believe all archaeology should serve). This working group is a great place to present your challenge of how to expose high school students to careers in archaeology and with whom to brainstorm solutions. That might or might not lead you to a guest lecture. If it does, you have a team in place that can help figure out who has the qualifications and qualities needed to deliver a lecture that accomplishes your collective goals. If the brainstorming leads to a different activity that may have more impact on high school students, that is even better.

Once you and your partners have conceptualized your program, you can move on to establishing what is needed to bring it to fruition. A basic spreadsheet will do the trick. Create workbooks or spreadsheet sections for personnel, facilities, supplies, and any other major categories relevant to

Figure 5.2. "Voices of Oklahoma" interns at a Sac and Fox Nation health fair. Each summer, "Voices" convenes high school students from backgrounds traditionally excluded from archaeology to learn and teach others about archaeology and how it can serve contemporary communities. *Courtesy of Kaylyn Moore, Oklahoma Public Archaeology Network*

your program (e.g., "transportation") (see appendix C). Then list everything you may need within each category in as much detail as possible. You are double-dipping here, by (a) creating a concrete guide to what your program will require that can (b) readily be turned into a program budget.

Work with your partners as you develop your spreadsheet, because they will think of line items relevant to their domains of expertise that are not apparent to you. Consider "hidden" program requirements; items that may be required as prerequisites for your more obvious needs (see chapter 6). For instance, if your program involves bringing high school students to your facility, you will need to list some form of transportation for them. Less obvious may be the background checks required for the drivers and others who will interact with your adolescent audience. Reach out to people who have previously hosted similar programs to see what you might be missing, rather than learning the hard way that you failed to account for x, y, or z. Once you and your partners finalize program needs, you can turn your attention to fulfilling them.

PROCURING COLLABORATORS AND RESOURCES

It is one thing to identify prospective partners; it is another to convince them to work with you. The key here is thinking in terms of *others'* currencies. What matters to you may not matter at all to them, and vice versa. In some cases, you and a prospective partner may very well have intersecting interests that can be leveraged such that by joining forces, you both get something that you value.

In our high school program example, why should teenagers, teachers, professionals, and community members even talk to you, let alone collaborate to devise a program to teach kids about jobs in archaeology? You cannot know everything that matters to communities other than your own (that is why you need their partnership in the first place), but you can make some educated guesses that will get you started.

Most teenagers are thinking about what they will do with the rest of their lives, and it is reasonable to expect at least some of them to be open to a career that blends the joy of outdoor physical labor with unraveling mysteries about the human past. Teachers are overworked and undercompensated, so they may be receptive to programs that shoulder a bit of their burden without creating new ones. Cultural resource managers need a constant supply of workers, and many also value the opportunity to reach and influence the next generation of professionals. Community members might like to see their kids presented with a career choice that can allow them to serve and preserve their own communities' tangible and intangible heritage.

The same principle of establishing the nature of "currencies" for prospective partners can also guide your procurement of the human resources needed to execute your co-created program. If you do land on a guest lecture as a desirable offering, what can you offer the person who you and your partners have identified as the perfect speaker? The more time you spend thoughtfully establishing your "pitch" (i.e., what is in it for the speaker), the more likely they are to agree to give the lecture you seek. Who in your working group is best positioned to make the ask? Someone with a prior relationship with the prospective speaker is likelier to get a "yes" than is a cold caller.

This is a good place to point out that students at various stages in their education make potent partners and project participants, and not just for those working in educational settings. For students, an opportunity to learn, add to their CV, and expand their professional network are discrete currencies. Students are also often financially challenged, so a cash stipend can be an important, literal currency.

Other less obvious currencies may also matter to students. For example, many young people seek social connections, so a program that provides an opportunity to expand their social network may appeal. Or perhaps they are members of a club or organization that requires them to earn service or internship hours. In fact, a single well-designed outreach program could tick all these boxes for prospective student staffers.

Public archaeologists in universities have an obvious advantage in terms of access to students to staff public outreach projects and programs. However, any organization with a college or university nearby can also take advantage of that labor pool. If you work in a small museum, reach out to faculty in allied departments, which could include anthropology, but also classics, history, geography, education, and others. Browse faculty and staff web pages for scholars who list outreach as an area of interest or expertise and start with them. Or ask a department chair about who on their faculty might be willing to partner with your organization (remembering when you contact them to think about what *their* currency as a department head might be; give them a reason to help you).

Non-Human Resources

Although people are the most important resource for any outreach undertaking, you will also need a location, equipment, and supplies to plan, execute, and implement it. Depending on your organization, space may or may not be readily available. Even if it is available, it may not be obvious how to reserve and access it. You also need to think from your audience's perspective; will everyone, including anyone with limited mobility, be able to park and readily make their way to the ninth floor or down a trail to find you?

Those in university settings should budget time and patience for navigating their institutions' facilities management and parking services. Beware that you may need to reserve a classroom sev-

Bonnie Pitblado and Alexandra Jones

eral months out from an event or, counterintuitively, there may only be a small window for doing so at a certain point after regular classes have been scheduled. Often, it can pay to host events off-campus. Universities are off-putting for many prospective visitors, for pragmatic or sometimes psychological reasons.

Public libraries can be superb places to host events, with free room use, ample parking, and a welcoming atmosphere. Outdoor venues like city parks can be similarly excellent for fair-weather events, although be prepared to navigate local requirements for insurance that may or may not be a deal-breaker. If you are affiliated with a university, such a request should go to your risk management office, which can direct you to the person who can provide you with a certificate of insurance.

If you think back to our suggestion to seek out "yes" people, the reality is that nearly anything is possible. If you and your partners dream up what seems initially like a pie-in-the-sky idea, do not be too quick to set it aside. It can be surprisingly easy to, say, rent out an entire movie theater for a showing—with treats—of some archaeologically themed film. The first theater you ask might refuse you, but the second might love to partner to sponsor an "Indiana Jones" matinee with a post-film discussion of what the movie got right and wrong about archaeology.

You will notice that we have not yet mentioned fundraising to cover the costs of your program. That is because once you have your spreadsheet list of everything you need, you should start checking off the items you have or can procure for free or as a "cost-share" from a partner. Collaboration gives you access to both your network of resources and to those of all your partners as well. The more partners you have, the more items on your "needs" list you will collectively be able to cover without using valuable time to procure external funding.

This process of gathering resources also goes for space, equipment, and supplies. Those in university settings or in organizations in a position to partner with people in universities are sitting on a gold mine of resources. It may not always feel that way; universities are notorious for their seemingly effortless ability to make even the simplest task complicated. But bear with them. Take the time to get to know folks who actively want to help you. Be strategic about this: who has been conducting outreach for thirty years at your local university? Call and ask if they would be willing to share how they get things done over a cup of coffee (coffee and companionship are themselves powerful currencies). Ask them straight up about "yes" people to seek out and "no" people to avoid. Remember, do not reinvent any wheels.

A certain fearlessness will take you a long way in the quest to compile your wish list of supplies and equipment. Even if it feels like a long shot that a theater department, itself probably strapped for cash, might want to donate scrap wood from set building so that you can create an educational activity for sixth graders, all they can say is "no," and they might say "yes." When you make an ask like this, always be ready with a follow-up question to the prospective "no," phrased something like, "I understand completely why you cannot help. Might you suggest a local business that would be willing to donate some of their scrap wood to our cause?"

On the nature of "the ask," keep in mind that (a) most people are busy most of the time, and (b) everyone has a preferred method of communication. This means you need to find a way to be adaptable and persistent without being off-putting. You may prefer sending requests via email, because that way you will not have to listen to a live "no." Some will welcome such interaction because they can attend to your request at a time that is convenient for them.

But sometimes, and nearly always when it is time to follow up on an unanswered email, a phone call works better. Some people prefer human contact and will answer a phone, whereas they might ignore an email. Others are simply conditioned to respond with more urgency to a ringing phone than to an email that can languish for months in an inbox. Throughout all of this, be polite and remember that the process is always as important as the outcome. Even if you get a "no" to whatever you are asking for this time around, with some intentionality in your approach, you can build a relationship that might yield a "yes" to a different request down the line.

Funding

Once you have exhausted your ability to assemble resources through your network of partners, it is—finally—time to seek external funding. At the most general level, that funding will come from grants and/or donors. This is not the place to exhaustively discuss all your fundraising options or tips for granting success because many excellent resources already exist to guide you through this. However, we will share a few broad-scale thoughts and suggestions.

Donations

First, private donations offer some advantages over money obtained through a formal grant application process. If you can establish a positive working relationship with a core donor or two who will write you a modest check when you need it, this will provide you with a level of flexibility and nimbleness that those dependent on grant funding do not have. While it may seem unlikely that people like this are out there, waiting to write checks for your offerings, they are. Your job is to identify and cultivate them using the same strategies we discussed previously: recognize what can be "in it" for them to work with you and build a relationship that realizes that value.

Keep in mind, too, that donations can come not just from individuals, but from businesses. Businesses, both local and larger, have good reasons for giving to nonprofits and universities in their communities; many have corporate giving arms and encourage their employees to volunteer and donate (through paid time off and/or donation matching). Often this is as simple as needing the tax break associated with donating to a cause. Many businesses have mechanisms in place to accept requests for cash or "in-kind" donations of materials they sell. So, for instance, you might find that your local big box store has a ready-made process for fielding requests for $100 worth of paper plates, cups, and other supplies for a reception at which their business can be credited for its largesse. Businesses want to know what is in it for them, so be sure this is part of your request.

Grants

If you must grant-write, choose your grant sources using a cost-benefit screening process. When considering whether a particular granting program is worth targeting, ask yourself how much of your remaining budget the source can fulfill, how long and involved the grant application is, and what is the typical rate of success. If you only need a small amount of money, you do not want to apply for a federal grant that will take eighty hours to write and promises only a 20 percent success rate. If you need a lot of money, you should not waste time with the small grant options. Save those for an undertaking of a scale that better matches their capacity. In pursuing a larger grant, consider who can be the recipient of the funding (nonprofit, government agency, university). If you or your institution do not qualify to apply, perhaps one of your partners does and can take the lead.

How does one go about identifying prospective grant sources? A Google search may get you started, but platforms dedicated to consolidating grant opportunities are powerful and offer a better way to identify opportunities. Some such services are free. For example, Grants.gov allows users to both search and apply for federal grants, cost-share agreements, and other awards. Others, such as GrantForward, are subscription-based, with fees typically based on the size of the organization. GrantForward and other databases like it can lead you to international, federal, state, foundation, corporate and various other grant sources that would be otherwise hard to find. Readers who work in university settings should contact their Sponsored Programs office to ask about subscriptions their university already has and how to obtain a user account. Faculty, staff, and often graduate students are usually entitled to such accounts, another reason for those outside of universities to seek university partners.

Contracts

Another increasingly common source of funding for public outreach is contracting in Cultural Resource Management (CRM). Section 106 compliance is a public process, conducted with public funding. Many agencies are recognizing the value of including outreach activities in project proposals, particularly for larger undertakings and creative mitigations. Such activities include project-focused public lectures, digital and print interpretive or educational resources, and K–12 classroom visits. Sometimes agencies approach their CRM partners about ideas for public programs. Other times, firms integrate a public outreach component into their proposals and budgets, which may get cut. However, if we don't ask and ask often, funding for outreach will never become the convention in compliance archaeology.

SUMMARY

We have tried in this chapter to provide advice that will help you get started in the world of public archaeology programming, an arena in which an "it takes a village" mentality carries the day. Partnerships allow you to do more with less, while also ensuring that the programming you develop serves its target audiences. We all dream of robust operating budgets, but most of us do not have the luxury of managing one. The antidotes are creativity, persistence, and a willingness to work with and understand the many organizations involved in your project. We particularly recommend paying close attention to others' currencies—what they value—and to interests you may share in common. Such knowledge will go a long way in helping you build relationships to create meaningful programs that enrich people in the ways you intend.

6

Embracing Logistics Planning

David A. Brown and Thane H. Harpole

The best public archaeology programs set aside time and energy to identify and implement essential logistical components before the first day. Those who are exceptionally disciplined will budget time afterward (and between projects) to renew, update, and improve these components. What are these mysterious essentials? We're talking about legal considerations like liability insurance and consent forms, budgeting, and marketing. These are your unsung heroes, your hardest working and often most foreign project elements. They help keep you from getting sued, going bankrupt, and wondering, "Why is no one attending my program?" These logistics seem boring but ignore them at your own peril. The work you invest here will keep your team focused. If done well, you will have peace of mind. If that voice in the back of your head is wondering if something is necessary, it probably is.

In this chapter, we break down often intimidating, obtuse, and misunderstood concepts and provide advice about when and how to implement various logistics. Remember, we are not lawyers, accountants, or marketing professionals. You may need to consult these experts before your project launches. We're just archaeologists who would rather you make new mistakes than the ones we've already made. We aim to introduce some basics to help prepare you to communicate knowledgeably with your project partners, hosts, and participants and converse with consultants who can help you craft the specific documents you need for safety, success, and sustainability. It is ultimately up to you to determine what is needed for your program.

LEGAL CONSIDERATIONS

Archaeological training does not typically include classes on mitigating risk or general liability, but we frequently hear stories about mishaps during field or lab projects, for example, the time "Timmy" got such a bad case of poison ivy that he looked like an MMA fighter after a match. Such stories are often the most memorable part of a class or project. Accidents happen, and many public programs benefit from an audience who is prepared for their experience, whether that entails doing manual labor in extreme environments and weather conditions, using sharp objects, or practicing an unfamiliar task in a classroom. Your job as the program planner is to ensure that you have protections in place for your audience and your team, such as permission forms, liability waivers, liability insurance, and other safety considerations.

Preparing and Protecting Participants

Program participants are your most important and least knowledgeable audience. They may be wholly unaware of your expectations for them or unfamiliar with the location, protocols, or equipment. Whether they are moving heavy buckets, handling delicate objects, or rotating through activity stations, you should spend significant time preparing them for the experience and setting reasonable expectations. This can be accomplished through orientations, tours, or a registration form that clearly lists potential hazards of participation. Place a limit on the number of participants per instructor to ensure your audience receives personal attention and supervision, timely answers to their questions, and guidance on how to successfully participate. Maintaining a small instructor-to-participant ratio elevates the experience and builds a relationship of trust. It also increases the likelihood of a positive takeaway that results in good "word of mouth" advertising and encourages returnees to bring friends and family to future programs.

For programs at active archaeological sites, an introductory tour establishes familiarity between the participant and the project team. It also provides time for safety briefings to cover frequently encountered problems. Registration forms are a familiar, convenient, often web-based resource that gives your audience permission to share with you information that will ensure their experience is a positive one. They are useful tools for any public programs where you need to limit participation, set advanced expectations, or notify participants of potential concerns. Most volunteers expect a form and understand that the experienced professional who created these forms has thought out the issues highlighted in each question, especially regarding youth-focused projects.

Preparing and Protecting Your Team

Your team and audience are equally important. Preparing your team for the program is essential because we are just as susceptible as participants to many of the issues highlighted above, even when we are a "team of one." Your team is essential to your program's identity. They will provide instruction and guidance and look out for potential problems before they happen.

Making sure your team is comfortable and prepared to assist your audience will result in their feeling more confident and capable. This can be done through training, creating a thoughtful physical

Figure 6.1. To ensure the best possible experience for participants, maintain a sufficient professional/volunteer ratio. During heavily attended events, choose an area that is well suited for controlling foot traffic when possible. Here, the public is separated from the dig by a brick wall. *Courtesy of The Fairfield Foundation*

David A. Brown and Thane H. Harpole

presence, and listening (and responding) to your team before, during, and after the program. Training is the most important and crucial first step. The team must be familiar with the site or location, the programmatic goals and outcomes, and the rationale for the methodology or procedures employed. Team members need to be allowed to improvise or innovate but should know their role and have a safety net of complementary staff support for when things go wrong. And things will definitely go wrong. Not everyone needs training in every area, but they must be patient and kind and believe in the benefits of public outreach. The best public archaeologists are prepared to be passionate, positive, and helpful throughout any program.

The team will operate best if you create a thoughtful physical presence by looking and acting like a cohesive unit. It doesn't have to cost much. Simple elements like matching T-shirts or name tags communicate professionalism and help your audience identify those who can assist or answer questions.

If you are in a rugged location, minor improvements to the site can create a safer environment that facilitates learning and focuses participants on the tasks at hand. Shade stations, bathroom facilities, coolers, first aid kits, chairs, and tables all provide relief for the audience and your team.

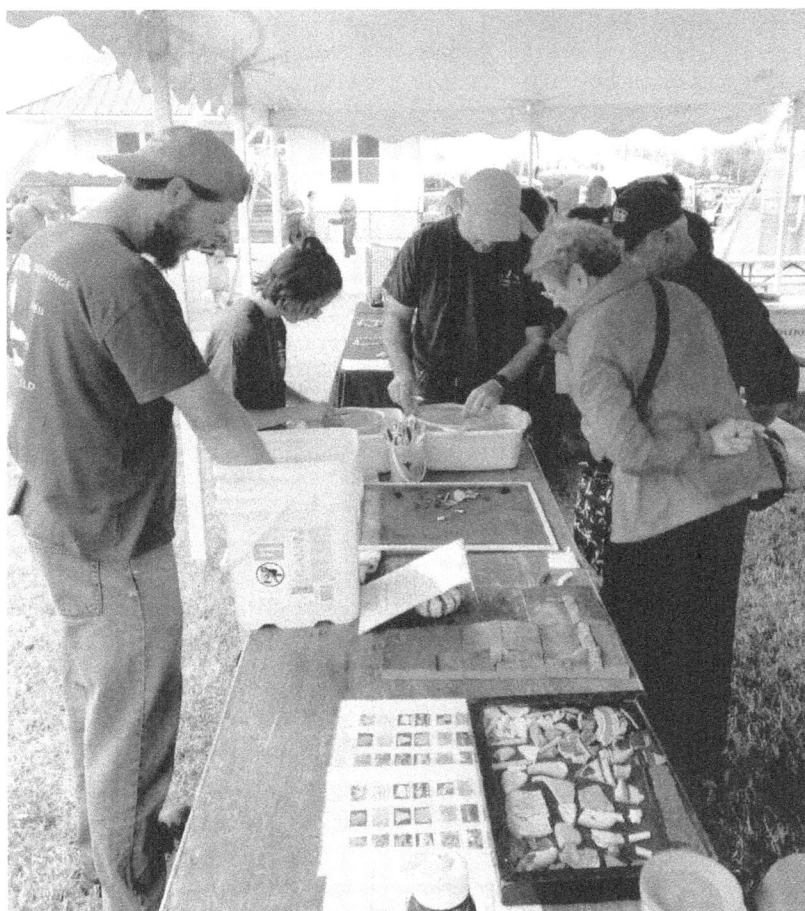

Figure 6.2. Processing collections with public assistance can be an excellent activity for those who cannot dig but still want to get their hands dirty. Providing washbasins, toothbrushes, and drying racks is important, but don't forget towels and other supplies for participants to help them feel comfortable. *Courtesy of The Fairfield Foundation*

Such amenities also encourage break times, conversations, networking, and camaraderie, which are essential to promote learning, avoid injuries, and sustain your team. It is also important to listen to suggestions and criticisms. No program is perfect, but involving your team in planning, implementing, and improving the program will lead to better results.

Liability Insurance and Waivers

Insurance is not a scam. It will give you, your team, and your stakeholders peace of mind. It is crucial because accidents do happen, no matter how well you've planned. Depending on the host location, program sponsor, or your place of employment, you may not be responsible for acquiring insurance, but you should investigate what/who it covers and when/where/how to proceed if any inadvertent situations arise. Working with a large corporation, agency, or university might lead you to believe certain logistics are covered, but it is best not to take anything for granted. Identify any gaps in the coverage. It is not always easy to find funding for full or supplemental coverage, so shop around for a good policy that covers what you need. It is your safety net.

Similarly, liability waivers are important. They acknowledge up front that there are risks: holes are deep, bugs bite, and laboratories are full of sharp objects and chemicals. Having a thorough understanding of potential risks will help participants be better prepared, and they will know that you take this seriously. Waivers also provide an opportunity in advance for participants to give consent to appear in photographs or video and the use of their likeness in promotional materials or on social media, rather than you having to track them down later (see below). See example templates in appendix D.

Waivers and insurance may not help or be necessary in every instance, but they are still very important considerations. It only takes one bad mistake to end your program and cause serious financial or career harm to you and your team.

Working with Minors

Before having direct contact with minors, check with your place of employment or academic institution and the host school or organization to identify their policies. There may be a required background check or training course to complete prior to a program. In formal educational settings in the United States, training on the Family Educational Rights and Privacy Act (FERPA) may also be necessary. Sometimes these requirements are dependent on your role in the program, like if you are the primary instructor for a camp at your site. Other times, there are requirements regardless of the supervision structure in place. These rules may also apply in certain distance learning situations involving live interaction on video. There are exemptions to these policies, such as when a child attends an event with a parent or guardian; however, these may also vary per organization. It is your responsibility to research the applicable policies and complete all requirements before you interact with children.

Photography and Video

It is always ethical, and often a legal requirement, to gain someone's permission before capturing their image. This includes all program attendees, as well as staff, students, and volunteers. Additionally, if someone is clearly identifiable in your footage, you need their explicit permission to use their image in academic presentations, marketing, publications, communications, or public display, including social media. Typically, your place of employment or school will have an established policy; if not, work with the appropriate experts to create a policy. Many academic institutions have a media release form or waiver template available to use or adapt. For those who do not wish to consent, provide instructions on how they can opt out. Maintain documentation on all approved and disapproved consent. Be aware of any specific moments during a program or event where you should not be taking photos or video. When working with a descendant community or other cultural or religious groups, ask about protocols ahead of time.

In public spaces or at large, open events, there are more limited expectations of privacy. If you want to take an intentional photo or close-up, that is the time to obtain permission. You can post a large, conspicuous notice at all entrances that clearly state photos and videos may be taken. When taking video, ask people being filmed to verbally express their permission on the recording. If your program or event is only open to registered or invited participants, notify them about media in advance on invitations or event announcements. Research how your state or country defines a private versus public place because consent requirements vary. For digital programs where people use webcams, all the rules about permissions for recording and use still apply.

Never take or use footage of a minor, in person or digitally, without obtaining and documenting explicit consent from a parent or guardian. Clearly communicate all possible uses for the image and anticipate some variability in the permissions. For example, some parents may be okay with their child's image appearing in an academic presentation or annual report but not on publicly viewable social media. In school classrooms or other school-sanctioned programs, teachers or administrators often document advance permission from parents for certain situations or events, in which case you do not need to collect individual forms. Always communicate with school staff ahead of time to determine what is or isn't permissible. In certain situations, photos or video of students are considered educational records and are protected under FERPA. There are also occasions when children are in protective care and cannot have their image circulated. The teacher will not point out those children, but they will make you aware of the situation.

MARKETING

Archaeology is cool. It is the one thing about our profession that is inarguable (yes, we are biased). But no matter how interesting and inspiring your public archaeology program is, no one will know about it unless you market it. This is not to say that every person you connect with will be interested. Your goal is to spread the word about your program, focusing on quality over quantity and effective and efficient engagement.

It is crucial to set reasonable expectations. Success is arbitrary and you need to define your marketing goals before you start. Ask yourself essential questions:

- Who is the program for?
- How many participants can you accommodate?
- What marketing strategies will most effectively reach your target audience?

This is where effective and efficient planning comes into play. You and your team have finite resources, including time, energy, and funding. Your challenge is to identify when and where to expend those resources. Strategies like print versus digital media or word of mouth versus direct solicitation are not always "either/or," and you may experience substantial trial and error. In most situations, you should choose options that have multiple benefits. For instance, while a standard press release may be limited to the media outlets in your local area, writing it is an excellent opportunity to concisely describe the program and solicit quotes from past participants or current team members. You can edit or expand the release to use for blogs, social media posts, radio pitches, or other needs.

Reaching Your Target Audience

Chapter 2 provides an overview of understanding your audience in order to effectively engage with them. Marketing also requires you to know your prospective audience and consider their motivations.

Having created an efficient description for your target audience, it is essential to ask yourself, "Is this effective?" and "Am I meeting them where they are?" Review what you've produced with an eye toward removing barriers and increasing accessibility. Use language that is easily understood, accurate, and positive, and provide details your audience needs to know. This information may be different than what you consider essential. Remember, your team can provide criticism and suggestions. A diverse team that includes individuals of different ages, nationalities, and identities can not only offer different perspectives on how to better reach various audiences but also help others feel more comfortable about participating in your programs.

Setting Expectations and Determining Success for Marketing

Chapter 4 provides an overview of setting intentions and determining success for your programs. It is important to return to these points when marketing. How will you know if your marketing communication is successful or if you will achieve your desired results? You might measure this based on overall reach, attendance, pre-registrations, or an increase in your social media followers or listserv members. Your marketing strategy should include a description of your target audience; which media format(s) will most effectively reach them; a budget that includes printing and shipping, advertisement space, and social media post promotion; and most importantly—your time.

The basic rule of thumb is to aim for quality over quantity while marketing. How many people can realistically attend your program? Do you want five hundred people emailing you about your one-week kids' camp? How many inquiries can you review and follow up with? Strategize where your target audience is most likely to see your marketing. An avocational society listserv, school newsletter, or local newspaper may get more traction than a social media post in some situations. Similarly, research audience demographics and analytics for your various social media channels—they do not all reach the same people.

Whether through a comment on social media or across your archaeology fair table, the most effective marketing includes testimonials that result from a positive experience. In our experience, the foundation of sustainability in public archaeology is built from organic marketing. People may tell others about the amazing program you offered that made a difference in their lives, no matter how small.

It is also useful to have a press kit for the news media, project collaborators, and other partners (see appendix E). Sharing such materials online or before the program can help keep everyone on the same page and prevent errors or misconceptions. We frequently encounter mistakes in news articles, like misspelled names or organizations, incorrect titles or affiliations, and misrepresented descendant community members. You want your program, your organization, and yourself to be represented as accurately as possible.

BUDGETING

Budgeting is about more than just money because time and labor are your most precious resources. Your plan should acknowledge the commitment necessary to host a successful program or event. Ultimately, the budget process is not designed to make you question the worth of your project (but it will). Its benefit is to help you recognize what is required to be successful.

Thinking Beyond the Big Day

The "day of" part of the program plan is easy to comprehend. For example, your public field day might require you to arrive by 8 a.m. and leave at 6 p.m. Trowels, dustpans, wash bins, toothbrushes, check. Three staff and two volunteers, check. Done? Nope. Not even close. Go back through your plan and imagine everything you might use and all the stuff you need to do this "right" (see appendix C).

David A. Brown and Thane H. Harpole

You will likely break much of it down between personnel, equipment, and supplies. Under "personnel," consider not only hourly rates but also fringe benefits and overtime. If staff or volunteers are donating their time and effort, document these contributions as an in-kind match. This will provide your future program plans with a more realistic cost estimate. Personnel also includes honoraria. Never overlook compensation for partners, collaborators, and consultants, including descendant community members and subject matter experts. While some may return it as a donation, others need these funds to continue their excellent work. This compensation reflects your commitment, recognition, and respect for those who are providing their time and knowledge.

Equipment (mostly permanent) and supplies (largely short-term and/or disposable) should almost always be budgeted at least 20 percent higher than your calculations, either because you may underestimate your needs or something will break or get lost during the program. Other common budget items include travel (vehicle rental, mileage, per diem, and/or accommodation for your team and possibly volunteers or community partners), venue rentals, and meals, snacks, and beverages.

Hidden costs are almost always incurred before and after the program. Some archaeologists ignore them or pay out of pocket. How many times have you paid for those end-of-day freeze pops or cold sodas? All program-related expenses should be considered and classified as such, no matter how insignificant they seem. Hidden costs leading up to a program include meetings and correspondence; creating program plans and agendas; preparing forms; recruiting staff, volunteers, and presenters; arranging travel bookings, venues, food, etc.; developing copy, marketing materials, and social media content; and purchasing supplies. Depending on your program format, you may have to acquire permits or prepare for field and lab work. Post-program costs include marketing your program success, doing program evaluation or assessment, paying bills, closing out budget lines, and completing grant or other funding reports. If the project is field-based, your event day(s) may be followed by site clean-up, artifact processing, cataloging, curation, research, and report writing. Costs like liability insurance and overhead start before your project and do not end with backfilling.

See appendix C for small and large event budget examples.

Overhead

Overhead is frequently ignored when budgeting. It covers recurring expenses (power, water, insurance, rent, etc.) that are difficult to assign to specific programs but are vital to your organization's success. Overhead costs are notoriously difficult to justify in proposals, but special programs do not exist in a vacuum. Your place of employment may already have a standard proposal budget that includes these costs, based on current or projected fiscal year rates. If not, pick a reasonable percentage to budget for overhead. It is universally accepted among businesses that charging for these costs is not only legitimate but a reflection of a professional organization that acknowledges what it takes to operate successfully.

Assessment and Evaluation

Evaluation and assessment are often forgotten, ignored, or compiled anecdotally after the fact. They are frequently cut from a budget when money is tight. They may be a costly addition to your budget but they are worth every penny. Done well, with thoughtful questions and accessible, well-timed engagement, assessment data will provide constructive criticism and encouraging feedback that may bolster your confidence in the program's effectiveness and document your success and impact. Consistently evaluating every public program will help you increase positive engagement and adapt future programs to the changing needs and desires of the audience. The process and the resulting data are rarely redundant. Use evaluation feedback and testimonials for future marketing, advocacy, and funding proposals. See chapter 12 for an in-depth overview of evaluation and assessment.

You Get What You Pay For

It is true that you can pull off a public archaeology program for little to no cost. Our recommendations are not meant to dissuade you from pursuing an amazing archaeology outreach program just because it might cost more than you thought. Your passion for sharing the past with the present for the future is not just a bumper sticker. The goal of this book is to help you create effective and impactful public programs. You deserve adequate equipment, a talented support team, and safety measures in place to lower risks and ensure the best chance at a positive and transformative experience for you and your audience. Outreach should not be an unpaid or underpaid add-on to other work or academic responsibilities; don't pay anyone less than a professional, living wage for this work. Invest the time to do it right from the start. People will notice, your peers included, and it will result in more opportunities and funding as others realize the vital nature of what you provide.

MANAGING THE NEXT STEPS

The lesson from this chapter is to embrace logistics planning. Some of what we described are elements you're undoubtedly aware of and likely completed as part of a prior program. You may have organized these logistics intuitively but did not acknowledge them as essential, or you did not consider them as interesting or high priority. We hope you recognize the importance of planning logistics and the time and effort required to reduce and mitigate risks. The advantage to embracing good planning is that it becomes exponentially easier with each new program, and this work will continue to inform and streamline your next event.

Think carefully about the overall structure of your program and avoid common pitfalls of forgotten planning logistics. This chapter is not your only resource; it is a comprehensive introduction. Because you're already interested in archaeology outreach, we know you are public-oriented. Be confident about reaching out to others to share what you know. There are others like you in various professions who will prove vital to your mastery of planning and implementing successful outreach programs. Reach out to lawyers, accountants, nonprofit managers, colleagues, and longtime volunteers to ask for input. Friendly advice is a low-cost opportunity for learning, but it can also build bridges across disciplines and forge mutual connections within your community. Connecting with other public archaeologists is also invaluable. Learning from their challenges and successes will prevent you from reinventing the wheel or making dire mistakes. These relationships will benefit your first program and all others that follow.

Implementing Public Archaeology Programs and Events

7

Fairs, Talks, Tours, and More

ALL-AGES PROGRAMMING

Stephanie T. Sperling, Meredith Anderson Langlitz, and Sara Ayers-Rigsby

While some public archaeology programming is designed for specific groups or demographics, most of our outreach is open to people of varying ages and backgrounds. Because we cannot anticipate who may attend our in-person or virtual programs, we need to create formats that are suitable for multiple publics. Any given event might attract multigenerational participants from a range of cultural, educational, and professional backgrounds, all of whom you will strive to engage and educate together.

Although sometimes challenging, all-ages events can be extremely fun and rewarding and align with your strengths, capacity, and outreach goals. In this chapter, we explore programs that are conducted virtually, at your own site, in public locations like libraries or festivals, or in areas of archaeological significance including parks, waterways, and historic properties. We include planning and implementation considerations and address common challenges.

Several approaches, including site tours, hands-on excavation and lab opportunities, or outdoor recreation events, attract visitors under the rubric of cultural heritage tourism. The National Trust for Historic Preservation defines this as "travel to experience the places, artifacts, and activities that authentically represent the stories and people of the past and present, including cultural, historic, and natural resources,"[1] although many people are drawn to explore places near their own communities. Other programs, like lectures, booths at fairs or similar events, and livestreamed or online programs could qualify as a different type of heritage tourism that brings archaeology to varying populations.

In all these cases, the National Trust's five principles for successful and sustainable cultural heritage tourism can be guiding lights when developing both in-person and virtual programming:[2]

1. *Collaborate*. Partnerships are vital to creating and implementing a strong, effective program.
2. *Find the fit*. Think about community needs and what works for you and your organization.
3. *Make sites/programs come alive*. Be creative, interactive, and find connections.
4. *Focus on quality and authenticity*. Make your program valuable and genuine.
5. *Preserve and protect*. Create a shared sense of responsibility to promote sustainable and responsible cultural resource management.

Keeping these principles in mind will help you create successful archaeological programs that will promote community awareness and understanding of local history, provide educational opportunities for people of all ages, and ensure diverse perspectives are considered and respected.

COMMON APPROACHES TO ALL-AGES PROGRAMMING

The possibilities are endless when it comes to all-ages programming. While public archaeologists have undoubtedly come up with more ways to engage the public than presented here, this section covers some of the more popular options, including lectures, virtual engagement, fairs/booths/roadshows, site visits and tours, volunteer field and lab days, and outdoor recreation opportunities.

Lectures

Lectures are a long-enduring and common form of public outreach. Nearly every archaeologist gives some sort of in-person or virtual presentation at least once during their career. We frequently present our research to the public at community events sponsored by local libraries, nature centers, civic organizations, and historical societies. At other times, you may be the event organizer and will need to solicit speakers and secure a venue. Regardless of the location and audience, public lectures should be conducted with learning outcomes, audience demographics, and accessibility in mind.

Setting up a lecture is fairly straightforward. If you are organizing the event, your primary logistics include identifying and reaching out to speakers and coordinating when and where. You may also need to plan a wrap-around event, book travel and accommodations, and do marketing. Prior to the lecture, arrive early to set up and test technology. Alternatively, you may be invited to give a presentation and should coordinate similar logistics with your host. In any case, this is your opportunity to tell a compelling and lively story to people who are very interested in what you have to say. Share your passion in a clear, honest, narrative style, and the audience will happily come along for the ride.

That said, lectures are not the most approachable form of public outreach, and they typically involve little engagement or one-on-one interactions. They tend to appeal to a limited audience, often consisting of highly educated older adults. If a lecture involves too much jargon and complicated slides or ignores accessibility considerations, it may bore or alienate many audience members (see appendix B).

Many presenters approach a lecture by focusing on what they want to talk about and not what they want their audience to remember. Even if a lecture is brief, it is still important to have learner-focused outcomes. Also, consider the potential audience type and adjust your pitch accordingly (see chapter 2).

If the lecture is recorded and shared publicly, obtain speaker permissions ahead of time. When livestreaming, choose a format that does not show your online audience unless you have explicit permission to share their identifiable faces. Ensure that you or the presenter have the rights or permissions to use the images included on presentation slides and provide proper credit lines. You will also need a mechanism for online distribution (i.e., YouTube) and providing closed or open captions.

Consider how the Q&A format will be managed. In a virtual setting, a moderator is useful to scan, select, and synthesize submitted questions before posing them to the speaker. For a hybrid lecture, plan how to incorporate audience members outside the lecture hall—assign someone to monitor the question feed so that those not physically in the room are not forgotten.

Budgets for lectures vary widely, as some groups can freely procure space, while others must pay for a venue. Think about other costs like AV setups, interpretation or captioning services, or after-hours staff salaries for evening talks. In many cases, it is customary to pay the lecturer an honorarium and reimburse them for their travel expenses. Your budget may also include a wrap-around event to provide additional networking or learning opportunities in a less formal setting, such as an invited dinner with the speaker, a bookend reception, or a classroom visit. Strategic partnerships may assist with funding, resources, or publicity. Offering a co-sponsorship to groups with similar interests is a great way to attract larger audiences.

Hosting an out-of-town speaker requires additional considerations. Speakers and hosts participating in the Archaeological Institute of America's National Lecture Program often exchange "pre-lecture forms" where contact information, event schedules, travel and local transportation arrangements, overnight accommodation information, audiovisual equipment needs, audience and venue information, and even local points of interest are exchanged.[3] Often, the highlights of hosting are found in social opportunities outside of the lecture hall, including conversations in the car on the way to and from the airport, sharing a meal, or exploring a local landmark together.

Other Types of Virtual Engagement

In addition to lectures, virtual engagement occurs in many forms, including online activities and contests, webinars or workshops, and social media campaigns. These may be timebound (a contest or an activity with a set schedule), passive (a self-paced activity or resource), or interactive (a crowd-sourced photo or trivia competition). If done properly, online programs also have the potential to bridge gaps in accessibility.

There are a multitude of platforms for hosting virtual events, including your website, online quiz sites like Kahoot, webinar streaming services like Zoom, or social media channels. Online platforms also give you the option to choose the extent to which your audience can interact. Your participants can engage through chat or Q&A boxes, and breakout rooms can enhance small group discussions. Depending on the situation, participants might interact synchronously or asynchronously from their own space, and your potential audience is not limited by geography.

While many online engagement platforms have a free tier, there may be hidden costs or subscriptions involved. If your program is particularly successful, you may need to pay for upgrades to accommodate your userbase or reach. Also consider what technology platforms or videoconferencing equipment and accessories you will need and what skills are involved in using them. Know who to contact and how to reach them for technical support. There may be technological glitches beyond your level of expertise!

Be aware that it is easy to get lost in the noise of the internet. Virtual engagement, particularly through social media, requires a well-planned and intentional content management strategy and an understanding of user types for each social media channel. It takes time and dedication to build an audience and a following, and your online engagement activities can get lost in the algorithms.

Without built-in mechanisms for feedback and analytics, you may know very little about how your content was internalized or received. Consider creating survey tools, collecting contact information for follow-ups, and providing ways for participants to connect with you. Piloting your program with outside participants before launching it online can help bridge gaps in engagement and participant connectivity. When collecting participant data, be aware of relevant privacy laws. While you may not be operating in Europe, the European Union's General Data Protection Regulation still applies to businesses collecting or using the personal data of European citizens.

Archaeology Fairs, Information Booths, and Roadshows

Archaeologists frequently participate in and organize informal public events where they create an informational setup for visitors who are there to learn, browse, and connect. These events include archaeology fairs, artifact roadshows, community festivals, and open houses. You might be identifying artifacts, offering short hands-on activities, or highlighting current research and local archaeology topics. This type of engagement involves opportunities for attendees to learn in an unstructured and self-paced environment.

Be strategic about partnerships, collaborations, and publicity efforts to positively impact attendance. If you are the organizer, cast a wide net for possible presenters. Reach out to Indigenous

Figure 7.1. Archaeologists engage bicyclists at an information booth set up during a statewide cycling event. *Courtesy of University of Iowa Office of the State Archaeologist*

communities, historical societies, museums, avocational archaeology groups, CRM firms, government agencies, and university clubs to solicit interest. Historical reenactors and craftspeople can also contribute to public understanding of the human past. Make sure the logistics, goals, and overall event atmosphere are clearly conveyed.

You may want to organize an archaeology-specific fair of your own. The goal here should be the ability for visitors to "learn about archaeology through multiple interactive activities and stations."[4] Whether you call it an open house, Archaeopalooza, or just Archaeology Day, these can be hosted by a single group but typically are collaborative efforts bringing many groups and related institutions together. They engage visitors through a series of brief interactions that include general knowledge about the profession, local and national cultural resources, and/or specific topics or themes.

Consider the need for volunteer assistance at your fair. Their tasks might include staffing booths, assisting presenters, helping with general setup and breakdown, facilitating First Aid/CPR, directing traffic, and troubleshooting any problems that arise. Remember, when so many people volunteer their time, energy, and expertise that smiles, thank-yous, and free food and/or drinks go a long way!

On other occasions, archaeologists set up informational booths at events unrelated to archaeology, like an educational fair or regional festival. Your booth might include hands-on activities, giveaways, artifacts or replicas, and visual aids to help tell your story during brief interactions. Remember, you may only connect with a visitor for a few minutes. Think about how to attract people to your booth and engage them most effectively.

These events appeal to a wide audience and provide positive and fun interactions with archaeology. They offer opportunities to expand awareness and knowledge of local cultural resources, encourage a preservation ethic, and network with fellow presenters and the community. Personal one-on-one interactions can be highly impactful and the informal atmosphere surrounding a fair can be more

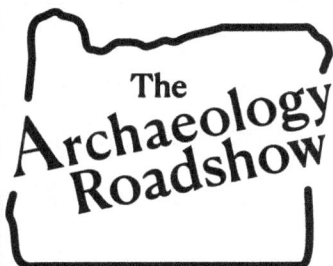

Figure 7.2. Archaeology Roadshow logo

Textbox 7.1. The Archaeology Roadshow

Lyssia Merrifield and Virginia L. Butler

The Archaeology Roadshow (archaeologyroadshow.org) is a large-scale, annual public outreach fair that is designed to promote stewardship of regional heritage and educate adults and children about the value of archaeology to all citizens. University faculty and students, Tribes, federal and state agencies, private companies, and avocational organizations host hands-on activities that relate to heritage, science, Indigenous history, and contemporary Tribal interests. The Archaeology Roadshow grew out of a 2012 public archaeology classroom project on the campus of Portland State University and has spread to several rural communities across Oregon, including Bend, The Dalles, and Harney County.

What are the best things about our project? Where are the challenges? What have we learned? Elsewhere we consider these questions in some detail.[1] Here, we want to highlight one key thing central to our success in rural Oregon: building partnerships with the arts community.

At our Portland events, we enlist the support of "typical" partners who are engaged with archaeology, heritage, and education. Because of its size, Portland has a critical mass of organizations and institutions—literally dozens—that we can call on to host temporary exhibits and activities. Rural areas of our state do not offer the same pool of cultural resources partners. One of our *Roadshow* sister communities, Harney County, located some three hundred miles southeast of Portland, is the tenth-largest county in the United States by area but has a population of only 7,500 people. How do you build support for an archaeology fair in a remote rural area?

Drawing on our professional connections with archaeologists in federal agencies based in the county and bringing students and colleagues from Portland and elsewhere, in 2017 and 2018, we hosted the Archaeology Roadshow in a large city park in the main population center of Hines-Burns. We attracted close to four hundred enthusiastic visitors one year, and the local community was pleased to host the event. While we might have continued focusing exhibits and outreach on archaeology and history topics during future Archaeology Roadshows, community members came to us with the brilliant idea of joining our celebration of heritage with the arts, especially traditional crafts and music. Harney County is home to several Oregon Culture Keepers, a juried set of artisans that keep traditional crafts alive through education and outreach.

So, in 2019, we launched the Cultural Crawl and Archaeology Roadshow. After a COVID hiatus, we unveiled the Archaeology & Culture Keepers Roadshow in 2023. Working together, our joint planning committees were able to share the load of organizing and implementing the large fair in a local park. Through broadening our frame, we attracted more exhibitors and visitors than we would have with a narrower focus just on archaeology.

In our newly configured public outreach that connected archaeology and the arts, visitors were invited to throw an atlatl spear, learn about important uses of native plants, and see demonstrations of skills such as saddle making and silver work, beading and basketry, and rawhide and horsehair braiding. Performances by local musicians and food carts offering Indian tacos and steamed dumplings enriched the experience. People of all ages came out for the day to learn about archaeology, heritage, and the importance of stewardship, but they also gained an understanding about Euro-American and Indigenous arts and crafts, showing what connects us all.

Note

1. Virginia L. Butler, Lyssia Merrifield, Virginia Parks, and Shelby L. Anderson, "Ten Years On: Engaging the Public through the Archaeology Roadshow," in "How Do We Reach More? Sharing Cultural and Archaeology Research with Others," ed. Darby C. Stapp and Julia G. Longenecker, *Journal of Northwest Anthropology, Special Publication* 4 (2021): 6–25, https://www.northwest anthropology.com/how-do-we-reach-more.

welcoming than a lecture or other more academic programming. These events also meet a diverse set of visitors at their level. Some may be learning about archaeology for the first time, while others are seeking career advice or ways to become more deeply involved in the discipline.

That said, most visitor interactions at table events are brief and your booth may be competing with countless others. A visually appealing, professional setup that invites people to stop and engage can be costly. Spend your money on fun (ideally sustainable) giveaways or nicely printed pamphlets that can be reused or repurposed at future events if the information is relevant.

Finally, at an artifact ID event, there could be a long line of impatient participants who want your attention. Advertise a maximum object limit for participants to bring and enlist specialists familiar with different artifact types and geological specimens. Be aware that some identifications can be a letdown for an enthusiastic or argumentative collector. It is helpful to provide resources, like books or websites, and to not dismiss unique noncultural objects. You ultimately want the collector to feel comfortable contacting you and sharing contextual information when they do find authentic artifacts and potentially unrecorded sites. As an ethical rule, a professional archaeologist should never provide a monetary value or appraisal resources for cultural artifacts. Politely decline to answer the question and provide a justification if asked (e.g., artifacts for sale are often fakes or traded illicitly, it promotes looting and the loss of contextual information, etc.).[5]

On-Site Public Visits and Tours

A 2023 poll conducted by Ipsos for the Society for American Archaeology indicated that most people in the United States learn about archaeology through television, museums, classrooms, movies, and print media; only 10 percent learn about archaeology at public events or parks.[6] Inviting the public to tour your active excavations can help increase that percentage. Such public days are great opportunities for people to see real archaeological work happening in their community and learn more about our methodologies.

Public days often occur at historical sites or parks. They may capture regular visitors who were unaware of the event and will view the archaeology as a bonus part of their day. In other cases, tours may be part of a special event for an academic field school or CRM project and attended by members of the press or the local community. These are often done in coordination with the contractor, property owner, and, when possible, descendant communities.

The biggest advantage of an excavation tour is capitalizing on an existing opportunity. You are already there conducting research! Share your enthusiasm for your discoveries with your visitors and show off your beautiful sketch maps and interesting artifacts. Excavations also have a "wow" factor. With consent from stakeholders, encourage participants to take pictures to share on social media, especially if they have an opportunity to do a little digging or screening of their own. Be mindful of anything that is culturally sensitive and help your visitors understand the science of archaeology. This is a unique opportunity to convey ethics, methodologies, and the need for careful but painstaking work.

That said, you may struggle to meet audience expectations during a site visit. They may be looking for King Tut, but you enthusiastically show them indistinct soil features and lithic scatters. Craft a story with jargon-free talking points to explain the excavation and demonstrate that your discoveries are crucial to our collective understanding of the past. Test your pitch on family and friends to determine whether you need to be more succinct or engaging.

It is easy during a site tour to inadvertently imply that excavation is the most important part of the archaeological process. Explain the research questions your team is hoping to answer and what you have already learned. Staging lab stations and showing research material or completed reports can emphasize parts of the process that take place before and after excavation.

Safety considerations are paramount. Conduct regular safety meetings with team members and consider installing caution tape or ropes to keep your audience away from open units and tools. Make sure your visitors are aware if the site is physically challenging to access. Provide shade and shelter for inclement weather and encourage hydration.

Volunteer Field and Lab Days

In contrast to excavation tours, archaeologists commonly organize public field or lab work events for volunteer participants. These can last a single day, a weekend, several weeks, or consecutive years. Participants might include families with young children, experienced volunteers, students interested in future archaeology careers, or adults with a lifelong love for archaeology. In any case, this is authentic, hands-on learning at its best. Participants will handle real tools and artifacts next to trained professionals who can engage and answer questions.

Volunteer field and lab events involve kinesthetic learning and engagement through physical activity and encourage teamwork. Participants are generally excited to help and connect with the past in a tangible way as they get their hands dirty. Participatory events also build relationships. You may develop a crew of regular attendees who will become future stakeholders, can accomplish meaningful work, and provide needed support for your organization.

A drawback of these programs is that participants may have romanticized expectations and find the real deal to be boring, tedious, or overly strenuous. Ensure the audience recognizes that archaeology is a multistep process which entails more than simply looking for cool stuff. Find ways to convey the tremendous amount of research and office time required to fully contextualize the artifacts and understand the people who created them. Also, ensure you have a plan for processing and curating the artifacts you and the volunteers will discover, in addition to writing up the results of your work. The same people who helped excavate in the field may be willing to assist with this part, as well!

Such events will add to your workload, and you cannot expect the level of speed and accuracy that you would get with a crew of professional archaeologists. Staff must patiently explain why each task is critical and often teach the same skill to several people at different times. They should be skilled in

Textbox 7.2. Engaging the Public in Research and Education

Constance Arzigian, Daniel Joyce, and Adam Novey

The Historic Indian Agency House (HIAH) in Portage, Wisconsin, is an important site of early nineteenth century Euro-American and Ho-Chunk interaction. A public archaeology program began in 2020 to simultaneously locate the treaty-mandated blacksmith shop and engage the public in the work. Since its inception, the program has involved over five hundred people. This project provides both research and a rewarding public outreach experience and draws participants from a wide area, many returning year after year.

Engaging young people and the public in meaningful research is often difficult. Visiting historic archaeological sites where everyone can see and help properly recover objects that they readily recognize not only engages them but sparks curiosity and enthusiasm for archaeology, history, and cultural heritage preservation. For those considering archaeology as a career, this can provide essential background information.

Project logistics include online registration for one-hour time slots over two consecutive summer weekends. This accommodates a variety of people. Individuals, including high school or college students, avocational archaeologists, or adults who "always wanted to be an archaeologist" can sign up for multiple hours or come all day on both weekends. Families with young children who may only have a one-hour attention span can also participate. Others just tour the excavations and ask questions.

A major benefit of having mixed ages and returning participants is that the more experienced people can teach the new arrivals. This doesn't always mean older folks teaching younger. We have many middle school students who effectively teach new participants how to trowel, keep level floors, and identify and bag artifacts. Volunteers draw floor plans and profiles and look forward to applying these drafting skills in real-world situations. Online registration is capped at ten individuals per hour based on available space and supervision capacity of around fifteen maximum participants per hour. Four archaeologists supervise in their own unit(s). This structure allows us to accommodate drop-ins and requests from those who want to continue digging beyond their registered time. Using an hourly framework for participant rotation, we engage substantially more attendees than if we used a daily model.

Staff and volunteers at HIAH coordinate with the archaeologists to place new arrivals in the excavation units. If there are new participants, a five-minute orientation is held at the top of the hour to provide historical context, the basics of archaeology, and site rules, such as keeping away from the edges of the unit. Archaeologists focus their attention on supervising participants while volunteers lead the orientation and pass out refreshments. Blacksmithing demonstrations offer participants something to do on digging breaks or while waiting for a spot to open. This has also proven helpful in cross-referencing blacksmithing debris and hand-forged items found in the ground.

Following the event, project archaeologists wash and catalog the finds, identify and photograph diagnostic artifacts, and tabulate all finds by provenience. Metal artifacts undergo electrolysis to aid identification. The HIAH museum permanently curates the artifacts and documentation. During each season's planning stage, we set aside funds to acquire long-term storage materials. We prepare excavation reports each season, including publicly shareable interpretations of our research questions. Reports are submitted to the Wisconsin Office of State Archaeologist for their permanent records and copies are maintained along with the artifacts in storage.

Figure 7.3. A volunteer bags artifacts during a public lab day at Mount Calvert Historical and Archaeological Park in Prince George's County, Maryland. *Courtesy of Stephanie T. Sperling*

working with the public and ensure a staff-to-volunteer ratio for new volunteers of 1:1. To protect delicate artifacts or resources, establish a sign-up process and assign tasks that are equal to participant ages and capabilities. Trained volunteers may be able to work with little supervision, but those with minimal experience will need a qualified archaeologist nearby to ensure they are not inadvertently destroying significant deposits.

It is your responsibility to ensure a safe working environment. There may be the potential for volunteers to encounter toxic material, like asbestos, a common building material often identified on historical sites. Ensure you have a plan in place for mitigating these hazards and that everyone is informed of the risks. Similarly, assess the outdoor conditions and inform volunteers of risks related to weather, temperature, and insects. Consult with the health and safety office at your institution before organizing the program (see chapter 6).

Finally, ensure participants feel valued and recognized, and follow up with them to share your findings. The most important thing anyone can give you is their time!

Archaeology and Outdoor Recreation

There are unlimited opportunities for archaeological education during organized hikes, paddles, bike tours, and more. Recreational activities naturally bring people together to be energized and revitalized. When framed using a cultural heritage lens, these experiences connect the past and present in unique and memorable ways.

As with many other types of all-ages programs, you may be invited to lead a tour, or you could be the organizer. These types of activities might entail hiking to an old farmstead, paddling through a cultural landscape, or biking on a former railway. For archaeologists, the human impact on the landscape may seem obvious, but others may have never considered how forests, fields, or waterways were made, used, and modified by people over time. Recreational tours provide opportunities to show people human aspects on the natural world that may otherwise go unnoticed.

The possibilities for conversations during outdoor tours are endless, and discussion topics could include environmental inequities or landscape changes over thousands of years. These tours may

Figure 7.4. Participants set off for a kayak tour of Jug Bay Archaeological Complex sites in the Patuxent River, Maryland. *Courtesy of Stephanie T. Sperling*

Stephanie T. Sperling, Meredith Anderson Langlitz, and Sara Ayers-Rigsby

promote a conservation and stewardship ethic by introducing people to places where they might not otherwise venture. They also strengthen connections between cultural and natural resources, inspire advocacy, and are a great way to elevate untold stories. Cultural heritage tours will attract people from inside and outside your local jurisdiction. Research shows that heritage tourists spend more money and time at their destination, resulting in positive economic impacts in the community.[7]

A successful tour requires an experienced guide who can interpret a vibrant picture of the past. The guide needs to project their voice to large groups of people, think on their feet, and adapt to teachable moments. They should be prepared to answer difficult questions or acknowledge when they do not have an answer. Extensive training is required not only to discern subtle changes within an ecosystem but also to effectively articulate those observations during a tour. Visual aids like artifacts, photographs, or maps are useful but can get cumbersome and should not be relied upon to make or break the event.

On outdoor cultural resource-themed recreation tours, give people space to enjoy their surroundings. They want to hear about your archaeological discoveries but also immerse themselves in the wonders of nature. Set aside time during the program for quiet reflection and conversation with other participants. Invite the audience to share observations, ask questions, and learn about the natural world and its relationship to history. These discussions can be more robust if you invite a tour co-leader with a different background and perspective, like natural resource managers or descendant community members.

Partners may also be necessary for access and infrastructure. Determine if you need shuttle transportation and a qualified driver or if your participants will meet at your starting point. Identify who will provide the necessary recreational equipment, such as bicycles, canoes, or personal flotation devices. Since you may be far off the beaten path, enlist a program partner who is trained in First Aid/CPR. Have a backup plan for inclement weather! With more partners involved, it may be easier to alleviate safety and logistical concerns.

Make the tour conditions and logistics clear on program descriptions and marketing materials (see appendix A). Clearly communicate the tour distance, time, and target audience—is it family-friendly or geared toward adults? Indicate whether any prior experience is required and if the tour involves ADA-accessible paved trails or potentially rugged natural surfaces. Setting parameters for participant abilities will help you create a sense of belonging on the trip.

SUMMARY

Public archaeology programs that are geared toward all ages will help foster a sense of shared cultural heritage, promote stewardship and ethical practices, and ensure that your research benefits and engages the broader community. They encourage conversation and critical thinking and can contribute to your local economy through cultural tourism. Finally, your program may erode the notion that archaeologists are gatekeepers by providing a platform for sharing research, interpretations, and stories in an accessible and engaging way. There may be challenges, but you and your participants will always have fun creating these memorable experiences.

NOTES

1. Robert McNulty and Russell Koff, *Cultural Heritage Tourism* (Washington, DC: Partners for Livable Communities, 2014), https://www.americansforthearts.org/sites/default/files/culturalheritagetourism.pdf.
2. Cheryl M. Hargrove, *Cultural Heritage Tourism: Five Steps for Success and Sustainability* (Lanham, MD: Rowman & Littlefield, 2017).
3. "Lecturer Resources," Archaeological Institute of America, accessed December 29, 2023, https://www.archaeological.org/programs/public/lectures/lecturer-resources/.

4. Ben Thomas and Meredith Anderson Langlitz, "Archaeology Fairs and Community-Based Approaches to Heritage Education," *Advances in Archaeological Practice* 4, no. 4 (2016), 465–78.
5. "Ethics in Professional Archaeology," Society for American Archaeology, accessed on December 11, 2023, https://www.saa.org/career-practice/ethics-in-professional-archaeology.
6. "New Poll Finds Continued Support for Archaeology in the US," Society for American Archaeology, updated June 29, 2023, https://www.saa.org/education-outreach/public-outreach/public-perceptions-studies.
7. Travel Industry Association of America, *The Historic/Cultural Traveler* (Northwestern University: Research Department of the Travel Industry Association of America, 2003).

RECOMMENDED RESOURCES

King, Eleanor M., ed. "Special Issue: Designing and Assessing Public Education Programs in Archaeology." *Advances in Archaeological Practice* 4, no. 4 (November 2016): 415–561. https://doi.org/10.1017/S2326376800001005.
"Lecturer Resources." Archaeological Institute of America. https://www.archaeological.org/programs/public/lectures/lecturer-resources/.
"Organizing an Archaeology Fair." Archaeological Institute of America. https://www.archaeological.org/programs/educators/more-resources/.
Pitblado, Bonnie, Bryon Schroeder, Matthew J. Rowe, Suzie Thomas, and Anna Wessman, eds. "Professional-Collector Collaboration: Moving beyond Debate to Best Practice." *Advances in Archaeological Practice* 10, no. 1 (February 2022): 1–128. https://doi.org/10.1017/aap.2021.43.

8

Engaging with Youth

CLASSROOM VISITS AND BEYOND

Elizabeth C. Reetz

Archaeology introduces students to the need to preserve and protect our shared cultural heritage, thus emphasizing respect, responsibility, caring, and citizenship. It is imbued with excitement and intrigue and can support curricular objectives in most subjects, including science, mathematics, social studies, and language arts, among others. Archaeology is also an ideal arena for cooperative learning, hands-on activities, and problem-solving.

Over the past several decades, knowledgeable and committed archaeologists and educators have spearheaded efforts to include archaeological topics in elementary and high schools by sharing information, developing teaching tools, and working to get archaeology incorporated into statewide standards for learning.[1] This chapter covers formal and nonformal educational programs that occur inside and outside of a K–12 classroom. We describe the most common program types where archaeologists interact with youth and introduce considerations for planning and implementing these programs.

Although there are different legal definitions for K–12 or the equivalent education in various countries, we define it here as the overarching educational system for primary or elementary and secondary school students in public, private, independent, or home schools, from approximately ages five to eighteen.

COMMON TYPES OF K–12 PROGRAMS

Regardless of the program type, preparing for a K–12 program involves organizing a plan, selecting topics/materials, and choosing appropriate instructional methods. Familiarizing yourself with the formats archaeologists use to engage with K–12 youth will help you to determine your interests and strengths and strategize for logistical challenges that may arise. These formats include in-person classroom visits, videoconferences, school assemblies and fairs, field trips, and camps or school break programs.

In-Person Classroom Presentations

Aside from field trips to museums and sites, most archaeologists interact with K–12 audiences as guest speakers in classrooms or after-school programs, often to share about careers or local archaeology.

Whether speaking to K–12 classrooms is a regular part of your job or you only plan on visiting once or twice, a familiarity with the typical format of these visits can help your presentation go smoother.

Classroom presentations can occur during a single class period to a limited group of students, or they may involve one or more presenters doing a talk or activity as part of group rotations. Individual presentation times typically range from about thirty to forty-five minutes, sometimes followed by a Q&A. When doing round-robin-type rotations, presentations with younger grades can be as short as fifteen to twenty minutes to align with attention spans. These in-person visits provide ample opportunity for hands-on activities, which is particularly important in a profession like archaeology that focuses on material culture and objects. They are also a great opportunity to use place-based education to foster curiosity and a connection to the local community (see chapter 1).

Videoconferences

Before the COVID-19 pandemic, archaeologists conducted occasional but infrequent videoconferences with K–12 classrooms. Some professionals participated in programs like Skype a Scientist, which connected them to students across the United States and internationally; however, many schools lacked the technology to offer live presentations. The COVID-19 pandemic prompted a large-scale pivot to online learning, and many teachers sought out guest presenters to engage students through videoconferencing. Although access to the proper technology is still an issue for many schools, it is now more conventional for teachers and scientists to use videoconferencing for outreach because of its cost- and time-effectiveness and access to non-local participants.

Digital presentations are well-suited for learners to gain awareness and knowledge of archaeological topics and processes. However, it is challenging to incorporate hands-on skills-building, unless the event is well planned and needed materials are circulated to participants prior to the teleconference. Although this requires more advance planning, it can greatly enrich the students' experience.

Encouraging engagement or dialogue during teleconferences is sometimes difficult. Communicate with the teacher about protocols for moderating participation, including when students should or should not be muted. Microphones and cameras add another layer of intimidation for some children to ask or respond to questions, making engagement tricky. No matter the age of your online participants, it is easy to miss body language or facial cues that communicate attention, confusion, or boredom. Although adults are used to lectures and discussions, younger children often have shorter attention spans and can easily get bored when no activity is involved. Be intentional about the length of time of your presentation and keep it shorter for younger ages. If someone's camera is off, you might miss engagement cues altogether. There are several reasons a student may not use video, and you should never force anyone to use this feature.

Assemblies, Fairs, and Special Events

In-school or after-school events occur at topical assemblies; Science, Technology, Engineering, and Math (STEM) fairs; career seminars, Parent Teacher Association (PTA) or booster club–organized activity nights; and standard after-school programs. These events are integrated into the school day as a break from the regular curriculum and to connect students from multiple grades, or they occur after the school day as special programs for students and families. These might involve one or more scheduled presenters, rotating activities, or educational booths.

Tabling a school fair is often less formal than being a front-and-center presenter. At open events, students or families stroll self-paced among the booths to do short activities or obtain information. If you provide an activity, plan for something that is accomplishable in the time provided and be cognizant of technology and supply needs. The advantage of this format is that you can potentially reach a large number of students, albeit often for a very short amount of time. One challenge is that it is difficult to predict attendance. Visitation could be a flop and you may be left wondering why you committed precious staff time and resources. On the other hand, your popularity may draw a crowd, making it difficult to give undivided attention to those seeking it. Most interactions may be brief, but others could be consuming of your time and attention. Busy events may also make it challenging to take short breaks, so be ready for anything!

Field Trips

Field trips provide students with a rare opportunity to see archaeologists in action. Many museums, parks, and similar visitor-focused organizations have a regular slate of field trip or tour options and well-established planning protocols, while other archaeological organizations might only host a field trip if an opportunity arises. Students may visit your facility or a site you are managing, or you may join the group on a visit to an external location. Depending on the location and amenities, your teaching method could include tours, lectures or discussions, hands-on activities, demonstrations, observation, and show-and-tell.

The biggest challenge with bringing students to your site or workplace is capacity. The number of students you can accommodate depends on your ability to staff and supervise them. It is important to coordinate the group size before the visit. You may have to turn down larger classes or find alternative locations to accommodate the group (often easier on a college campus). Multiple tour stops sometimes affect timing if, for example, one stop goes over time, the bus cannot find parking, or several children need a bathroom break. You also need to consider your co-workers' responsibilities and deadlines. A troop of children moving through the lab can be disruptive, regardless of instructions to use inside voices. Or if on-site, your co-workers may be working on something that is sensitive or requires undistracted focus.

Figure 8.1. Students assist an archaeologist with screening for artifacts at a historical archaeological site. *Courtesy of University of Iowa Office of the State Archaeologist*

Teachers sometimes cold call (or email) to ask if you can coordinate an opportunity for their students to visit an active archaeological excavation. On the rare occasion that an opportunity is within a reasonable distance of the school, you must coordinate with your site supervisors, landowners, and contractors to learn about any insurance or liability needs, hazards, safety gear, and logistics involving buses, parking, and accessible travel to the site area. Factor in bathroom facilities and an inclement weather backup plan. Keep your number of participants small for safety, supervision, and engagement purposes.

Because field trip groups often visit excavation and curation or collections facilities, adequate supervision is essential to prevent accidents and broken objects. Unfortunately, materials have been stolen during school field trips. Maintain an inventory of your teaching supplies before and after the event. Also, accidents do happen. Use personal protective equipment for high visibility or safety when handling sharp objects, as your situation requires. Refer to chapters 6 and 7 for more on logistics and site visits.

Summer or Seasonal Programs

K–12 children participate in day camps and residential camps during school breaks or as special enrichment programs. Archaeologists commonly participate in programs organized by local school districts, colleges, universities, museums, community or nature centers, or nonprofits that often involve groups like Scouting America, Girl Scouts of the United States of America, Upward Bound, YMCA, various "college for kids" groups, and similar organizations. The types of programs and the youth they serve vary, but archaeology can be integrated into nearly any camp setting. If you are a guest presenter, you will probably provide similar activities to those done during classroom visits or school fairs.

Residential camps or programs that occur over multiple days or weeks offer opportunities to engage with youth for longer periods of time than field trips and school visits. Educators can provide

Figure 8.2. Girl Scouts at a residential summer camp record observations about a precontact structure in Utah. *University of Iowa Office of the State Archaeologist*

in-depth experiences and a structured curriculum that moves beyond a basic understanding of archaeology and do more conscientious assessments. Although camps typically involve a small number of participants, you can reach higher levels of learning and participation and engage students in ways that shorter programs cannot. Camps present an avenue for archaeologists to help children build practical and intellectual skills, inspire a deeper interest about past people and cultural resources, and foster citizenship values and stewardship ethics.

While these experiences can have an incredible impact and might influence future generations to value conservation and stewardship, camps require the most investment of time and resources. In addition to instructional time, you will probably spend weeks planning logistics and curricula and preparing materials and activities. Sometimes, the background planning and organization are done by the host organization, and all you must do is show up at a location with your supplies. Other times, you may be required to help with logistics beyond your student contact time, like registration, transportation, or permissions. If you are planning to organize your own camp from scratch, realize that it takes an incredible amount of planning, preparation, and resources, as well as liability and legal considerations. It can be done, but partnerships and collaborations will be crucial.

INTENTIONAL PREPARATION TO IMPROVE THE EXPERIENCE

> "I'm gonna wing it."
>
> —me, about something I most definitely should not wing (internet quote, no credit)

Make a Plan!

It is not unusual for a scientist to feel they can just show up to a school program or welcome field trip visitors and wing it. This might appear to work, or at least check a box, but what is the value or impact of doing that? Regardless of the type or duration of K–12 programs, the most effective experiences will result from having a clear plan (see chapter 4). Optimize your activities to align with goals, outcomes, audience needs, and assessment methods, even if you perceive your program as straightforward or simple. Also, expect the unexpected! Things may not go perfectly or always be in your control, but having a plan gives you a reference point to return to when you feel off-path.

Before you establish your goals and outcomes, find out what the classroom instructor needs. Your mere presence in the class does not guarantee a successful or valuable educational experience, particularly if there is not adequate communication prior to your visit. Teachers may be working on curricular topics that relate to your expertise and looking for engaging ways to enhance that content or provide a real-world perspective. If this is the case, find out if they are trying to meet any specific standards. Alternatively, they may be seeking an activity with no specific curricular tie-in to fill a scheduling gap, provide a break from planning, or simply offer something fun to their students. Do not make assumptions but clarify details and adapt your program accordingly.

Communication with the teacher leading up to your participation as a guest speaker is imperative. Teachers do not often have an opportunity to read or respond to emails regularly during the school day, so your correspondence may be delayed or infrequent. Do your due diligence to check in and keep the conversation going, and make sure you adequately express your most pressing needs, questions, or concerns.

Choosing Appropriate Topics or Activities

Classroom activities created by archaeologists, teachers, and interpreters are readily available online. Without reinventing the wheel, many of these can be adapted to different settings and topics. If you are a first-time presenter or an archaeologist who wants to improve your K–12 outreach, seek out a seasoned educator for resources or advice. Also, be wary of how your program might perpetuate stereotypes or misconceptions, like treasure hunting or reinforcing the myth of the "Vanishing Indian" by speaking about them only in the past tense. This negates the experiences and dynamic cultures of Indigenous peoples today.[2]

It is helpful to review your presentation ideas with the teacher to ensure your content and activities are in alignment with the students' ages, learning levels, and other accessibility needs, or if any topics might be sensitive or taboo for certain students. Your program may involve presenting to multiple grade levels at the same time. If you are unfamiliar with adapting a lesson for grades above or below its intended audience, teachers can suggest modifications to reach both younger and older students. As a reminder, Piaget's theory of cognitive development emphasizes that we must align instructional methods and content with how students develop cognitively (see Chapter 2).[3] The majority of elementary school-age children still think concretely or may be only beginning to cognitively process the abstract associations between tangibles and intangibles. Archaeology is laden with abstract ideas and intangible concepts. What seems like an obvious relationship to you may not make sense to an elementary school student. Making connections to familiar concepts, like shelter, food, family, or technology helps to make unfamiliar ideas about the past relevant to their daily lives (see chapter 1).

You may need to familiarize yourself with a school's alignment to educational standards. These change often, so ask a teacher to direct you to current resources. It is generally thought that teachers are required to teach topics or curricula with little flexibility, but a survey jointly conducted by the Society for American Archaeology and the Society for Historical Archaeology suggests that social studies teachers have a fair amount of agency to choose topics and resources as they see fit.[4]

To Dig or Not to Dig?

Whether or not to involve children in authentic excavations and the debate on the efficacy of simulated or "sandbox" digs will always be a hot topic in the profession. While fun for children, many archaeologists would agree that sandbox excavations require a lot of work for an inauthentic experience. You may spend hours or even days preparing stratigraphic levels in dig boxes only to have children rapidly bore to the bottom seeking treasures. Digging also perpetuates a misconception that it is the only thing archaeologists do. Through assessment, evaluation, and rigorous study, archaeology educators are learning that when digging is involved, most other information about the archaeological process or past peoples is not retained by teachers or students![5]

Authentic excavations have potential to provide highly impactful experiences for children, but only in the right situation. You need to determine if you have the staff and capacity to provide an adequately supervised experience that maintains scientific rigor. Understand that you still need to go through the entire compliance process, from consultation to permits to lab processing to reporting. Also realize that the tediousness of archaeology suits some children, but it can be too slow-paced for others and leave them feeling bored or left out.

Children can still have authentic fieldwork experiences at archaeological sites without excavating. Pedestrian surveys, documentation of aboveground features, traditional mapping, sketching, note-taking, GPS data collection, photography, and analysis of cut banks are potential experiential activities appropriate for children. These activities can also be done inside the school, on school grounds, in parks, and on local trails.

Textbox 8.1. Excavating with Kids: Affordances and Constraints

Jeanne M. Moe

Archaeology educators have long raised questions about the ethics and educational value of both simulated excavations and student participation in real excavations. However, literature about excavations and their educational value is scant.

In 2017, an archaeologist colleague asked me to evaluate the efficacy of student excavations conducted in the playground of a historic elementary school. Over two days, approximately fifty-four fourth-grade students participated in the excavation of five one-by-one-meter units to a depth of twenty centimeters below the surface. The archaeologist presented students with background knowledge about the history of the school using historic photos and records and assisted students with interpreting some of the artifacts in a "laboratory" scenario.

For the assessment, I developed research questions, an assessment instrument, and interview protocols for the students and the teacher following the excavations. I received forty-four written assessments, interviewed seventeen students individually and two focus groups of five students each, and interviewed the teacher. The case study revealed some interesting information.

Most of the students thought that the purpose of the excavations was to learn about the past. Some of these students mentioned the human past. Three students thought that the purpose of the excavations was to learn about their own school and three thought the purpose was to compare past and present. Two students thought that the purpose was to answer questions about the past, while two thought they were excavating because the public wanted to see the artifacts. Similarly, one student thought the purpose was to teach others about the past.

The eleven misconceptions uncovered provided important insights into student learning. One student thought that the reason for excavating was because the local historical museum wanted more artifacts. One student thought that we were digging up "ancient humans" and another thought that the excavation told us everything we needed to know. Three students understood that excavation destroys a site, but it was okay because the archaeologist was going to put the artifacts back in the ground. Three students were concerned that excavation destroyed the "land" but did not connect that destruction to the archaeological site.

Students certainly enjoyed the experience and will probably remember it for many years. Generally, they understood that archaeology is "more than digging." It is a process requiring time, teamwork, and great care, and its purpose is to learn about the past. They understood that archaeological sites should be left unexcavated unless there is a good reason to dig. The teacher, however, interpreted the act of excavating as *the* archaeological process and the only true inquiry-based component of the experience. Because the students had dug, they did archaeology. Background and history content and artifact interpretation were not as important as excavation. Research shows that teachers mistakenly conflate process with inquiry.[1] Interestingly, by focusing on the process of archaeology rather than the content, we reinforced the common misconceptions of what inquiry-based instruction and learning really are.

Was it worth the time and effort? While students did learn something about archaeological processes for collecting data, I think that time would have been better spent using proven inquiry-based materials in the classroom. Process and content should be well-integrated to provide students with real information about the past and how archaeology can be used to build knowledge about past cultures and lifeways.

Note

1. Lynn Rankin, "Lessons Learned: Addressing Common Misconceptions about Inquiry," Foundations 2 (2020), 33–37, https://www.nsf.gov/pubs/2000/nsf99148/pdf/ch_5.pdf.

Figure 8.3. A middle school student documents the dimensions of a 1940s barn foundation. *Courtesy of University of Iowa Office of the State Archaeologist*

LOGISTICAL CONSIDERATIONS FOR PLANNING AND IMPLEMENTATION

Group Size

Be cognizant of the group size to ensure an effective ratio of instructors to students. No one is going to have a great experience if there are too few educators and too many children—especially the educator! If you cannot control the group size, adjust your program type to accommodate. Although it is not optimal for several types of learners, age-appropriate lecture-type presentations, show-and-tells, or Q&A sessions can work for larger groups and a single instructor. If you are including hands-on activities or group discussions, aim for smaller class sizes.

Generally, more complicated hands-on activities require fewer students and more instructors. Younger age-groups may require more instructional supervision than older students doing the same activity. Unfortunately, there are no standards for the "best" instructor-student ratio. You need to recognize your staffing limitations and when you need to enlist additional help.

It is not uncommon for teachers to invite additional classes or grades after you are scheduled to visit a school as a guest presenter. It's exciting for their students to learn from an archaeologist, and they want to expand the opportunity to as many students as possible. Other teachers might hear about your visit and ask to participate. Due to rigid schedules or instructional needs, it may not be possible to repeat a program over multiple class periods to accommodate all teachers. If your programs require fees, the teachers may not be able to afford the extension needed to cover your time. Don't be afraid to set boundaries and limitations for yourself—you can say no. Or be prepared

Elizabeth C. Reetz

to pivot. Sometimes this change in participant size is organized well in advance, but other times it can balloon at the last minute.

Legal or Privacy Concerns

If you work in government or higher education, check with your human resources representative to determine if your workplace requires training or certifications before working in person or digitally with minors. If you are unaffiliated with a workplace that offers internal training, school administration can likely point you in the right direction. Additionally, ensure you meet all the criminal background checks required of the K–12 organization. A teacher or other adult supervisor may need to be present during any videoconference, even if it involves holding a career discussion with one student. Depending on the situation, you may have to pass a training on the Family Educational Rights and Privacy Act (FERPA).

As emphasized in chapter 6, do not post photographs of minors on social media or use them in promotional materials or even professional presentations without permission. Schools each have different rules, so always check with the teacher. In some circumstances, photographs or videos of students may be considered an "education record" and protected under FERPA, or students may have legal protections regarding their identifiable image. Teachers should have records on file regarding privacy or security concerns for their students. In other scenarios, obtain permission directly from a parent or legal guardian.

The adoption of digital outreach brings new challenges and considerations, particularly with security and/or privacy concerns of minors. Schools protect students' data from being tracked by utilizing school accounts, but many students also use home devices. You can take extra precautions by using the waiting room or lock meeting features to ensure no unwanted guests access the session. When possible, allow the teacher to set up the meeting and send you an invite.

Classroom Management

Do not assume that teachers will be engaged or participate in classroom management during your visit. While many teachers are active participants during guest presentations, there are instances when teachers focus on other responsibilities, check out, or temporarily leave the room. One disruptive student can detract from the learning experience of others and throw off your concentration. Although this does not happen often, set your expectations with the teacher ahead of time and communicate about their involvement during your visit.

TIPS FOR IMPROVING K–12 PROGRAMS

It's Not All About You

When presenting to K–12 youth, avoid lectures where you give facts and answers. Allow participants to discover their own answers, and do not forget to take a back seat at times and become a learner like everyone else. Be conscientious about your interactions. You do not want to create a learning atmosphere where you are positioned front and center because it can be intimidating. Situate yourself among the students, and when possible, conduct introductions and group discussions in a circle where participants and instructors are equal.

Jargon

As with any audience, watch your jargon and avoid acronyms (see chapter 2). Even terms that you do not consider professional jargon may be unfamiliar to students! Be intentional with your language and know the learning level of your students. Their grade level might not be representative of their actual learning level, as you may find out when communicating with the teacher during planning.

Be Accessible

Ask your contact about classroom and student needs. Determine the accessibility of your activities and supporting materials and consider more inclusive options or alternatives. Also, be cautious of allergies, especially if your activity involves cookies or peanut butter (for the classic cookie or sandwich excavation!). There are several other considerations, as outlined in chapter 3.

Validate Answers

Students will be more willing to participate in discussions if they feel their perspectives are valued. Let them know you see where their answers are coming from. If a question has a specific answer that does not allow for much interpretation, do not respond with a negative. Modify your response like, "That is a good answer, and I can see how you might think that because of . . . , but there is another answer I am looking for."

Ongoing Assessment

Review and evaluate both throughout and at the end of the activity. Question the students about the experiences you are helping to facilitate. Try using investigative, exploratory, or inquiry-based questions as much as possible, such as:

- How would you describe this?
- What do you think about . . . ?
- Do you observe any differences among . . . ?

Refer to chapter 1 for more in-depth information on inquiry-based learning and chapter 12 for assessment strategies.

Wrapping It Up

Build in discussion time near the end of a visit or activity to bring students together to debrief and expand on ideas from discussions that occurred throughout the experience. Try to relate some of the discussion to your objectives to show that the group made collective achievements and learned something new. Encourage their interpretations, as well. Students may be reticent to share their thoughts while talking to a group or to someone they do not know, so do not feel offended if discussions do not flow well.

NOTES

1. Karolyn Smardz and Shelley J. Smith, eds., *The Archaeology Education Handbook: Sharing the Past with Kids* (Walnut Creek, CA: AltaMira Press, 2000), 19.
2. "The Impact of Words and Tips for Using Appropriate Terminology: Am I Using the Right Word?" Native Knowledge 360°, National Museum of the American Indian, accessed December 2, 2023, https://americanindian.si.edu/nk360/informational/impact-words-tips.
3. David C. Engleson and Dennis H. Yockers, *A Guide to Curriculum Planning in Environmental Education* (Madison: WI Department of Public Instruction).

4. Elizabeth Pruitt, e-mail message to author, December 15, 2021.
5. Jeanne Moe, "Kids and Excavations: Affordances and Constraints" (PowerPoint presentation, 84th Annual Meeting of the Society for American Archaeology, Albuquerque, NM, April 12, 2019).

RECOMMENDED RESOURCES

Chiarulli, Beverly A. "Let's Find a Barn and Put on a Show: Ten Lessons Learned from Designing Public Programs. *Advances in Archaeological Practice* 4, no. 4 (2016): 550–55. https://doi.org/10.7183/2326-3768.4.4.550.

"Project Archaeology: Discover the Past—Shape the Future." Southern Utah University. https://projectarchaeology.org/.

Smardz, Karolyn, and Shelley J. Smith, eds. *The Archaeology Education Handbook: Sharing the Past with Kids*. Walnut Creek: Altamira Press, 2000.

9

Community-Based Heritage Management Programs

Samantha R. Rubinson and Sarah E. Miller

Stewardship is the first principle in the Society for American Archaeology's Archaeology Code of Ethics. Principle No. 1 states, "It is the responsibility of all archaeologists to work for the long-term conservation and protection of the archaeological record by practicing and promoting stewardship of the archaeological record. Stewards are both caretakers of and advocates for the archaeological record for the benefit of all people; as they investigate and interpret the record, they should use the specialized knowledge they gain to promote public understanding and support for its long-term preservation."[1]

The principle not only states the ethical responsibilities of archaeologists, but also calls for professionals to ensure that they work to further public understanding of cultural resources and encourage their preservation. Yet, the principle does not say how. In this chapter, we introduce various formats of heritage management programs that rely on public participation and provide examples of effective programs. We aim to help you identify interested communities and volunteers and choose a program type that best suits your needs.

Figure 9.1. African-American community members participating in data recovery in Cosmo Cemetery. *Courtesy of Florida Public Archaeology Network*

Archaeology outreach programs focus on sharing information with the public and bringing resources to the community. These programs often occur as lecture series, tours, fairs, etc. (see chapter 7). They may require local volunteers, although not on a recurring basis. Conversely, volunteer-based heritage management programs are designed for active participation on a recurring basis. Trained volunteers can monitor heritage and archaeological sites, give tours, do site condition assessments, conduct site clean-ups, and other tasks.

Whether your program is focused on outreach or recruiting volunteers, your success or failure depends on integrating community priorities and building an interest. Participants and volunteers like to learn new things and work autonomously on tasks they have been trained to do. Ultimately, they need to enjoy what they do if they are to participate sustainably.[2]

GETTING STARTED

Questions to Consider Prior to Planning

Every community is different. A program that is successful in one location may not work in another. Regardless of the level of community involvement in your program design, begin by getting to know the people you hope to engage and recognizing the relationship they have with their cultural resources. Consider the questions below and let the answers guide you in developing your community-based heritage management program.

Community. Which communities are best suited to your program? This selection is vital. If your program needs experienced hikers with four-wheel-drive vehicles, look to engage seasoned groups that already have the skills and equipment. If your program needs volunteers who will work weekdays, advertise to groups that don't have weekday jobs. If your program is designed for K–12 students, reach out to classroom teachers or youth groups. If the community is known, continue working through the questions below.

Knowledge. Does the community know about local cultural resources or archaeology? If not, you may need to provide educational outreach opportunities about local resources and your program. Appreciation builds from education. Establish a baseline of archaeological literacy that you expect your community participants to achieve.

Appreciation. What does the cultural resource mean to the community? If they do not care about it, you may have to advocate for its importance. If they do care, it is easier to recruit assistance for the formation of a program. A good starting point is to ask the community about the economic, cultural, and social value of the site from their perspective.

Stewardship. Does the community have a volunteer ethic? If not, communicate your message by participating in community events and providing materials to encourage them to contact you when they feel like the resource is being disturbed. You can also create passive displays like interpretive signs at or about the resource to convey information the community can observe or follow. If they do have a volunteer ethic, we find citizen scientists are often already engaged with other programs you may be able to partner with, such as Sierra Club or 4-H groups.

Accessibility. Does the community have easy access to the resource? If not, you will need to find creative ways to bring the resource to the community. Transportation and economic barriers affect participation. Some auxiliary organizations assist with transportation costs or workshop development through grants or donations.

Cultural sensitivity. Are there Sovereign Tribal Nations with ancestral ties to the landscape? Are there descendant communities or families with long cultural or historical ties to the resource? Program developers need to consult with those who are connected to the area and invite them into the planning process. This should be an open invitation (no expiration date) to participate when and how they see fit. Some may choose to be involved and some may not, but it is important to ask. Be sensitive to the fact there are sacred places that Tribes do not want anyone to visit. Similarly, descendent communities may not want visitors, especially in rural areas. When in doubt, put people first. After all, you want your program to do more good than harm.

Communication. How does the community communicate with each other? To promote your program, first investigate where to advertise most effectively (see chapter 6). In addition to social media or local newspaper articles, try sending notices to churches or community centers to reach new volunteers you may not otherwise encounter. When contacting schools, look for approval from the school district to place notices in virtual newsletters or announcements. And never underestimate word of mouth; encourage volunteers to invite friends and family!

Previous efforts. How successful were previous outreach programs in the community? Learn from other efforts to make improvements or prevent repeating mistakes. Contact similar organizations in the area to learn from their experiences with marketing, outreach, and fundraising. Although your

Textbox 9.1. We Learn, They Learn: Working Together to Protect Cultural Heritage

Dawn Suzanne (Wanatee) Buffalo and Julie Spotted Eagle Horse Martineau

Involving avocationals and the interested public in active archaeological practice with professionals is, in our opinion, a natural developmental stage to what archaeologists and Tribes should be doing to protect cultural resources. Though this may increase the complexity in communication and collaboration between Tribes and archaeologists, we believe it is worth it to the entire community. We all rely on private landowners and citizens to inform us of archaeological finds or damage to resources connected to our Tribal communities. Avocationals and the interested public bring increased knowledge and information to some of our discussions, and the more they participate in these discussions, the more they feel empowered to speak up at civic meetings about archaeological discoveries and preservation. No one is the enemy here; we all gain from learning each other's perspectives.

At a local level, we see it as beneficial to Tribes when others learn about Native Americans and the contemporary issues that Tribes deal with. Too often, there is a disconnect where people freeze us in the past, unaware we exist today, and this is dehumanizing. We are *from here*, not somewhere else, and we're *still here*. Heritage management programs should make connections between the past and today and invite archaeology into the present with us.

Archaeology is about people, not just the artifacts. When Tribes are involved in heritage management programs and Tribal perspectives are emphasized in educational resources, the public come to understand the complexity of culture and objects. Through these programs, the public can learn how objects come into collections, how to properly care for them, and how to see them from different perspectives. For example, corn is not always just corn, it is symbolic. Artifacts are not just collector's items. It is critical to educate the public on the importance of provenience and why certain objects, such as grave goods, are not for display.

Public archaeology programs that promote collaboration among Tribes and the public provide a way for us to connect with our Elders. They also have the potential to introduce Native students to historic preservation issues and career fields. Additionally, Tribal members can learn about historic preservation practices that benefit us and get to know people at the agencies and organizations who advocate for cultural resource protections. Also, it doesn't matter if Tribal lands are expansive or limited. If Tribes fail to adopt protective practices, we leave our cultural sites open to being looted. This endangers our shared heritage. When Tribes, archaeologists, and the interested public get involved in the preservation process together, we increase the level of protection for our cultural resources.

program might vary greatly from other community programs, your time and resources are valuable. Don't reinvent any wheel unless absolutely necessary for the success of your program.

Tips for Selecting Cultural Resources

Selecting a site or cultural resource in your community to anchor a program requires thought and consideration. First, find a resource that is relevant and interesting to the local community. Remember, the passion that archaeologists have for a resource may not be shared by the public. To gain public buy-in, emphasize why their local resources are interesting and significant on a community, state, or national level. For example, a historical cemetery may not interest some members of the public until you connect it to, for example, regional fishing, turpentine, or railroad history.

Second, make sure the property owner consents to visitors and that the site is accessible. If reaching the site is difficult, provide orientation and training to ensure safe entry and exit. Money, time, and physical ability may limit the range of volunteers who participate, but the community you select for engagement may be drawn to activities such climbing, off-roading, or diving in addition to heritage management and are prepared for the journey.

Last, be aware that public lands are subject to laws that limit access to information about cultural resources (e.g., the Archaeological Resources Protection Act of 1979 [ARPA]) for sites on federal land. These laws require careful sharing and tracking of site information. Bringing the public to archaeological sites may require permission from land managers, permits, and training of volunteers about preservation laws to ensure confidentiality.

TYPES OF COMMUNITY-BASED HERITAGE MANAGEMENT PROGRAMS

The program formats covered here include archaeology certification programs, historical cemetery programs, and statewide site stewardship programs. We describe each program format, provide advice on program planning and implementation, and include examples of successful programs from the larger public archaeology community.

Archaeology Certification Programs

Archaeology certification programs train non-professional community volunteers to do site inventories, excavations, and condition assessments. These programs differ from site stewardship programs as the volunteers participate in supervised projects with finite timelines, not recurring, long-term site monitoring. Rather, certified volunteers assist land managers/owners with preservation projects when funding, time, and staff are limited. Without degrees in archaeology, the volunteers do not meet the Secretary of Interior's standards for archaeology;[3] therefore, a professional archaeologist must supervise the work to uphold scientific standards.[4]

Certification programs are often connected to local archaeological societies and are created to enrich the lives of volunteers and/or to assist archaeologists with their legal and ethical duties of care. Partnerships with local societies or nonprofit "friends of" groups are critical to, for example, federal and state archaeologists who often lack adequate funding for staff positions.

As the program lead, establish a consistent schedule of classes covering key topics such as local cultural history, artifact identification, site recording, forms and documentation, field safety, and ethics. The effectiveness of your volunteers is directly tied to the quality of their training, so seek feedback on classes and make necessary updates to enhance proficiency. Conduct hands-on training sessions for tasks like pedestrian survey and unit excavation, with volunteers fulfilling a checklist of requirements and dedicating a specified amount of time for certification. Ensuring they acquire the

Samantha R. Rubinson and Sarah E. Miller

necessary experience is no easy task. As we mentioned, archaeologists must ethically adhere to the scientific method and archaeological process that requires background research, implementation, data collection and processing, interpretation, publication, and finally, curation or storage of artifacts and documentation. A comprehensive training program must adequately cover the entire archaeological process, with a particular focus on understanding and completing required forms.

Volunteers need to feel useful and needed. Prepare your site(s) and/or survey area for volunteers before the training. Ensure that your paperwork and documentation forms are in order. During the training, advise volunteers on what to wear, bring, and expect so they are ready to work on day one. Complete all necessary legal documents like volunteer agreements and liability waivers prior to beginning field or lab work (see chapter 6). Have sufficient staff in place to supervise all volunteer activity to ensure the quality of work and data collection. Providing a diversity of projects will keep certified volunteers interested and active.

One of the best examples of an archaeology certification program is the Archaeological Technician Certificate Program, available to Archaeological Society of Virginia members.[5] For over thirty years, volunteers have contributed thousands of hours of work annually at a variety of sites, including Jamestown, Mount Vernon, Poplar Forest, and Montpelier. Applicants attend a series of classes on Virginia culture history, artifact identification and analysis, and laws and ethics. Course instructors assign readings in addition to classroom work. Certificate students must complete sixty hours of lab work, sixty hours of survey, and sixty hours of excavation for a total of 180 hours. Before graduation, students must conduct twenty hours of public outreach, record two archaeological sites, and pass lab and written exams. The training is rigorous and is approaching one hundred graduates.

Archaeological certificate programs are not limited to terrestrial sites. Specialized diving groups that focus on submerged resources have similar rigorous training and contribute thousands of hours to archaeological study. Diving with a Purpose (DWP) is an international organization of divers who specialize in assisting in African Diaspora projects.[6] Their flagship program, Maritime Archaeology Training, is a weeklong course that builds skills in mapping shipwrecks underwater. They also sponsor Youth Diving with a Purpose in partnership with Biscayne National Park. To date, DWP has trained five hundred divers who have documented eighteen shipwrecks in six countries and donated over 18,000 hours of service.

Working in Rural Communities

People in rural communities are often wary of outsiders, particularly government officials. However, fostering trust is vital to achieving local cooperation on archaeological projects. Hiring someone from or respected by the community when possible often fosters trust. Additionally, a program developer should assess the priorities of community members regarding the resources, encourage local participation, and support ongoing work. Offer volunteers an honorarium, access passes, or something they see as a privilege for their service.

When seeking volunteers in rural communities, consider that there is a limited pool of people who likely live a significant distance apart and may only gather for special events, religious activities, work, or school. To engage such communities, start by attending community events and getting to know community leaders. These connections will help you find the best strategies for advertising to dispersed people.

The Arizona Site Stewardship Program established an advisory committee to work in collaboration with rural communities. Because Arizona is a large state, the program manager is unlikely to have local knowledge of the preservation priorities of every community, so local officials, Tribal representatives, and federal and state land managers assist in making decisions and providing support on a local level.

Textbox 9.2. Citizen Stewardship—Breaking Barriers

Rayette Martin

Rural community members and off-road enthusiasts are two often untapped allies for helping manage cultural sites on public lands. Through community participation (riding off-road, participating in the rodeo, hosting booths with free activities at community events, and engaging with locals), I broke into both the rural and off-road communities and learned that they want to both preserve their access to and assist in preserving cultural sites. However, formal programs do not work.

These communities rarely participate in preservation programs like the state-run Nevada Site Stewardship Program (NSSP) because of restrictions placed on volunteers, like sharing site information, riding off-highway vehicles, and carrying firearms. A lack of trust in federal entities, especially the Bureau of Land Management (BLM) in western states, complicates matters. For example, 90 percent of NSSP's archaeological sites are managed by federal entities and require signed agreements with the agency for stewardship.

To address these barriers, citizen stewardship was developed and is being promoted by the nonprofit Nevadans for Cultural Preservation. Anyone can report damage to cultural sites in Nevada through a web page managed by NSSP. Individuals decide when and where they are going and report only when finding damage. Citizen stewardship provides a valuable opportunity for these communities to participate in preservation.

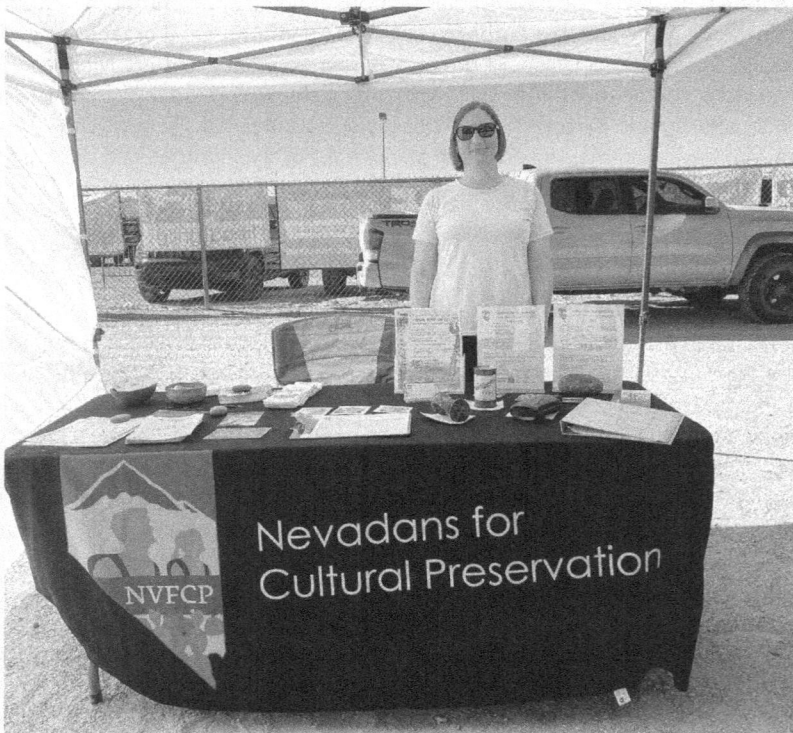

Figure 9.2. NFVCP outreach booth at an annual off-road event, Hump-n-Bump, in October 2022. *Courtesy of Nevadans for Cultural Preservation*

Samantha R. Rubinson and Sarah E. Miller

Historical Cemeteries

In 2011, the Florida Public Archaeology Network (FPAN) held its first Cemetery Resource Protection Training (CRPT) workshop.[7] Historic cemeteries, particularly African American cemeteries, are endangered cultural resources vulnerable to demolition by neglect. CRPT was developed to train local communities with management strategies to help keep cemetery features aboveground and in place for another one hundred years. The workshop begins with participants building a "Cemetery of Us," adapted from the "Museum of Us" introductory lesson to Project Archaeology, where they draw their final resting place to share with the class.[8] The activity begins a daylong conversation about cemeteries as a section of a population, what people buried in a cemetery have in common, and the different management strategies we could use for what becomes a very diverse paper landscape on the wall. The workshop continues with an overview of historic cemetery management, a presentation on cemetery laws for the state where the workshop is taking place, detailed descriptions of how to record historic cemeteries for the official state inventory (e.g., the Florida Master Site File), and the need for monitoring historical cemeteries with repeat visits at least once a year. Workshop participants also travel to a local cemetery to practice documenting and assessing headstones. Participants especially enjoy headstone cleaning, where they scrub and wash away biological growth with a D/2 solution recommended by the National Center for Preservation Technology and Training (NCPTT).

You will find volunteers interested in cemeteries nearly everywhere. Many people love history and genealogy or have family members in local cemeteries. FPAN has trained over one thousand volunteers since CRPT began and has held four conferences for program graduates. In 2023, CRPT traveled to Kentucky to conduct two workshops in different counties, thus demonstrating the template does easily transfer. To start a cemetery stewardship program, it is highly recommended that you attend an NCPTT workshop on cemetery maintenance and become familiar with the organizations commonly involved in cemetery preservation like American Gravestone Studies chapters, state and local historical societies, and genealogy groups. Veterans are another great resource for information, and they are often willing to dedicate volunteer hours to document military headstones.

Site Stewardship Programs

Site stewardship programs use volunteers to monitor and document changes to cultural resources. These volunteer-based programs require cooperation between land managers and participants, and they are often developed by concerned citizens in response to damaged cultural resources resulting from human impacts such as high visitor traffic, looting, graffiti, and erosion. Additionally, the land manager may not have the personnel or funds to monitor, protect, or mitigate the cultural resources that are susceptible to damage. Many of the larger site stewardship programs in the United States were formed by merging small-scale local efforts with management assumed by a larger entity like a state government.[9]

Stewardship programs have three essential components: training, repeat monitoring, and a central location for information storage. Like the archaeology certification programs, volunteers receive training in culture history, artifact identification, damage assessment, forms, reporting, safety, and ethics. However, stewards place an emphasis on repeat visits to a single site and focus on site assessment strategies. The scope can vary from a single site or community to an entire state or region of the country.

In 2022, stewardship program managers across the United States were surveyed on three major topics: program structure, funding, and technology.[10] The structure of a program is influenced significantly by demographics, resource availability, and the involvement of land managers/owners. While program structures vary, they share common foundational principles. In the western United States, many programs used the Arizona Site Stewardship Program as inspiration. In the eastern United States and the United Kingdom, some organizations were inspired by the Scotland Heritage at Risk Program (SCHARP), developed by Scottish Coastal Archaeology and the Problem of Erosion (SCAPE).[11]

It is important to establish a long-term funding source prior to program launch. The eight oldest and largest stewardship programs in the United States are managed and funded by their state's State Historic Preservation Office (SHPO). Consistent and reliable financial support at the state level directly correlates to the size of the programs. Other forms of funding for stewardship programs include grants, federal assistance, private support, and fundraising. If this is not secured before the launch of a program, sustainability will be an ongoing issue.

In the last ten years, technology has become vital to stewardship programs. You will need to establish a database for monitoring documentation, including site assessment reports and photos, to record how sites change over time and track incidents of damage. It is ideal for volunteers to directly submit their reports and to provide land managers access to the data. Smartphone applications are another option to consider. A custom-built app like ShoreUpdate used by SCAPE for SCHARP is expensive to set up and a challenge to update for iOS and Android. Third-party apps like Field Maps or Survey 1-2-3 can be integrated with existing databases to reduce the costs of developing and updating applications unique to your program.

To run a stewardship program, you must provide training and ongoing support, and assign archaeological site(s) to monitor. Consider offering other ways to volunteer, and always give people recognition for accomplishments. The data they collect can be used by land managers and law enforcement to preserve and protect sites. Conversely, the educational message of stewardship can be integrated into other forms of public outreach. Documentation and photos showing site damage can send a strong message to the public about the illegal destruction of sites and the importance of preservation activities.

In 2018, the Utah state legislature created the Utah Cultural Site Stewardship Program (UCSSP) in response to increasing visitation and damage to cultural resources in the state's numerous national and state parks. The Utah SHPO manages and funds the program. The program structure was intentionally designed to be similar to programs from surrounding states, including Nevada and Arizona. This involved developing a database and smartphone application to aid in data collection, reporting, and archiving. As of 2022, the UCSSP is one of the largest in the country, with 237 trained stewards monitoring 523 sites. UCSSP has assisted in the prosecution of vandals under ARPA, and the long-term results of this program are promising.

FPAN created the Heritage Monitoring Scout (HMS Florida) program in 2016 to engage the public in assessing sites that will be impacted by climate change.[12] The program was relatively easy to start. Staff and volunteers researched similar programs and piloted a beta submission system for site assessment forms and photos. The original Google Doc database migrated to an open-source Arches platform. Subsequently, the program became more formalized, and a formal manual was published as part of the 2019 HMS Florida Special Category Grant funded by the Florida Department of State. During that project, volunteers and staff completed over five hundred assessments of archaeological sites across Florida. HMS Florida volunteers receive training about basic climate change literacy, recognizing and documenting changes to sites over time, and submitting monitoring forms and photos in Arches.

Samantha R. Rubinson and Sarah E. Miller

Textbox 9.3. Heritage Awareness Diving Seminar (HADS)

Nicole Bucchino Grinnan

Archaeology along Florida's coastline tells a prolific narrative of the state's past. Challenges to protecting and preserving submerged cultural resources, however, are significant. The twentieth-century culture of treasure hunting, established with the advent of recreational scuba, has fueled popular romantic perceptions of shipwrecks and shipwreck diving. Many residents and visitors are likewise unaware that submerged cultural resources are generally protected by federal and state laws. Such circumstances often lead to a "perfect storm" in which Florida's submerged cultural sites are both knowingly and unknowingly looted, resulting in loss of knowledge about the past and the destruction of the marine habitats that grow on these sites.

As recreational scuba diving is one of the primary ways that people can access submerged cultural resources, it is surprising that internationally recognized standards for scuba certification across training agencies do not include any references to cultural resource preservation. While new divers are taught to not interfere with or harm marine life, there is no standard that requires instructors to discuss legal or ethical issues surrounding disturbing cultural resources.

The Florida Public Archaeology Network (FPAN) developed the Heritage Awareness Diving Seminar (HADS) to fill the gap in education about submerged cultural resources that is perpetuated by recreational scuba training standards. With over 2.5 million active scuba divers in the United States, and nearly 6 million worldwide, the task of teaching them about the importance of preserving cultural resources is monumental.[1] For this reason, HADS targets dive professionals: those individuals who can impart their understanding of the importance of underwater historic preservation to all the divers they meet or train during their careers. During two classroom sessions, HADS participants learn about maritime archaeology, shipwrecks, and underwater heritage tourism; maritime artifacts; issues in conservation; and laws pertaining to submerged cultural resources. To conclude the course, participants join FPAN staff on dives to two distinctly different shipwreck sites. One site is selected because it has been heavily looted and has little marine life. The other site is selected because it is relatively well preserved, has a vibrant marine ecosystem growing around it, and is an exciting place to bring divers.

For over a decade, HADS has sought to instill a strong preservation ethic among Florida divers, both for the preservation of cultural and natural resources and for the sustainability of Florida's sizeable underwater heritage tourism economy. Buy-in from agencies like the State of Florida's Division of Historical Resources and NOAA's Florida Keys National Marine Sanctuary helps HADS to be successful. Representatives from these agencies regularly co-teach HADS with FPAN staff, a show of solidarity in messaging from both the state and federal government. While HADS has faced some challenges in scheduling courses for busy dive professionals, regular communication with dive shop leadership and virtual training opportunities via Zoom have helped boost attendance. Course benefits and resources also attract new participants. For example, all participants are eligible to become Heritage Awareness Diving Specialty instructors with three of the major scuba training agencies upon completion of HADS. Participants also receive access to up-to-date PowerPoints and scripts for teaching the specialty (or for integrating HADS messages into other scuba training).

Although HADS was initially designed to meet what FPAN perceived to be a need in Florida's recreational scuba industry, the training has found much broader appeal. Dive professionals and cultural resource managers in other states and countries have adopted HADS as the framework for their own submerged cultural resource diver training programs. Similarly, non-divers like museum specialists and educators regularly attend HADS to add to their knowledge about Florida's rich submerged archaeological record.

Learn more at: FPAN.us/HADS

Note

1. "2023 Diving Fast Facts: Fast Facts on Recreational Scuba Diving and Snorkeling," Diving Equipment and Marketing Association, accessed on July 14, 2023, https://www.dema.org/store/download.aspx?id=7811B097-8882-4707-A160-F999B49614B6.

Figure 9.3. HADS Instructor Dr. Della Scott-Ireton on the Mystery Wreck shipwreck site in the Florida Keys National Marine Sanctuary. The Mystery Wreck is a relatively unknown site to divers and, as a result, is extremely well-preserved. *Courtesy of Florida Public Archaeology Network*

SUMMARY

Engaging communities in heritage management programs based on cultural resources can be a powerful experience for both program personnel and volunteers. It is often said, "With education comes appreciation," but appreciation also begets preservation. Training volunteers to participate in preservation and stewardship is both good for the cultural resources and good for the community. With a little training and encouragement from an archaeologist in their community, local residents can make a big difference.

NOTES

1. "Ethics in Professional Archaeology," Society for American Archaeology, accessed on July 14, 2023, https://www.saa.org/career-practice/ethics-in-professional-archaeology.
2. Sarah Miller and Laura Clark, "Heritage Monitoring Scouts (HMS Florida): Archaeologist and Citizen Scientists Respond to Climate Change" (PowerPoint presentation, 10th International Conference on Climate Change: Impacts and Responses, Berkeley, California, 2018.
3. Department of the Interior, "Archaeology and Historic Preservation; Secretary of the Interior's Standards and Guidelines," *Federal Register* 28, no. 190 (1983): 44716-4470.
4. "Ethics in Professional Archaeology."
5. "ASV Archaeological Technician Certification Program," Archaeological Society of Virginia, accessed on July 14, 2023, https://virginiaarcheology.org/archeological_tech_cert_program.
6. "Diving with a Purpose: Restoring Our Oceans, Preserving Our Heritage," Diving with a Purpose, accessed on July 14, 2023, https://divingwithapurpose.org/.
7. Sarah E. Miller, "Cemeteries as Outdoor Museums," *Advances in Archaeological Practice* 3, no. 3 (2015): 257-90.
8. Cali A. Letts and Jeanne M. Moe, *Project Archaeology: Investigating Shelter*, rev ed. (1998; repr., Bozeman: Montana State University, 2012).
9. Sarah E. Miller and Samantha Rubinson, "National Site Stewardship Survey," OSF. 2023 osf.io/qxm3d.
10. Miller and Rubinson.
11. Sarah E. Miller, "Community Engagement in the 21st Century" in *Handbook of Global Historical Archaeology*, eds. Charles Orser, Pedro Funari, Susan Lawrence, James Symonds, and Andrés Zarankin (New York, Routledge, 2020), 150-78.
12. Sarah E. Miller and Emily Jane Murray, "Heritage Monitoring Scouts: Engaging the Public to Monitor Sites at Risk Across Florida," *Conservation and Management of Archaeological Sites* 20 (2018): 234-60.

10

Navigating the Unexpected

Stephanie T. Sperling and Elizabeth C. Reetz

If you have made it this far in the book, you have learned how to effectively prepare, plan, and implement a variety of programs that will engage and excite people of all ages and abilities. What could possibly go wrong?

Spoiler alert—the answer is "everything." To paraphrase the old adage of Murphy's Law, if anything can go wrong, it probably will. Unexpected problems will arise, and you should anticipate challenges, no matter if this is your first time leading a tour or your hundredth elementary school presentation. Unpredictability is the name of the game.

The authors of this book and our colleagues could undoubtedly fill an entire volume with our own "whoops" moments. Some of our greatest hits include the times when:

- A senior manager fell out of his kayak during a tour on a chilly October day,
- Four hundred people showed up for a public tour when the organizers anticipated twenty-five or fewer,
- Four people attended a talk in an auditorium with capacity for 150 (leaving 146 empty seats),
- A group of forty Scouts and their families showed up to a volunteer dig day that had capped pre-registration at twenty participants, and
- An evening STEM event limited to groups of fifteen fourth-graders turned into a pre-K free-for-all with dozens of toddler siblings who were brought along by their parents.

This only scratches the surface.

It is easy to get frustrated at setbacks, especially when you have invested your heart, soul, time, and money into a program. A stressful event could even make you question the point of all these endeavors. But the connections you make may have unexpected and lasting impacts, in addition to providing an excellent opportunity for learning and growth (not to mention a potentially hilarious story).

When the unforeseen happens, it is imperative to respond calmly and effectively to minimize the impact on attendees and the overall success of the event. Develop a plan to deal with urgent concerns like injuries or cultural insensitivity, and delegate responsibilities and tasks to team members based on their expertise and strengths. Stay calm, assess the situation, and always prioritize the safety of your audience.

Textbox 10.1. No Leathers? No Demonstrators!

A. Gwynn Henderson for the Living Archaeology Weekend Steering Committee

Living Archaeology Weekend (LAW) is Kentucky's longest continuously running archaeology education program (www.livingarchaeologyweekend.org). This award-winning, immersive event is held annually in eastern Kentucky's archaeologically rich Red River Gorge. Over the course of two days, more than 2,000 school children and public visitors experience American Indian and Frontier Kentucky lifeways by doing and observing their technologies. Visitors also are exposed to archaeological interpretation and site preservation.[1] The LAW program goes beyond the two-day event, demonstrating the parallels between ancient and modern technologies and highlighting connections that stretch through millennia.

In 2023, LAW celebrated its thirty-fifth birthday. Given such longevity, the LAW Steering Committee has experienced its share of "situations" that have upended event programming, forcing us to pivot in real time. For example, there was the year unexpected torrential rains forced us to move everything indoors . . . at the last minute. And routinely, a school bus (or two) is late, and this throws off our carefully crafted schedule *completely*.

But none of these "Oh No!" moments come close to the "No Leathers" year.

At the event the previous year, Tribal demonstrators had voiced their concerns about insensitivity in our programming. White demonstrators were wearing leather outfits, an act perceived by Tribal people as an appropriation of Native cultural elements. This practice was a passive holdover from an earlier version of the event, but that was no excuse for it to continue.

The LAW Steering Committee "pivoted" in response. We sent out an email, which included guidelines for demonstrating at LAW, to all non-Native demonstrators. In it we explained that, out of respect for Tribal peoples, they could no longer wear leathers at the event. This was also in keeping with their role as third-person interpreters, who do not dress in character. To the committee, this request seemed like a small change to make.

The fallout from non-Native demonstrators to this "small" change was immediate and not at all positive. From their perspective, the ban was upending a tradition. Their feelings were hurt. They felt disrespected.

LAW Steering Committee members were shocked at the response, although upon reflection, *why* we were so surprised is difficult to explain. Out of the blue, with no warning and with no conversation or discussion, the committee had told the demonstrators, most of whom had been LAW demonstrators for over fifteen years, to adjust their presentations.

The committee "pivoted" a second time, scrambling to address the non-Native demonstrators' concerns in a meaningful way with the respect and integrity all parties deserved. We acknowledged their feedback and recognized their need to feel "heard" as significant contributors to the program. We explained again in an email why we had made the decision, but our decision was nonnegotiable: they could not dress in leathers. One-on-one discussions were held with several demonstrators.

There were tangible repercussions. LAW lost a couple of demonstrators—voluntarily or were not asked back by the LAW Steering Committee. But the valuable lessons the committee learned—specific ones and ones that were broadly focused—more than made up for those losses.

The situation forced us to truly see the demonstrators: they were equal partners, not passive content providers. Now the committee considers the multiple groups who make LAW what it is—demonstrators, the LAW Steering Committee, volunteers, sponsors—as collaborators.

Figure 10.1. Pump drills are a popular hands-on activity at Living Archaeology Weekend
Courtesy of D. Applegate (2013), used courtesy of Living Archaeology Weekend Steering Committee

The event also improved enormously. Now:

- Tribal peoples know we are responsive to their concerns.
- The event is not stereotyping Native peoples as exclusively skin-wearers through historically inaccurate clothing.
- White demonstrators are not impersonating Native peoples.

But perhaps most importantly, the "No Leathers" year provided the impetus for needed changes. Our perception of the event expanded. We reflected on the true purpose and goals of the event—and how well we were adhering to them—not just on what the audience was learning, for that had been our primary concern up to that point. In the end, we discovered that "Oh No!" moments are often really "Ah Ha!" moments.

Note

1. A. Gwynn Henderson, Darlene Applegate, Wayna L. Adams, Tressa T. Brown, and Christy W. Pritchard, with Eric J. Schlarb and Nicolas R. Laracuente, "Living Archaeology Weekend: Building a Bridge to the Past through Technology," in *Y la Arqueologia Llego al Aula: La Cultura Material y el Metodo Arqueologico para la Ensenanza de la Historia y el Patrimonio*, 3rd ed., eds. Alejandro Egea-Vivancos, Laura Arias Ferrer, and Joan Santacana (Gijón, 2018), 253–89; Linda S. Levstik, A. Gwynn Henderson, and Youngdo Lee, "The Beauty of Other Lives: Material Culture as Evidence of Human Ingenuity and Agency," *The Social Studies* 105, no. 4 (2014), 184–92, https://doi.org/10.1080/00377996.2014.886987.

In all cases, good communication is crucial. Even if the crisis is somewhat minor, like a technology failure during a hybrid lecture, keep your attendees informed. Transparency builds trust, even in challenging situations. If the issue caused inconvenience or disruption, acknowledge the problem and apologize if necessary.

Above all, learn from the experience. Conduct a thorough debrief with your team to process what went wrong and use this knowledge to improve future programs. Follow up with collaborators and attendees, gather feedback, and address concerns. If appropriate, share your insights and experiences with peers or mentors and keep a healthy sense of humor and humility. It is easy to get frustrated and discouraged, but remember that the benefits of sharing the joy and wonder of our archaeological past far outweigh the challenges.

THE COVID-19 PANDEMIC

The most disruptive force in recent memory was the COVID-19 pandemic that began in early 2020. Millions of lives were lost, and countless other people endured fundamental changes to their livelihoods. The pandemic shuttered businesses, disrupted supply chains, and compounded a health crisis with an economic crisis. Despite some monetary support from governmental programs, almost every industry was deeply impacted.

Public archaeology was no exception. Prior to COVID-19, our outreach largely focused on in-person experiences. With an emphasis on tangible material culture and experiential learning, our underfunded programs seldom ventured to virtual formats. We also lacked the technology and capacity to shift away from the status quo. But like so many others, public archaeologists rapidly pivoted to digital platforms. We adapted our programming and learned how to approach different formats of outreach. This tragedy challenged existing norms and practices but also provided opportunities for growth and innovation.

We hit the ground running, often stumbling, to increase our programmatic scope. At the beginning, many of us found ourselves unprepared for the privacy, security, and accessibility concerns that came with virtual outreach. While some of our efforts failed, we were able to share our discipline with far-flung audiences, experiment with new technologies, embrace openness and inclusivity, and adopt digital accessibility best practices. Later, social distancing inspired new ways to connect with vulnerable communities. These initiatives required flexibility, ingenuity, and endless last-minute adaptability.

Although there is no substitute for the hands-on learning afforded by field and lab opportunities, some of our pandemic-era formats are here to stay. Virtual presentations are now standard offerings for schools and communities where technology was updated using government-issued pandemic funds. We can quickly pivot to such a format when conditions are unsafe to travel to an in-person program. Other times, virtual programming is more economical. Gone are the costs for transportation and accommodation to participate in a one-hour program across the state! To an extent, we now know what we didn't know before the pandemic, and if anything, we know we still have a lot to learn.

While accessibility was often an afterthought prior to the pandemic, public archaeologists now seek ways to be more inclusive to vulnerable individuals and people who cannot travel. These efforts build a broader community, allow for a more diverse range of participation, and promote social equity (see chapter 3).

To explore the effects of the pandemic on public archaeology, the editors of this book organized a 2022 Society for American Archaeology (SAA) conference symposium called "How will COVID-19 Shape the Future of Public Archaeology?" The diverse methods and approaches highlighted in the symposia later inspired this publication. Twenty archaeologists participated in the Chicago session and shared their experiences with the socially distanced, vaccinated, and masked crowd at the first in-person conference many of us had attended in years. Ironically, one of our participants tested positive for the virus the morning of the session and was unable to attend. She took the lessons learned from the previous two years and quickly recorded her presentation in her hotel room, which was then presented to the in-person audience a few hours later.

The presentations highlighted the disruptions and innovations that public archaeologists encountered. Nearly all the speakers described their pivot to digital programming, with varying speeds of adaptation. The Archaeological Institute of America (AIA) was no stranger to virtual outreach, but the pandemic forced them to adapt and scale up by launching Listening Sessions, Tweetathons, and online ArchaeoCons, along with transforming the 124-year-old national lecture program into a series of over two hundred webinars.[1]

Crow Canyon Archaeological Center launched a "Discover Archaeology" webinar series, which ran for over eighteen months.[2] This work was complemented by a series of K–12 educational videos to use in conjunction with mailed kits of hands-on material. Meanwhile, the University of New Mexico provided for hands-on learning with an undergraduate "Introduction to Archaeological Method and Theory" hybrid class. The professors distributed "lab kits," including ceramics, lithics, and owl pellets, in advance of two in-person outdoor lessons.[3]

Some archaeologists sought new funding to develop programs. The University of Iowa Office of the State Archaeologist (OSA) received an Institute of Museum and Library Services grant under the Coronavirus Aid, Relief, and Economic Security (CARES) Act to co-develop "Connected for Life: Object-based Digital Programming to Foster Active Minds for Senior Living Communities."[4] This project offered accessibility-minded synchronous virtual programs to older adults using objects curated at the OSA. Project Archaeology acquired National Endowment for the Humanities (NEH) funds to implement "Voices of the Ancients: Archaeology and Oral Tradition in the American Southwest."[5] Upper elementary, middle school, and high school teachers from over thirty states convened at Southern Utah University to engage with archaeologists and Tribal Elders. The summer institute emphasized the importance of including Native voices in American history narratives and provided educators with the tools and knowledge to transfer their learning about Fremont history and culture to their students in classrooms across the nation. The Vermont Archaeological Society led an NEH Landmarks of American History and Culture Workshop that was designed to be held in person but was ultimately transformed to virtual in the summer of 2021.[6] This challenged them to teach place-based education fully online. Their innovative use of technology helped to deliver a successful and highly reviewed workshop that was, in many ways, more usable for teachers than the in-person version may have been.

Partnerships were vital during the pandemic. At Virginia Commonwealth University, the Virtual Curation Lab teamed with several cultural heritage organizations across the Mid-Atlantic region to scan and digitize sites and artifacts.[7] These were presented as online 3D renderings used for various creative initiatives by the National Park Service, SAA, and Germanna Archaeology. In other instances, universities searched for ways to maintain and foster relationships with local communities during the pandemic. The University of Hawaii West Oahu 2021 field school used community-based participatory research to develop a collaborative venture that was done with, by, and for the community during the Kalaeloa Heritage Park Project.[8] They established ways to monitor sites in the park and update their site management plan before conducting a traditional site survey with a small group of socially distanced participants.

The pandemic also enabled worldwide connections, particularly during quarantine. The University of Minnesota Morris, located in rural west-central Minnesota, created global opportunities for students during this time.[9] Larger classrooms were made Zoom-ready, several students attended major online conferences, and anthropology classes welcomed international archaeology speakers. The public archaeology projects around the site of Las Huacas in the Chincha Valley of Peru were also forced to adapt during COVID-19.[10] In 2019, the Proyecto de Investigación Arqueológica las Huacas

(PIALH) began to develop public archaeology programs around the site of Las Huacas and laid the groundwork for community connections. During COVID-19, site history was retold online for children ages six through thirteen using both synchronous and asynchronous content. Students learned about the possibilities of working in cultural heritage and engaged a wide range of professionals. However, attention spans varied, and it was difficult to coordinate cell phone use for the kids. That said, their work demonstrated the potential of digital content but also highlighted the need for local collaborators. Distribution and communication about these events would have been extremely difficult and less successful without these partners.

In Colorado, the Program for Avocational Archaeological Certification (PAAC) continued its work during the pandemic.[11] This program facilitates public service and the protection of archaeological resources in Colorado through education, research, and on-the-ground management. While they were able to engage with hundreds of people through online classes, people craved in-person field and lab work. A hybrid format was eventually established as post-pandemic protocol. In Prince George's County, Maryland, archaeologists with the Maryland-National Capital Park and Planning Commission, Department of Parks and Recreation had varying degrees of success with pandemic-era programming.[12] They created and produced short videos, implemented virtual summer camps, developed outdoor lab events, and organized hybrid conversation circles. While some of the outreach efforts continue, most were abandoned or heavily modified when in-person programming resumed.

The passion and dedication of these archaeologists is admirable. Professionals in our field are noted for their problem-solving ability, and the conundrum of creating programming during a pandemic presented a rare challenge. We experienced successes and failures. While the COVID-19 pandemic may fade into memory, we should reflect on how it impacted public archaeology. Through flexibility and trial and error, we made the big pivot. The lessons we learned will shape the future of public outreach for years to come.

The following chapter provides an in-depth look at how a private company dedicated to archaeological education and outreach modified and innovated numerous programs during the pandemic to stay in business and engage communities across Ireland and beyond. The founders were able to navigate challenges and emerge with a renewed approach to their mission. By learning about the company's experiences, successes, and challenges, we hope you will gain valuable insight into the resilience of archaeologists in the face of unforeseen obstacles. Moreover, the chapter underscores the importance of adaptability and perseverance in sustaining educational endeavors, ultimately highlighting an enduring commitment to fostering a deeper understanding and appreciation of cultural resources through community-based archaeology.

NOTES

The following citations were presentations at the 87th Annual Meeting of the Society for American Archaeology, Chicago, Illinois, April 2, 2022.

1. Meredith Langlitz and Ben Thomas, "Online Activities and Content, Networking, and the Importance of Community: Lessons from Presenting Public Programs in a Pandemic."
2. Tayler Hasbrouck and Tyson Hughes, "From the Landscape to the Living Room: Making Public Archaeology Virtual."
3. Genevieve Woodhead and Asia Alsgaard, "Helping Hands and Hands-On Learning."
4. Elizabeth Reetz, "An Overview and Assessment of Virtual Object-based Archaeology Programming for Older Adults in Senior Living Communities."
5. Jeanne Moe and Samantha Kirkley, "Voices of the Ancients: Providing Safe, In-Person Teacher Workshops during a Global Pandemic."
6. Angela Labrador, "Revolutionary Past Meets Digital Future: Going Virtual with Place-based Teacher Training."

7. Bernard Means, Ashley McCuistion, and Mariana Zechini, "Can't Touch This: 3D Archaeology and Public Outreach during a Global Pandemic."
8. Kirsten Vacca, "Community-based Participatory Research in the Era of COVID-19."
9. Rebecca Dean, "Stuck in the Middle (of Nowhere) with You: How the COVID Disruption Brought Educational Opportunities to Rural Minnesota."
10. Jordan Dalton, Bryan Núñez Aparcana, Mary Avila Peltroche, and Sol Donayre Pachas, "Community Archaeology in Peru during COVID: Taking a Site-based Approach Digital."
11. Rebecca Simon, "'PAAC Tales': The Past, Present, and (Hopefully) Future of the Program for Avocational Archaeological Certification."
12. Stephanie Sperling, "Innovate, Adapt, and Pivot: Creating Flexible Public Programming during a Global Pandemic."

11

The Effects of COVID-19 on Public Archaeology

A VIEW FROM IRELAND

Denis Shine and Stephen Mandal

This chapter presents a personal account of one Irish company operating in the public archaeology sphere during the COVID-19 pandemic. The Irish Heritage School (IHS) is a private company offering university-accredited heritage research and training courses for Irish and international students, typically on projects deeply embedded within local communities. All IHS programs and projects focus strongly on public archaeology (referred to as community archaeology in the United Kingdom and Ireland) with a core ethos that attempts to facilitate "engagement and meaning of the past in the present."[1]

Writing this reflective paper three years on from the height of the COVID-19 pandemic is challenging and cathartic in equal measure, revisiting as it does traumas left by a near-unprecedented global emergency, the true impacts of which might not be understood for many years to come. Ireland, as a Western country with an extremely high vaccine uptake (90.8 percent of the population received at least one dose of the vaccine[2]), dealt with the pandemic as well as could be hoped. However, the virus's consequences were still substantial and might be crudely summarized as having three major impact groups:

1. Those impacted directly during COVID-19 by death or serious illness.
2. Those impacted economically through loss of employment, business closure, etc.
3. Those impacted socially and emotionally by the impacts of the virus and its associated public health measures (for example, lockdowns).

Our experience falls firmly in groups two and three, with our main revenue-generating activities effectively shut down from March 26, 2020, to July 19, 2021. We present a synopsis of our story immediately prior to and during this "lockdown period" as an example of a public archaeology response to a virtually unprecedented global health crisis.

THE IHS IN A PRE-PANDEMIC WORLD

Pre-COVID-19, we had a long-established commitment to public archaeological practice in Ireland and internationally.[3] Since our first community-based field school at the Black Friary in Trim, County

Meath, in 2010, the IHS has long recognized the potential that field schools have as exemplars of community archaeology practice.[4] The role of field schools has perhaps additional importance in Ireland as community archaeology is much younger than in other countries and, while growing in popularity, remains poorly defined and under-practiced.[5] As such, field schools in an Irish context have significant scope to advocate for and facilitate greater community participation in the archaeological process.

Following principles that argue that archaeology's relevance, in fact, depends on public engagement, the IHS runs all their field schools (in Wexford in southeast Ireland and, more recently, in the Irish midlands) in a manner that maximizes the potential for direct and indirect community engagement with their heritage.[6] Most typically, this included regular public outreach events such as open days, children's camps, pop-up museums, lecture series, community workshops, community excavations, etc. Pre-pandemic, these public outreach events were facilitated and financed by international students working at our schools, who pay a fee to earn academic credits and gain in-field training.

A tangible ancillary economic benefit of our field school model to the host community is that students stay with local families during their time on the project. Besides giving the students a more meaningful and immersive cultural experience and providing revenue for local families, in our experience, "homestay" also serves to draw families into their heritage. It is one thing to attend a lecture or site tour by an academic, it is another to have a student come home every evening filled with enthusiasm for what they are doing and learning. The enthusiasm of the students breaks down barriers to the research element of our work and encourages greater participation amongst the local community. The economic benefits of students visiting a community are, of course, not only restricted to the homestay hosts but extend to local hospitality, tourism, catering, and other business sectors.

A good example of the multifaceted community benefits of one of our larger ventures is the recent Digging the Lost Town of Carrig project, which was based on excavations (from 2018 to 2022) at the site of Carrick, the first recorded Anglo-Norman castle in Ireland (dating from 1169 CE).[7] The site is located within the Irish National Heritage Park (INHP) in County Wexford, in southeast Ireland. The INHP is the largest open-air museum in Ireland, consisting of thirty-five acres of natural forestry that recreates nine thousand years of history through a series of replica structures. IHS commenced

Figure 11.1. An aerial shot of Carrick immediately prior to excavations commencing in 2018. *Courtesy of Irish Heritage School*

Denis Shine and Stephen Mandal

Figure 11.2. An aerial shot of St Mary's Abbey immediately prior to excavations concluding in 2023. *Courtesy of Dan O'Meara Photography*

an excavation and education project at the site in 2017 and provided both the local community and visitors with numerous immersive opportunities to engage with the site's archaeology. These included tours for the sixty-thousand-plus annual park visitors, open days, children's camps, experimental archaeology activities, and immersive weeklong community excavations.

A second research project in County Wexford, Discovering St. Aidan's Monastery, was also founded in partnership with the local community shortly prior to COVID-19. This project commenced with a set of community-run geophysical surveys at Clone, an early medieval enclosure near the medieval town of Ferns. These surveys were followed by two seasons of community excavations at Clone and a series of archaeological surveys in Ferns itself;[8] collectively, these activities paved the way for the marquee excavation around St. Mary's Church, a circa 1160s Augustinian Abbey in Ferns.[9] Like Carrick, the goal of the Discovering St. Aidan's Monastery project was to run a best-practice archaeological research program while providing economic and heritage value to the local community. The project was administered with a clear partnership approach and offered walks, talks, open days, pop-up museums, family days, school visits, community publications, archaeological camps, successive seasons of community excavations, etc.

THE IHS IN A PANDEMIC WORLD

The COVID-19 virus reached Ireland in February 2020, with a lockdown beginning in March 2020 that subsequently proved to be the longest in Europe. Successive lockdowns in October 2020 and late December 2020 were also collectively amongst the strictest in the world. Responding to the threat posed by COVID-19 and wishing to provide surety to all partners at each of our field schools, we made the difficult decision to cancel all our 2020 field programs on March 26. This decision was not taken lightly, as all our community outreach work was either directly dependent on or indirectly funded by fees from our educational programs. However, we felt a full closure was the wisest course of action to protect the well-being and safety of our staff, students, partners, and, crucially, the communities we worked with. However, being the first to shut in our sector in Ireland gave us more time to plan for COVID-19, allowing us to initiate a creative and positive three-pronged approach:

1. Create an online community, including community-based educational programming, which we call the Virtual Heritage School (VHS).
2. Migrate our field projects and their community outreach online.
3. Commence accredited online student programming. This programming would be followed by blended programs, which would mix real on-site research (facilitated by community volunteers as restrictions allowed) with online collegiate courses.

Each of these initiatives was established with multiple contingency plans, which would allow the IHS to react to ever-changing restrictions and public health advice.

Virtual Heritage School (VHS)

Our first response, as with most organizations worldwide, was to go virtual, and on March 27, 2020, a day after canceling all our field schools, we launched the VHS. Launching a virtual school immediately after closing our main revenue streams was obviously the culmination of a long process of development and contingency planning, with the VHS being the quickest and easiest initiative to launch as it required no external input or permissions. Retrospectively, being the first in our sector to migrate online not only helped secure our survival through COVID-19, but also helped the IHS recover more seamlessly in a post-lockdown environment.

The VHS was originally conceived as a short-term solution, keeping us connected to local community members, field school alumni, and the wider heritage sector. It featured online lectures and talks, archaeological book and television reviews, heritage-themed children's activities, video tutorials and tours, online coffee mornings, and more. However, it quickly became apparent that dedicated community-focused educational programs for both adults and children could be provided under the VHS umbrella, leading to two of our most successful pandemic initiatives, the Dig it Kids workshops and the Know Your Locality courses.

Dig it Kids Workshops

Dig it Kids was co-founded by IHS director Stephen Mandal in 2010 (becoming part of the IHS group in 2023) with the aim of inspiring children's love of learning and sense of awe of the world around them through fun, hands-on activities and storytelling. Pre-pandemic, all Dig it Kids activities were held in person. In recognition that young children and their parents needed support during the lockdown, the Dig it Kids team designed and presented a series of free online workshops every Saturday morning from March through May 2020. These two-hour sessions combined fun facts, crafts, and stories and had a regular attendance of over two hundred children from Ireland, the United Kingdom, France, Spain, Dubai, and the United States. The success of the online workshops resulted in a Community Heroes Award from the Irish national radio station Newstalk. Subsequent to this award, we were approached and partnered by the Irish Heritage Council through their Heritage in Schools Scheme to assist a small group of heritage specialists in delivering a pilot virtual program for primary (elementary) schools in counties Donegal and Kilkenny. Over a six-week period, we virtually visited over fifty schools, undertaking archaeological crafts and telling stories on Irish prehistory and history. In total, from our virtual school visits through to June 2021, we reached over 250 classrooms (some 6,500 children). These school visits were also complemented by virtual events for several county libraries throughout the country across a similar timeframe.

Know Your Locality Courses

In February 2021, with funding from Ancient Connections (a cross-border program between Pembrokeshire in Wales and County Wexford to help develop shared arts, heritage, trade, and tourism), we conceived and delivered a free online adult educational program, called Know Your Locality. This course was envisioned as a community archaeology initiative that would equip participants with archaeological research skills, ultimately permitting them to explore monuments within five kilometers of their home (the maximum permitted travel distance allowed by the stay-at-home directive at the time). The pilot was attended by over 500 people from throughout Ireland, as well as from as far afield as the United Kingdom, Europe, the United States, and Canada. Arising from the success of the free pilot program, Offaly County Council approached us to prepare a custom county-specific course in March 2021. Since that initial county-specific course, we have prepared and delivered over twenty similar community courses for twelve county councils throughout Ireland, all of which have engaged and enthused communities on their local built and cultural heritage.

Migrating Field Projects Online

As stated, when COVID-19 arrived in Ireland, our marquee archaeological project was Digging the Lost Town of Carrig, while Discovering St. Aidan's Monastery had only just commenced. Our primary concern after shutting these projects was to keep the archaeological and local communities engaged as wholly as possible—an objective made easier through strategic partnerships and support from both Wexford County Council and Ancient Connections.

For our Carrick project, we created a series of online specialist master classes on topics such as ceramics, bioarchaeology, zooarchaeology, and geoarchaeology, each being a specialism that underpinned our understanding of Carrick specifically, but also medieval Irish society at large. Each of the five master classes consisted of forty- to fifty-minute-long professionally produced videos with one of Ireland's foremost archaeological specialists, followed the next day by a live online lecture and Q&A with that specialist. Collectively, the video and lecture were intended to replicate as closely as possible an "in-person" expert tutorial. The videos were recorded during an initial relaxation in COVID-19 lockdown measures in September 2020 and were made available on a free subscription basis throughout October and November 2020.

The master classes proved a fantastic success, with 300-plus attendees for many of the lectures from Ireland, the United States, the United Kingdom, Europe, Australia, and elsewhere. The audience was an eclectic mix of Wexford locals, students, enthusiasts, and even several Cultural Resource Management professionals who chose to attend the classes as part of their continuing professional development.

During COVID-19, the IHS and INHP also produced a virtual hour-long tour of the heritage park with the park's media consultants, Crannóg Media. As the only authentic archaeological site in the park, Carrick was a central aspect of this virtual tour. Arising from this initial production was a site-specific tour featuring the excavation within its wider medieval landscape. This tour was recorded as a thirty-minute guided video with segments at each of Carrick's most important monuments, several of which are in private ownership and closed to visitation, even outside of pandemic restrictions. The tour meant the "visitor" could tour the castle, the borough, the later demesne, or any part of Carrick they chose to explore, and remains a useful teaching aid to this day. These longer tour videos were complemented by several more accessible video shorts (three to five minutes in length), which showcased the project's research.

While the Discovering St. Aidan's Monastery project in Ferns was not as advanced as Carrick at the start of the pandemic, concerted efforts were made to highlight it digitally, such as through the preparation of similar professionally produced video shorts. However, unlike at Carrick, the main aim

Figure 11.3. Recording taking place for our master class series, during a relaxation in COVID-19 lockdown measures. *Courtesy of Irish Heritage School*

at Ferns was to produce more interactive educational programs that could be accessed by international and Irish students and, as importantly, by the local community. The first of these was a free online forensic anthropology course covering burial excavation techniques, osteological profiling, and skeletal pathologies. The success of this pilot program subsequently saw it adapted as a fully accredited university course.

Online and Blended Programming

The success of our pilot forensic anthropology course reinforced that opportunities still existed for online third-level study abroad courses, as well as potentially in blended learning. Following the June 2020 pilot, we adapted our online educational materials and with our partners, Maynooth University, one of the largest universities in Ireland, we commenced delivering our accredited online Dead Men Do Tell Tales course; this program ultimately ran three times, in November 2020 and March and June 2021, before travel restrictions were finally lifted, and students and community members alike could resume attending our projects in person. The Dead Men Do Tell Tales course was delivered as a combination of professionally pre-recorded tutorials, laboratory sessions, and workshops, which were supplemented with live lectures, "Q&A" sessions, and guided independent research time. Each day, participants were provided with instructional videos (ten minutes to one hour in length), which they were required to watch in advance of the next day's live online instruction. Students were then sent assignments, such as field assessment sheets and site journal entries, which were evaluated in online group feedback sessions. One benefit of participants watching videos and completing self-directed learning overnight, before formal instruction the next day, was that exercises could be undertaken at an individual's own pace. Buoyed by the success of the forensic anthropology course, the IHS also successfully established a two-week accredited online "excavation" program using several of the methods described for the forensic program.

After producing our first two online courses, we attempted a more ambitious blended program, which in April 2021 was formally accredited by the Institute for Field Research. This program was unique, combining local community volunteers undertaking excavations at our Carrick and Ferns sites with third-level students who would attend remotely. The community volunteers provided the required workforce, while the students, paying fees for an accredited course, would fund the excavation. The production of such an ambitious program followed market research by the IHS that showed that nearly half (44 percent) of our target market would be happy to accept blended learning as an alternative to field-based research in the event of travel restrictions continuing. Thus, The Medieval Landscape of Ferrycarrig and Ferns: A Model in Blended Learning, was founded. The course, focused on excavation skills and bioarchaeology, also featured training in experimental archaeology, public archaeology, survey, and post-excavation techniques. As with previous COVID-19 programs, the online component of the course included standard online lectures and pre-recorded videos, but with the crucial addition of "trench training" sessions, whereby online students would join the site on a live feed for daily discussion of the excavation findings, thus allowing online and field participants to attend excavation in live time together!

Time differences were an obvious challenge, particularly for North American students, so the online excavation was scheduled from 1 to 5 p.m. Irish time. Online students also joined our "Custard Cream Chats" (named after every dig crew's favorite biscuit/cookie)—an informal lunchtime discussion on the excavation, where so much field school learning actually takes place.

The blended program, perhaps more than any other initiative we undertook during COVID-19, best exemplified how a creative and adaptable approach to the pandemic could potentially surmount seemingly insurmountable obstacles, like contributing to an excavation from the other side of the world!

Thankfully, we could revert to our pre-pandemic model in late summer 2021 with strict social distancing measures in place. While the blended program did not continue, its production represented a new level of creative thinking and innovation within the organization. Creating the course also resulted in a range of video tutorials, which have since proven invaluable to both our field students and community volunteers as revision aids and preparatory educational materials.

REFLECTIONS

Once the travel restrictions lifted, we found, rather predictably, that there was a high demand for both community and third-level excavations. From the easing of travel restrictions in July to the end of the 2021 season, we hosted two international field schools and facilitated three community excavations. Other pre-COVID-19 community events also quickly resumed, from tours of the sites to larger marquee events such as our Carrick Open Day, which pre-pandemic had been one of the INHP's largest-ever recorded attendances.

While COVID-19's impact was, of course, most devastating and tragic from a public health point of view, it also obliterated businesses' income streams overnight and sundered established community connections. For the IHS, as with any business related to travel, it was a time of great uncertainty, where our primary concern was to protect our incomes (and those of our staff) while trying to secure our business' future in a forced closure that lasted some sixteen months.

However, despite the ravages of COVID-19, we also found it elicited remarkable kindness, resilience, adaptability, and creativity from both organizations and individuals. Our greatest challenge was how to remain connected while remaining safely at home—a challenge that was best met with flexibility, innovation, and a good sense of community. Like most organizations, we migrated online, finding that this not only kept us connected but also offered new mechanisms by which to engage local people with their past!

Well-practiced community archaeology has always incorporated diverse strategies to facilitate the involvement of local people.[10] The pandemic simply prompted this range of strategies to expand, with online initiatives allowing us to engage a wider community. The ever-changing nature of the pandemic also demanded incredible flexibility and reflexivity. Our engagement strategies needed to constantly evolve with the pandemic, with several responses never reaching full fruition, despite considerable planning. Conversely, other ventures (such as our online adult and children's community programming) proved incredibly successful, with the IHS continuing to maintain these programs post-pandemic. With the benefit of hindsight, the most successful ventures were those that involved the greatest consultation with local communities and academic partners. The need for rigorous consultation has long been recognized in community archaeology, partly to counter historical criticisms of archaeology as being elitist and non-responsive to community demands.[11] Throughout the pandemic, we remained in constant contact with students, community members, alumni, and local groups, listening to how best we might support them in a highly volatile environment and/or change our practices to best meet the challenges posed to our sector. It was this partnership approach that helped ensure our digital successes.

The pandemic also permitted valuable time to reevaluate our personal and professional pathways, as well as our company's strategic direction. Although the pandemic caused significant financial stress for the IHS, it permitted time to succeed in other areas and initiate long-term planning. For example, during the pandemic we were awarded a significant community grant, allowing us to expand our experimental archaeology activities in partnership with the INHP. The work undertaken with this grant undoubtedly contributed to our being the only Republic of Ireland site nominated for the Outstanding Archaeological Achievement award in December 2021. More significantly, almost immediately after our first lockdown was implemented, and still in the early stages of the pandemic, we commenced an innovative project restoring a set of historic buildings in Birr, County Offaly, as our headquarters—a project that is a thirty-year commitment by us to the town of Birr to see these buildings returned to both educational and community use. Now two years on from the pandemic, these buildings are central to all our third-level and community projects.

To conclude somewhat philosophically . . . perhaps we should not be surprised by the innovation COVID-19 inspired? Historically, some of our greatest works of literature, art, and science have been inspired during social distancing. Shakespeare is argued to have penned several of his great plays (such as *King Lear*, *Macbeth*, and *Antony and Cleopatra*) while plague repeatedly ravaged London in the early seventeenth century. Mary Shelley is thought to have written *Frankenstein* while on lockdown because of the "Volcanic Winter" caused by the eruption of Mount Tambora, while Isaac Newton is believed to have formulated some of his greatest ideas while social distancing to combat an outbreak of bubonic plague in 1665. Only time will truly tell what societal responses COVID-19 elicits, including for practitioners of public archaeology! Certainly, for the IHS, it caused financial and emotional stress, but it also encouraged new and innovative community archaeological practice, which ultimately has seen the IHS develop as a more diverse and resilient organization that is better equipped to engage Irish communities in their local heritage.

NOTES

1. Dydia DeLyser, "When Less is More: Absence and Social Memory in a California Ghost Town," in *Textures of Place: Exploring Humanist Geographies*, eds., Paul C. Adams, Steven D. Hoelscher, and Karen E. Till (Minneapolis: University of Minnesota Press, 2001), 24–40.

2. "COVID-19 Vaccination Uptake in Ireland Reports," Health Protection Surveillance Centre, accessed 29 August 2023, https://www.hpsc.ie/a-z/respiratory/coronavirus/novelcoronavirus/vaccination/covid-19vaccinationuptakereports/.

3. Sally K. May, Denis Shine, Duncan Wright, Tim Denham, Paul S. C. Taçon, Melissa Marshall, Inés Domingo Sanz, Faye Prideaux and Sean Paul Stephens, "The Rock Art of Ingaanjalwurr, Western Arnhem Land, Australia," in *The Archaeology of Rock Art in Arnhem Land*, Terra Australis 47, eds. Bruno David, Paul S. C. Taçon, Jean-Jacques Delannoy, and Jean Michel Geneste (Canberra: ANU Press, 2017) 51.

4. Stephen Mandal and Finola O'Carroll, "A New Model for Site Preservation and Archaeological Practice," *Archaeological Institute of America Site Preservation Program: Heritage, Conservation & Archaeology*, 2011; Stephen Mandal, Ran Boytner, Denis Shine, Danny Zborover, D. and Madeleine Harris, "The Carrig Field School: A Model for the Benefits of Field School Education," in *Carrick, County Wexford: Ireland's first Anglo-Norman Stronghold*, eds. Denis Shine, Michael Potterton, Stephen Mandal, and Catherine McLoughlin (Dublin: Four Courts Press, 2019).

5. Christine Baker, "Community Archaeology: More Questions than Answers," *Archaeology Ireland* 30, no. 3 (2016), 37–40; Christine Baker, Finola O'Carroll, Paul Duffy, Denis Shine, Stephen Mandal, and Michael Mongey, "Creating Opportunities and Managing Expectations: Evaluating Community Archaeology in Ireland," in *Transforming Heritage Practice in the 21st Century: Contributions from Community Archaeology*, eds. John H. Jameson and Sergiu Musteață (Switzerland: Springer, 2019), 5–28; Ian W. Doyle, "Community Archaeology in Ireland: Less Mitigator, More Mediator?" in *Shared Knowledge, Shared Power: Engaging Local and Indigenous Heritage*, SpringerBriefs in Archaeology, ed. Veysel Apaydin (Springer Cham, 2018), 45–59; Paul Duffy, "Resurrecting Monuments—A Year in the Life of a Community Archaeology Group," *Archaeology Ireland* 30, no. 1 (2016), 11–14; Thomas Kador, "Public and Community Archaeology: An Irish Perspective," in *Public Participation in Archaeology,* eds. Suzie Thomas and Joanne Lea (Woodbridge: Boydell Press, 2014), 35–48.

6. Kelley M. Berliner and Michael Nassaney, "The Role of the Public in Public Archaeology: Ten Years of Outreach and Collaboration at Fort St. Joseph," *Journal of Community Archaeology & Heritage* 2, no. 1 (2015), 3–21; D. Clark Wernecke and Thomas J. Williams, "From Maya Pyramids to Paleoindian Projectile Points: The Importance of Public Outreach in Archaeology," *Journal of Archaeology and Education* 1 (2017), 1–34.

7. Denis Shine, Stephen Mandal, Christopher Hayes, and Madeleine Harris, "Finding Carrig," *Archaeology Ireland* 32 no. 2 (2018), 35–40; Denis Shine, Michael Potterton, Stephen Mandal, and Catherine McLoughlin, *Carrick, County Wexford: Ireland's first Anglo-Norman Stronghold* (Dublin: Four Courts Press, 2019).

8. Denis Shine, Barry Lacey, Chris Corlett, Ian Elliott, and Stephen Mandal, "Clone, Ferns: A Meadow of St Aidan?" *Archaeology Ireland* 34, no. 4 (2020), 24–29.

9. Stephen Mandal, Michael Potterton, and Denis Shine (eds.), *Discovering Medieval Ferns, Co. Wexford* (Dublin: Four Courts Press, 2023).

10. Stephanie Moser, Darren Glazier, James E. Phillips, Lamya Nasser el Nemr, Mohammed Saleh Mousa, Rascha Nasr Aiesh, Susan Richardson, Andrew Conner, and Michael Seymour, "Transforming Archaeology through Practice: Strategies for Collaborative Archaeology and the Community Archaeology Project at Quseir, Egypt," *World Archaeology* 34, no. 2 (2002), 220–48.

11. Amy Treble, Gavin Smithies, and Hannah Clipson, *The Wider Community's Perception of Archaeology—Elitist or Accessible? Evaluating the Grosvenor Park Excavation* (Chester: University of Chester, 2007); Faye Simpson and H. Williams, "Evaluating community archaeology in the UK," *Public Archaeology* 7, no. 2 (2008): 69–90, https://doi.org/10.1179/175355308X329955.

Section III

Understanding and Communicating Impact and Success

12

Approaches to Assessment and Evaluation

Elizabeth C. Reetz and Rebecca Dean

> Just because we teach some piece of content, and even if we teach it well, we cannot know what learners understand unless we ask them—and ask them we must.[1]

Assessment and evaluation are natural partners to public archaeology and provide informative, data-rich stories about your participants. The terms "assessment" and "evaluation" are sometimes used interchangeably, as they both require data collection, analysis, and interpretation. For our purposes, we are defining assessment (also known as assessment of student/participant learning) as a measurable way to increase the quality of a program with a focus on the individual learner. A public archaeologist could collect assessment data at an event, during a classroom lesson, or after a lecture to determine what their attendees learned. Evaluation (sometimes called program assessment) is typically more in depth and is project- or program-focused. It makes meaning of assessment data, allowing you to judge the quality or effectiveness of a program by looking at how or why it works. For example, you can review your learner-focused assessment data from consecutive years of an ongoing event as one component of an evaluation to help determine what is or is not working and strategize improvements for future iterations.

Assessment and evaluation are challenging, and they require extra planning, effort, time, and funding that may be hard to come by. However, they have the potential to provide many benefits to both individual programs and public archaeology at large, including programmatic improvement, stronger impacts, and positive public relations. Evidence gained from your data can be used to promote programs and services, increase participation, communicate with stakeholders, and emphasize value and benefits to a community. This evidence also strengthens applications for funding opportunities. Many organizations require assessment or evaluation plans for grant-based projects, and having a proven track record for carrying out such plans will strengthen your application.

We also help each other when we share or publish our results (see chapter 13). If we communicate about successes and challenges, we provide opportunities for other professionals to streamline their resources, prevent ourselves from continuing to reinvent the wheel, and offer inspiration for new programs or outreach methods. Most importantly, we help ourselves and strengthen our network of public archaeology practitioners.

Keep in mind that assessment and evaluation done for human subjects research with an intent to publish the results requires ethical approval conducted by an Institutional Review Board (IRB) (see chapter 13). No IRB approval is necessary to collect assessment data to use internally (e.g., keeping records, providing feedback to stakeholders, improving content and instructional methods, etc.).

Considering the limited time and funding typically available for public archaeology programs, it is vital to understand if our efforts are worthwhile. Assumptions and anecdotes are not enough to prove anything, and they do little to convince administrators that these efforts are worth funding. Assessing public programs is ethical archaeology, just as archaeologists have been saying for decades about doing public archaeology.[2] Simply put, it is good science. If we measure our success and impacts, we strengthen our tools for advocacy and the protection of cultural resources, justify funding for public programs, and positively impact public perceptions of preservation and heritage.

ASSESSMENT

What does assessment look like?

- At the end of a public archaeology program that engaged a descendant community, participants are asked to write for ten minutes reflecting on their experience, what they learned about themselves and their community, and the value of archaeology. These notes are compared to a similar writing activity that occurred at the beginning of the program. The testimonials are included in a scrapbook with pictures and mementos for the donors.
- A public archaeologist gives a presentation to elementary students. She then observes the students as they participate in a related activity to see if they use the new vocabulary and concepts she introduced. Their application of the vocabulary is used as evidence of learning in her report on the importance of the classroom program.
- Before a lecture at a local historical society, a three-question survey about archaeology is handed out to all attendees. A QR code is included on the slides to link to an electronic version. When the lecture ends, the same survey is redistributed. The survey results reflect changes in the audience's interest in archaeology before and after the lecture. The public archaeologist uses this increase in interest to argue for more funding for public lectures.

As discussed in chapter 4, establishing strongly defined goals and outcomes is foundational for any successful public archaeology program, and these goals and outcomes are directly tied to assessment (see appendix F). Establishing the intended knowledge, skills, and attitudes for participants informs the creation of the learning outcomes that guide the selection of program activities. To ascertain learner progress, direct inquiry is essential. During a program, we might assume that the audience understands us if they nod in agreement, or we consider a classroom visit a success if the children participate. But how do we *really* know if they were paying attention or engaged? We cannot determine what our learners gained unless we ask them.

Similar to designing programs, crafting goals and outcomes and outlining a strategy is crucial in assessment. This will guide your focus and help to determine effective data collection methods. Just like when you conduct archaeological research, the appropriate data and methods to answer your questions are determined by the goals of your assessment. Testimonials and impact stories might be more appropriate if the goal is to convince private donors to support the program. If your aim is to assess student learning, you might analyze participant essays and reflections. If your project is grant-funded, the grantor may have specific requirements for assessment that will provide a focus.

Ideally, assessments should be implemented before, during, and after a program. Pre-assessments allow you to determine the baseline knowledge of your participants. For example, a program could begin by asking the participants to spend two minutes writing (or discussing) what they know about local archaeology. This type of assessment is an essential building block in the educational process. You must assess what your audience understands before you can build on that knowledge,

Elizabeth C. Reetz and Rebecca Dean

Textbox 12.1. Making Assessment Quick, Easy, and Effective

Elizabeth Pruitt

Pre- and post-program surveys may seem too demanding for young students, but formal questionnaires aren't the only way to gauge understanding and collect feedback. In 2018, when I was the Society for American Archaeology's manager of education and outreach, I assessed participants in a weeklong after-school program using a simple questionnaire and sticky notes.

At the beginning of the first day, I asked students (ages eleven to fifteen) to respond verbally to initial questions. These included "What is archaeology?," "What do archaeologists do?," and "How would you describe an archaeologist?" I wrote their answers on sticky notes and attached them to the wall. In the back of the room, I made table space, pens, and sticky notes available throughout the week and explained to students that anytime they had an opinion about an activity or learned something new, they could independently write it on a note. When students experienced "aha!" moments, I encouraged them to write it down. Doing so highlighted the moment as a part of science that should be celebrated and documented.

At the end of the last day, I again asked the same questions from the first day, wrote down their responses, and added them to the wall in a new sticky note cluster. Compared to the students' original understandings of archaeology, these answers showed greater detail, specificity, and accuracy. Reviewing each day's sticky notes was a quick and uncomplicated way to assess which activities were most engaging. It underscored which topics "stuck" most with the group.

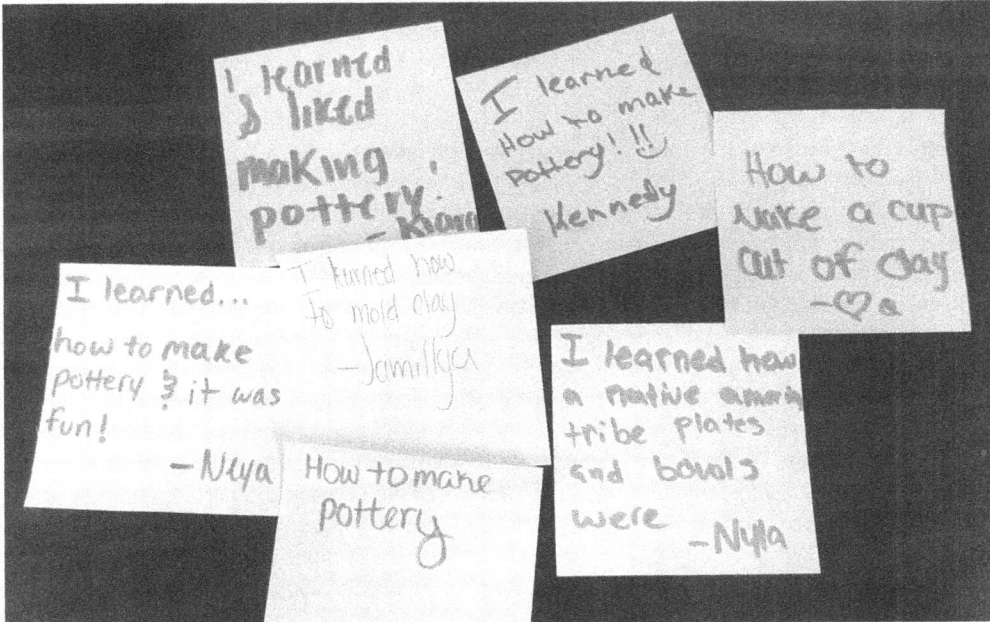

Figure 12.1. Examples of students' sticky note responses. *Courtesy of Elizabeth Pruitt*

and you cannot proceed with teaching more complex concepts unless you assess comprehension of the basic concepts needed to move forward (see chapter 1).

Ongoing or formative assessment takes place throughout a program and allows you to improve participant learning by making course corrections to better reach success. Additionally, students may be more motivated to continue learning if they receive ongoing feedback about their progress. It is often useful, for example, to ask all participants to write at least one anonymous question, concern, or comment on a card and drop it into a box after an activity. Those comments can then be used to modify the activity or address points of confusion the next time the participants meet. As another example, an excavation project might define success as training 90 percent of participants to have a basic level of competence in artifact identification. The program directors could introduce regular assessments of participants' proficiency. If these identify a weakness in, say, the identification of lithic materials, then that could become a focus for the next session. Assessments that are embedded within the program are easier to conduct and give better information, but they must be carefully planned.

Finally, summative assessment occurs at the end of a program. These assessments show how much growth or added value came from the program. This is an excellent way to show funders that the program was impactful or to impress potential donors. For example, a collaboration with a local Scout troop might use the number of Scouts successfully earning badges as evidence of programmatic success.

Assessment strategies can be direct or indirect. Direct assessment of learning occurs when participants' knowledge, skills, or attitudes are recorded and compared to a predetermined metric of proficiency or success by the program director or staff. Indirect assessment is a participant's self-reported learning or skill development. For example, direct assessment would be observing a program participant correctly sort lithic artifacts from unmodified rocks. Indirect assessment would be asking program participants how confident they are with distinguishing differences between lithic artifacts and unmodified rocks. Both have a place in assessment, although direct assessment tells us more about participant learning.

EVALUATION

What does evaluation look like?

- An archaeological society wants to restructure a decades-old avocational certification program to better meet the needs of students and instructors, revise lesson content to reflect current methods and research, and create more ways for people in rural communities to participate. The society conducts a needs assessment to solicit feedback from former program participants, potential future participants, professional archaeologists, and the society's Indigenous partners. Based on the evaluation data, the society applies for a grant to develop self-paced eLearning modules that align with stakeholder needs.
- An archaeology educator observes naturalists who adapted her lesson on archaeology and human impact on the landscape for "Archaeology Day" at a weekly outdoor program. One program component involves building simple shelters with driftwood to discuss low-impact land use during the Ice Age. The archaeologist notices that students immediately start building, without the naturalists providing any interpretation about the Paleoindian time period. The archaeologist documents her observations for the program supervisor and recommends modifying orientation and training on "Archaeology Day" so that naturalists use the provided educational materials to contextualize archaeology and emphasize evidence of human land use.
- An agency's long-standing public archaeology division is under threat of elimination due to budget cuts. The staff hires a consultant to perform a summative evaluation for an unbiased analysis of the program's impact over the past ten years. Evaluators review the agency's annual reports and program files to calculate the total number and types of outreach programs conducted, the

Elizabeth C. Reetz and Rebecca Dean

Textbox 12.2. Intentionally Assessing Archaeological Career Interest Development among High School Students

Carol E. Colaninno and Susan M. Kooiman

As archaeological educators, we engaged thirty high school students in archaeological learning at the Gehring site, located on Southern Illinois University Edwardsville's (SIUE) campus in the summer of 2022. Our goal was to expose high school students from historically marginalized communities to careers in archaeology and increase interest in the field. We used an intentionally designed assessment to determine if the program met our goals.

In collaboration with SIUE's Upward Bound Math and Science program, students learned and engaged in fieldwork, including setting up units, mapping, recording, excavating, screening, and identifying artifacts. Afterward, they worked alongside the undergraduate field school students and applied what they learned. The program culminated with a panel discussion by local archaeology and heritage management professionals.

To assess whether the program successfully increased students' interest in archaeological careers, we administered pre- and post-surveys to the students. We wanted to determine if the programs fostered students' interest in outdoor learning, along with their self-efficacy and career interest in archaeology.

We derived and modified the outdoor learning interest items from Lamb et al.'s science interest survey.[1] With this validated instrument, we modified items designed to assess students' science interest in both informal learning spaces and the classroom.

Self-efficacy—one's belief in their abilities to accomplish a certain task or perform a particular skill—is a variable that correlates with a student's career interest. For our students, we hoped to build their self-efficacy in archaeological tasks and skills to help them envision archaeology as a career. For this assessment, we modified four items from the science community integration survey by Estrada et al.[2] We also modified six items from Kier et al.'s career interest survey.[3] In accordance with our approved Institutional Review Board (IRB) protocol (SIUE protocol #1609), we obtained informed consent from twenty-two of the student participants and their parents.

The results of the eighteen-item survey showed statistically significant increases in interest in archaeological and outdoor careers. Although there were observed increases in mean scores in all but two of the other categories, these increases were not significant.

Assessment plays a crucial role in evaluating the effectiveness of educational and outreach initiatives, shedding light on successes and areas in need of improvement. The Gehring project successfully achieved our primary objective of enhancing students' interest in archaeology, while also revealing a need for bolstering self-efficacy. The results offer tangible evidence that can be leveraged to secure essential structural and financial support from funding agencies and institutional administration. Armed with this data, we can establish a robust foundation for sustainable outreach, education, and community programs by creating the necessary support systems and infrastructure.

Notes

1. Richard Lawrence Lamb, Leonard Annetta, Jeannette Meldrum, and David Vallett, "Measuring Science Interest: Rasch Validation of the Science Interest Survey," *International Journal of Science and Mathematics Education* 10 (2012): 643–68.
2. Mica Estrada, Anna Woodcock, Paul R. Hernandez, and P. W. Schultz, "Toward a Model of Social Influence that Explains Minority Student Integration into the Scientific Community," *Journal of Educational Psychology* 103, no. 1 (2011): 206–22.
3. Meredith W. Kier, Margaret R. Blanchard, Jason W. Osborne, and Jennifer L. Albert, "The Development of the STEM Career Interest Survey (STEM-CIS). *Research in Science Education* 44, no. 3 (2014): 461–81.

geographical range of these programs, and the total number of participants reached. They circulate surveys and conduct interviews with program partners, collaborators, and attendees. Participants self-report how the agency's public programs impacted their awareness and knowledge of archaeological topics and attitudes about stewardship and preservation. Agency staff submit the summative report to administration as justification for continued funding and support.

Evaluation is assessment that is project- or program-focused, rather than learner-focused. Program evaluations are more in depth and time-consuming than other types of assessment, often taking months or even years to complete. Because they are so detailed, evaluations provide rich, data-driven information that can be used for program development, improvement, and relevance. Although evaluation is more involved, planning and implementation are like a basic assessment. In addition to collecting new data, evaluations often involve looking at existing information and resources.

There are three types of programmatic evaluation. A front-end evaluation, sometimes referred to as a needs assessment, guides the development of a program. These evaluations take an in-depth look at how a program would best operate, determine the needs of your potential participants and stakeholders, identify learning gaps, and inform the creation of programmatic goals and outcomes. Formative evaluation is conducted during a program or pilot, and the information gathered is used to make improvements or assess progress toward goals and outcomes. It identifies what is working and what is not working. Summative evaluation, like summative assessment, is done at the completion of or toward the end of a program and looks at whether outcomes were achieved. Used to determine value, success, or justification for a program, summative evaluation results are often provided to decision-makers.

IMPLEMENTING ASSESSMENT AND EVALUATION

Making a Plan

Whether you intend to do a brief assessment for a short activity or a comprehensive program evaluation, make a plan and outline your strategy. Explain the criteria used to determine if your participants successfully met the outcomes and use an appropriate measurement strategy. For example, if your objective is for the participant to gain knowledge, ask them to explain something. If the objective is learning a skill, the assessment should require demonstration of that skill. Your assessment could be as simple as noting skills to observe or questions to ask your participants during discussion. Other strategies will produce documentation and recordable metrics.

You can also use a logic model. This is a planning and evaluation tool used to visually outline your program, identify the sequence of evaluation activities, and see relationships among the program's resources, activities, and outcomes. Logic models evaluate a program as a whole and examine specific activities or elements. In this framework, you begin by contextualizing your problem, goal, or situation. Often, evaluators include underlying assumptions about why and how the program should work. Components of a logic model include inputs (staff, funding, materials, etc.), outputs (activities and participants), and intended outcomes or accomplishments. The latter can be broken down into short-term or immediate outcomes, medium-term or intermediate outcomes, and long-term impacts. There are many ways to format a logic model and adapt it to your needs. We provide an example in appendix H.

Strategizing assessment and evaluation early in your program planning process will help carry out your best intentions. Assessment is easy to overlook or get cut or rushed because you ran over time and your participants are headed out the door. If you truly want to collect and document data, adequate preparation is imperative.

Elizabeth C. Reetz and Rebecca Dean

Collecting Data

Although assessment and evaluation differ in situation and purpose, there is overlap among assessment strategies and data collection tools. A quick or simple assessment of your audience may employ only one strategy if that is what your capacity allows. Programmatic evaluation will use several assessment strategies to generate different types of data.

Methods used to measure success can be either learner-focused or program-focused. Data collection tools can be structured to generate either quantitative (numbers-based, measurable, countable) data or qualitative (descriptive, interpretation-based) data. If your aim is to determine how many or how often, use quantitative approaches like closed-ended questions (multiple-choice, yes/no, true/false, etc.), rating or Likert scales, and observation checklists or tallies. If you are interested in questions such as how, why, or what happened, or are seeking information on someone's behavior, motivation, opinion, or experience, use qualitative tools such as open-ended questions, one-minute papers, journals, or field notes to get descriptions or reflections.

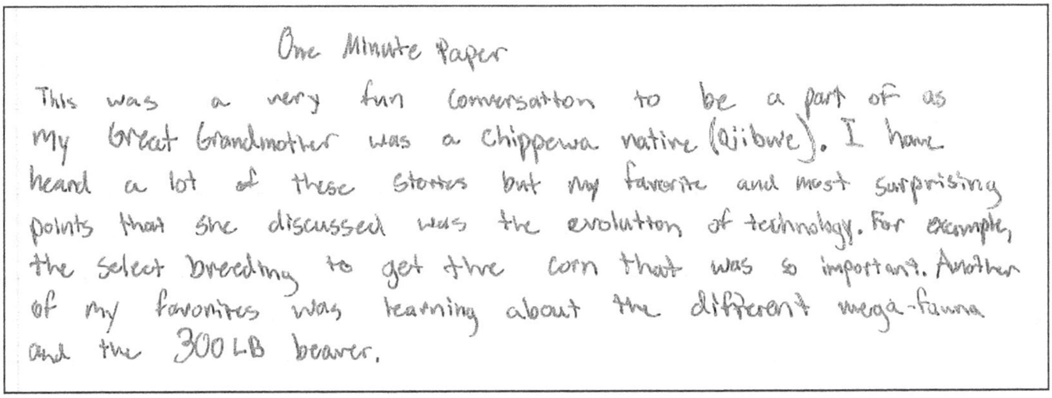

One Minute Paper

This was a very fun conversation to be a part of as my Great Grandmother was a Chippewa native (Ojibwe). I have heard a lot of these stories but my favorite and most surprising points that she discussed was the evolution of technology. For example, the select breeding to get the corn that was so important. Another of my favorites was learning about the different mega-fauna and the 300 LB beaver.

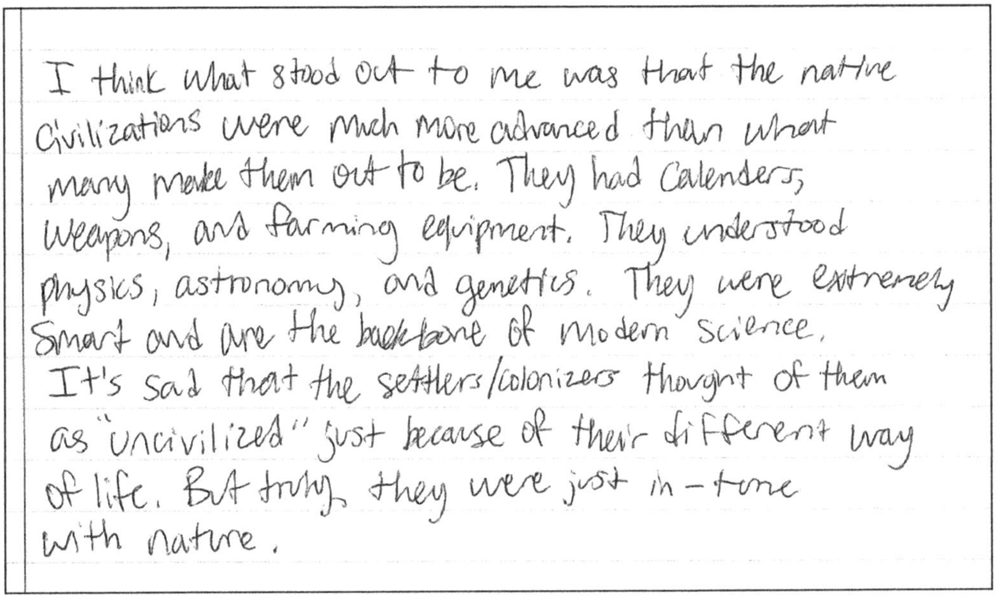

I think what stood out to me was that the native civilizations were much more advanced than what many make them out to be. They had calenders, weapons, and farming equipment. They understood physics, astronomy, and genetics. They were extremely smart and are the backbone of modern science. It's sad that the settlers/colonizers thought of them as "uncivilized" just because of their different way of life. But truly, they were just in-tune with nature.

Figure 12.2. Examples of one-minute paper responses. *Courtesy of University of Iowa Office of the State Archaeologist*

Common Tools and Methods for Data Collection

What is the task? Do you have the right tools for the task? Are you using these tools properly? Do not limit yourself to questionnaires. Look at your goals and objectives and research different strategies to ascertain what data each strategy will generate and how that data will be used to answer the questions in your assessment plan. Table 12.1 defines some common assessment strategies and data collection tools, suggests better practices for implementing them, and explains common ways they are used to learn about participant learning. Examples of some data collection tools used in public archaeology programs are included in appendix H.

Determine if there are any potential gaps among various assessment strategies or what level of nuance each provides. Combining different tools and strategies, also known as triangulation, will offer more in-depth data and a richer understanding of your impact, but note that competing strategies can affect the data collection. Also, build in time to pilot your data collection tools! You may find that your participants answer a particular question in a completely different way than you anticipated, and you need to rephrase or revise. Diversifying your strategies will help you understand which works best for various programs, and you can continue to refine and improve to ensure you collect quality data.

Using Existing Data

Determining the effectiveness of a lesson or program does not always require collecting new data. Programmatic evaluations almost always involve looking at existing information and resources. A good place to start is to document what you already know.

In a perfect world, we would all have archived records with plans, procedures, feedback, or reflections from previous programs. Since this is not the case, an internal review is a great way to reflect on a program and determine necessary adjustments or improvements for a repeat or similar program. If archived records do not exist but you know your workplace participated in a specific program, seek out institutional knowledge and document it. You may know of a peer or colleague who could advise you and share their thoughts.

An often-overlooked source of feedback about events and programs is social media. If someone either really enjoyed or disliked an aspect of your program, they might add a comment or reply to an event page, announcement, or news article. Likewise, they may ask questions or express concerns leading up to a program, which allows some limited pre-assessment. Screenshot and archive these comments to serve as testimonials.

Challenges

Due to lack of funding and resources for outreach, we are often stretched thin. We stretch ourselves even further to incorporate basic assessment and evaluation, and further still to create and implement a thorough evaluation plan. Thus, it is no surprise that many scientists-turned-public outreach practitioners have not had opportunities to develop the necessary skills to assess the learning of their participants or evaluate the effectiveness of their programming. This has created a dissonance that makes it easy to cut any proposed or planned assessment if time or funding runs out.

Creating and implementing an assessment plan is not easy. There will always be factors one cannot easily control. Your lesson or program may run long, and your post-assessment gets rushed or cut as people begin to depart. You might only get a few responses or people willing to participate in your assessment. Some of this can be mitigated by incorporating pre- and ongoing assessment; however, these are sometimes difficult to conduct because many of us do programs solo because of funding, personnel, and capacity. It is helpful to ask another person to assist with assessment or make observations while you are presenting or instructing. The fact that assessment can be frustrating is

Elizabeth C. Reetz and Rebecca Dean

Table 12.1. Examples of Assessment Strategies and Data Collection Tools

Data Collection Tool or Strategy	Description	Better Practices	Common Uses
Quiz, Survey, Questionnaire	A set of questions about participant knowledge or opinion/belief. Can be given before, during, and/or after an activity, program, or experience.	Use paper (like sticky notes) or an electronic platform Qualtrics, Google Forms, etc. Keep it short (under five minutes) during in-person programs to maintain participant attention. Participants are more likely to complete a survey when it is multiple-choice or Likert-scale and less than five questions. Use simple, clear language.	As a summative assessment to check post-program knowledge or attitude of participants. Can also be used for self-reported skill assessment. Given both pre- and post-program or activity to show changes. As an ongoing assessment to check for comprehension.
Discussion	Can be moderated, large-group discourse or small breakout conversations that take place at any point during a program.	Be clear on the rules of engagement before discussion begins and enforce them to keep the program safe for all participants. Provide written questions or prompts to guide discussion. These can be provided during and/or before the activity. Give opportunities for everyone to speak, particularly those unwilling to speak up in public, through small breakout groups or a number/email to submit directly to program leaders. Online discussions can be useful! Live Zoom chats tend to shut down the usual monopolizers of conversations and asynchronous discussion boards allow participants to think and reply thoughtfully to each other.	As a summative assessment to get a general idea of the attitudes and level of knowledge of participants near the end of a program/activity. Gives more in-depth data than a quiz but does not give as good information on each individual participant. Evaluated as an assessment of teamwork, cross-cultural communication, and other group-based skills. Short discussions can be used as ongoing assessments to check for comprehension, concerns, and unmet needs.

(continued)

Table 12.1. *Continued*

Data Collection Tool or Strategy	Description	Better Practices	Common Uses
Reflection, Exit Ticket, One-Minute Paper	A short period of informal writing (one to five minutes) that can take place at any point during an activity or program. When it is labeled a "reflection" it is usually summative and reflects upon the material covered. Writing can be stream-of-consciousness, bullet points, or thoughts with doodles. May be done anonymously.	Provide paper, pencils, and someplace to write. For reflections, provide one short, thoughtful writing prompt with some flexibility. For example, "What was the most important thing you learned from today's activity?" Lower the stakes so participants feel less intimidated about responding (e.g., give out small cards for writing and clarify that it is informal and/or anonymous).	Knowledge—more in depth and meaningful than multiple-choice. Attitudes—more in depth and meaningful than Likert scales. Pre-assessment—excellent for word or concept definitions. Summative assessment—can be compared with pre-assessment for value added. Retention of knowledge. Feedback for ongoing assessment.
Observation, Skill Check	Asking participants to perform or watching participants as they demonstrate skills or knowledge in context while participating in the program (e.g., while excavating or working in groups).	Use a rubric or checklist. Share with participants. Embed in your "usual rounds."	Mostly for skills assessment (e.g., skill development over time, skill level at end). Ongoing assessment to see where problems arise.
Interview/Focus Group	Should be moderated individual or group conversations with around two to twelve participants. Can occur at any point during a program.	Provide written questions or prompts to guide discussion. These can be provided during and/or before the conversation. Conversations can be organic; moderate to stay on topic. Obtain and document informed consent before recording any video or audio.	Interviews can be a formative or summative assessment to understand comprehension, impressions, attitudes, or experiences or to learn more about participants' answers collected with another tool. Focus groups are primarily summative or front-end and can explore in-depth topics through a small group discussion.
Document Review	Organizing and analyzing archived program data or metrics. Literature search or meta-analysis.	Maintain records and files for events and programs that include participant counts, notes, testimonials, assessment data collection tools, inputs and outputs.	A summative assessment to investigate what was done in prior situations; look for patterns or information to inform future programs. Gather information on how a project operates without interrupting the project.

what keeps many from attempting to carry it out, but the more we document and communicate our successes and challenges, the better we and others can prepare, adapt, and improve our initiatives.

Likewise, programmatic evaluation is time- and resource-intensive. It can take weeks to months or longer and requires comprehensive planning, data collection, analysis, interpretation, and reporting. If an evaluation is conducted internally, our familiarity with our own programs may impact how we interpret subjective feedback. Also, we do not always have the proper skills or expertise to analyze and interpret this type of data. That does not mean we should not do internal evaluations; however, it is important to acknowledge and communicate any limitations. Hiring an external evaluator may provide more objective or unbiased interpretations of the data, but this is often beyond our means. If your organization is considering an extensive overhaul of services and programming or building a program from scratch, an external evaluation that is independent of the program could provide greater credibility and validity of the findings. Plan for this in grants or contracts, if possible.

Finally, assessment and evaluation may require asking questions we might not want answered, and could, for better or worse, hurt our egos. We could find out that our trusty and reliable slate of programs developed after years of effort does not actually produce the impacts we want and need. What if we have accidentally been perpetuating misconceptions? If people leave our community lectures bored and ambivalent about what we discussed? That we are failing to convey that archaeology isn't just digging? Acknowledging a lack of success is a hard pill to swallow, and the status quo is comfortable. But the truth is, we need to know, and we need the data to support our findings.

NOTES

1. Jeanne M. Moe, "Conceptual Understanding of Science through Archaeological Inquiry," (EdD diss., Montana State University, 2011); Jeanne M. Moe, "Best Practices in Archaeology Education: Successes, Shortcomings, and the Future," in *Public Engagement and Education: Developing and Fostering Stewardship for an Archaeological Future*, ed. Katherine P. Erdman (New York: Berghahn Books, 2019), 216.
2. Elizabeth Reetz, "Event Review: 'Archaeology Education: Building a Research Base,' *Journal of Community Archaeology & Heritage* 6, no. 3 (2019), 229–31, https://doi.org/10.1080/20518196.2019.1625190.

RECOMMENDED RESOURCES

Ernst, Julie A., Martha C. Monroe, and Bora Simmons. *Evaluating Your Environmental Education Programs*. Washington DC: North American Association for Environmental Education, 2012.

Giancola, Susan P. *Evaluation Matters: Getting the Information You Need From Your Evaluation*. Alexandria, VA: US Department of Education, 2014.

Walvoord, Barbara E. *Assessment Clear and Simple: A Practical Guide for Institutions, Departments, and General Education*. 2nd ed. San Francisco: Jossey-Bass, 2010.

13

Building a Research Base

Elizabeth C. Reetz

As a result of hard work in recent years, practitioners in archaeology education are gaining traction in their decades-long efforts to institutionalize and professionalize the field. Some of these efforts include the founding of the *Journal of Archaeology and Education* (*JAE*), The Heritage Education Network (THEN), and the Institute for Heritage Education (IHE), as well as conferences and thematic journal volumes exclusively focused on public archaeology and archaeology education. To strengthen that momentum, we cannot understate the importance of doing assessment and evaluation to improve our public programs, increase our public impact, and build a research base (see chapter 12). Conducting and publishing research to share that knowledge is one of the most impactful ways to benefit the profession.

THE IMPORTANCE OF COMMUNICATING ABOUT OUR PROGRAMMING

Why do we tend to deliver public programs, from lectures to classroom visits, without consideration for best practices? Ellenberger and Richardson point out that many professional archaeological organizations in the United States and the United Kingdom are quiet on the matter of evaluation and outcomes of public archaeology in their ethics statements, particularly regarding community collaborations, and no organization explicitly mentions the need to evaluate public projects and share best practices.[1] Respectively, this work is underrepresented in published academic work. Although archaeology and heritage education do not yet have formally identified learning goals and benchmarks,[2] researching individual learning experiences and identifying optimal practices will contribute important evidence-based insights. A growing library derived from assessment and evaluation also offers models to create and implement effective public programs aligned with research.

To prevent that dreaded reinvention of the wheel, the development of any public archaeology program should involve research into work done by others. A simple internet or social media search will reveal examples, but often there is no documented record of impact, effectiveness, or challenges. Without this information, it is not possible for other practitioners to adapt, revise, or improve methodology, pedagogy, or logistics. Additionally, sharing knowledge with other practitioners will save time, effort, funding, and other resources used to develop and implement programs—all of which we have in short supply.

UNDERSTANDING RESEARCH DESIGNS FOR ASSESSMENT OF PUBLIC PROGRAMS

A good scientist would never carry out a study without understanding comparative literature and creating a well-thought-out research design structured to test hypotheses and interpret evidence. Archaeologists know this well; learning to create a research design is an integral part of collegiate study and a vital task undertaken by professionals. However, when it comes to human subjects-based educational assessment or evaluation, many believe they do not have the skill set to perform such studies. That isn't true! There are many parallels. Although the following is only a cursory overview, the intention is to provide a basic understanding of some research designs and methods that are most applicable to studies with participants of public archaeology programs.

Most archaeologists understand a research design as a plan of action to carry out field, laboratory, or curatorial projects. These involve context, research questions, methods for data collection and analysis, and dissemination plans. Research on public programming follows essentially the same format, only the tools, methods, and forms of analysis for the social sciences are different.

In the social sciences, the term "research design" sometimes also refers to the overall strategy and analytical approach. Each of these have different parameters for the treatment or intervention (your program or event), variables (the attributes or characteristics you are trying to measure or study), treatment and/or control groups (participants and non-participants), participant sampling, data collection tools and methods, and timing. Table 13.1 outlines some typical approaches in social sciences research that could be used to study public archaeology programming.

Of these, experimental research is the least applicable design for assessing public archaeology programs and events because it requires both a control group and treatment group, with participants that are randomly assigned before beginning. This is difficult or impossible in our field, considering that people typically self-select to attend or participate in our public programs or events. However, it is sometimes considered the strongest research design because the results are attributable to the program and not to external factors. Quasi-experimental research involves a control group that cannot be randomly assigned. One example of a public archaeology scenario that falls into this category would be administering questionnaires to test student knowledge *before* and *after* an archaeology unit. The same methods would be used to collect data from a control class at the same grade level that was not taught the same unit.

Most research on public archaeology programming is non-experimental. We generally seek specific information about knowledge, skills, attitudes, or awareness resulting from a program, and only the people who attended can provide that source of information. Thus, the results apply only to the group or situation in the study and cannot be extended to the population at large. This research is difficult to replicate with another group or situation, but the methods and findings can inspire others to do their own similar studies or make adaptations in their programs. On the other hand, such studies may have varying degrees of transferability, which is the extent to which the effectiveness of an intervention could be achieved in another sample or setting.[3] Transferability has value to the reader of the research, who can make connections between the results and their own situation or experience.

The majority of published research on public archaeology programs is in case study format. This design is well-suited to our situations, capacity, and feasibility, but in order to look at our impact in different ways, we should consider other types of research. A case study can provide information on what further research is needed and create opportunities to build on existing projects. For example, a series of similar case studies on the efficacy of avocational certification programs in several states could help improve learning outcomes for new participants enrolling in a program. Or a series of case studies of nonformal learning at museums could provide a basis for comparing outcomes in different regions or among different age levels.

In addition to publishing the results of program and event initiatives, there are helpful ways to contribute to this growing research base through other types of studies that do not include human

Table 13.1. Potential Designs for Use in Research Studies of Public Archaeology Programs

	Research Design	Purpose
Experimental	True experimental	Investigate a statistical relationship between two variables with an ability to manipulate those variables; cause and effect. Must involve both a treatment and control group; random assignment of participants is essential.
	Quasi-experimental	Evaluate cause and effect between two variables without randomization. Typically involves both a treatment and control group; random assignment of participants is not possible. In between a true experimental and correlational study.
Non-experimental	Case study	Examine details of a particular situation in a real-life context to understand participants, experiences, projects, etc. and explain how or why.
	Correlational	Describe a relationship between two or more variables.
	Descriptive	Describe a situation or phenomenon. No random assignment of participants, involves only one group.
	Observational	Answer a research question based on observations, with no intervention or forced change to the experience. Can be descriptive (see above) or analytical where the focus is on the data.
	Longitudinal	Making repeated observations over time after an experience to describe patterns of change and study variables that might explain why a change occurs. Involves a single group of participants with data collected at regular intervals.
Non-human	Ex post facto	Examine past occurrences or conditions; a look back at what took place, with no interference from the researcher; uses data collected before a hypothesis is formed.
	Historical/Literature Review	Investigate past evidence (secondary sources, primary sources like archives, official records, reports, etc.) to establish facts; explain the cause of events and their effect on the present. Sources must be authentic and valid.
	Meta-analysis	A systematic, statistical review of data from independent studies on the same subject to examine overall trends.

subjects, such as literature reviews and meta-analyses. Published research on archaeology and heritage education is found in a myriad of locations, some of which may be unfamiliar or simply unknown to us and our colleagues. These include international, national, and regional books and journals on archaeology, anthropology, heritage studies, history, education and its various subfields, psychology, cognitive psychology, environmental education, outdoor education, and interpretation. There may be analogous studies focused on different subjects that provide overviews of methods, techniques, and learning theories that could inspire or strengthen public archaeology programs, and there is a need to synthesize this information and communicate it to the archaeological community.

OBTAINING ETHICAL APPROVAL FOR PUBLISHING RESEARCH

Prior to starting a research study using feedback or data from any interaction or intervention with human participants, you must receive informed consent from any participants and obtain an ethical review and approval from an approved board or committee. Depending on the country, ethical approval for human subjects research is conducted by an Institutional Review Board (IRB), Independent Ethics Committee (IEC), Ethical Review Board (ERB), or Research Ethics Board (REB) (referred to as IRB going forward). The Principal Investigator (PI) can use any approved board or committee in the host country. Different countries have different laws and requirements. For example, in the United States, oral history reviews are exempt from IRB approval. Some countries only review clinical health research. Review the protocols in the country where your study takes place and identify alternatives for ethical review if necessary.

Finding an Ethical Review Board

Many colleges and universities have IRB committees. IRB staff are typically well-informed, helpful, and happy to work with you. If you have questions about any part of the process, or whether a review may be needed, reach out to them. They may host educational sessions to support researchers and often have instructional resources on hand.

If you are an independent researcher or your institution does not have an IRB, you can seek out a project collaborator who can apply on behalf of their affiliation as a PI. Your PI does not have to be listed as the first author in your publication, and it is always beneficial to have additional eyes reviewing research plans, data entry, and data analysis, particularly with coding and theming qualitative data. If you cannot identify a partner, there are commercial consulting firms willing to serve as the IRB of record for a fee. Alternatively, you can contact other nearby universities or institutions that have an ethics review board and inquire if they are willing to oversee the pertinent aspects of your study.

Preparing for the Process

You and every collaborator must meet your institution's review requirements. You may be required to complete training before you can be listed as a researcher on an IRB. In the United States, the CITI program is typically used for this training.[4] It is free for those affiliated with most colleges and universities, or available to independent researchers for a fee.

Some ethical approval boards have a screening process, questionnaire, or quick decision tool that assists in determining if a study should be defined as human subjects research and undergo the full approval process. Often referred to as a Human Subjects Research Determination (HSRD), this process reviews your project purpose, description of study procedures, and data collection plan or source of existing data. It also requests information on whether your project involves obtaining data through an intervention or interaction with living individuals and if that data may be identifiable.

For those who regularly collect programmatic data or participant feedback (e.g., for grant requirements) for internal review and to archive with your program or project data, you can possibly use this for a later research study. If your participant data was anonymous or cannot be tracked back to an individual, the review may be quick, and the study may be exempt from the full review process. If the HSRD determines your study is, in fact, human subjects research, you will be required to go through the full IRB process.

Before you start the ethical approval process, ensure you have the following in place:

- project title, summary, and description
- research questions, study aims, or hypotheses
- research background or significance; potential benefits
- relevant literature
- team members and affiliations
- funding source, if applicable

Elizabeth C. Reetz

- estimated number of research subjects and how you will access, recruit, or enroll them
- description of the study population
- materials to obtain/document informed consent
- data collection, sampling, and analysis methods
- finalized data collection tools
- summary of potential risk to the study participants and your plan to minimize that risk
- plan for privacy, security, confidentiality, and anonymity (if applicable) when collecting and storing data

Any participant's informed consent should include consent to the study and to publish data they provide. Make the risks to the individual very explicit. In public archaeology programming, these could include physical harm or discomfort, psychological trauma such as anxiety or shame, or privacy violations like a leak of personally identifiable information. There may also be risks for various types of discrimination or social stigmatization, depending on your project. Certain population groups are considered "high risk" in human subject research, including children, students, and people who are elderly, economically or educationally disadvantaged, or those with disabilities. A person's age, culture, language, and health status may also impact their risk in the study.

The ethical review process could take months, so plan accordingly. You will not be able to submit a project for review and then start collecting data the next week, probably not even the next month. Many committees meet infrequently, and they may have hundreds of projects to review. The IRB may require you to provide additional information or make modifications to your application, especially the consent forms, during the review process. It is not unusual for them to request clarifications, and the process can be back and forth. Be patient. It will be worth it! If your study passes an ethical review, include evidence of this when you submit your publication. If your study was considered exempt after the HSRD, you should explain the reason for the exemption.

PLANNING A RESEARCH STUDY

When strategizing a research study, it is helpful to draft a purpose statement and create a table or outline of the following questions (see appendix H):

1. Research questions: What do you want to know?
2. Indicators: How will you know it? What will the information look like?
3. Information sources: Who/what can provide the information needed?
4. Tools: How will you gather the information needed?
5. Design and sampling: When and from whom will the data be collected?

If you created a logic model for program planning or evaluation, use it to provide the basis for developing a research design (see chapters 4 and 12). This will assist in research question development, identifying and describing different participant or stakeholder groups, and generating data collection questions and indicators.

Remember that intentional planning that includes strong programmatic goals, outcomes, and assessment is key (see chapter 4). When you create a program plan using an educational framework like Understanding by Design (UbD) (see chapter 1; appendix G), it can be used in a research design. UbD begins by establishing exactly what you want your participants to know; the enduring understandings can translate into research questions. Your UbD assessment strategy provides your indicators of success and data collection tools.

Additional components of your research plan that you should establish before beginning are your methods for data analysis, interpretation, and communication or dissemination. There are several different techniques for analyzing quantitative and qualitative data (see chapter 12), but only certain methods may be appropriate. For qualitative data analysis, it will strengthen your results to have multiple researchers review, code, and theme the data independently. The degree of agreement between the researchers who assign codes or categories is called "inter-rater reliability." Your research plan should include these people.

Data Collection Factors

The previous chapter introduced various strategies for collecting assessment and evaluation data. Often when we decide we want to collect data from program participants, we almost immediately jump to writing a survey or questionnaire to frantically distribute at the end of a program. This is the wrong approach, and it may not be the most appropriate data collection method for your study. Crafting a survey before establishing research questions could mean you are soliciting feedback that may not provide appropriate information. Developing your data collection tool(s), no matter the strategy, should be one of the last steps in the preparation phase.

Many different methods may be appropriate for the study, but choosing data collection tools requires careful consideration. Your research questions, indicators of success, and information sources will begin to help narrow down your choices. Other considerations include capacity, time, funding, personnel, and the expertise of those analyzing data. Plan when the information is being collected and from whom. For example, if you are looking for an increase or gain in knowledge, skills, or awareness, document the baseline of what participants know before the program starts and collect the same information after the program ends by using a pretest-posttest. If you want to learn if your program was the influential factor in any gain or increase, you must include a control group.

When collecting data, it is necessary to define a population of interest, which is the group of individuals you aim to draw conclusions about. A single study might include multiple populations (e.g., professional archaeologists and avocationals). If the number of participants is small, it probably is not necessary to sample, and it is likely possible to get feedback from everyone depending on the data collection methods. With larger group sizes, data collection methods may drive the sampling methods or vice versa. For example, if a study is seeking rich, qualitative information that can be derived from interviews or focus groups, but the program involves fifty participants, it would be too challenging to collect information from the entire population. Alternatively, if 1,000 people attend an archaeology fair and the researcher seeks to collect information from as many participants as possible, an expedient data collection tool would be a wise choice. Ultimately, choose the tools that align with your sample population and can most effectively help answer research questions.

No matter your data collection tool, the way you phrase a question will yield different data and require specific analyses. Beware of leading questions. As much as possible, pilot your data collection tools with colleagues, volunteers, students, or anyone available to weed out and redraft questions that elicit confounding or biased responses or ultimately do not address your research questions.

SEEKING MENTORSHIP AND ADVICE

Archaeologists and educators who are publishing human subjects research recognize the importance of this work and encourage others to conduct and communicate assessment. The contributors to this book; those affiliated with the *JAE*, IHE, and THEN; and archaeologists in the educational and public outreach arms of our professional organizations may be willing to share challenges and tips or provide perspective or ideas. We all have a lot to learn from each other. As we grow our research base, we will expand our collective knowledge of evidence-based practices for high-impact programs and start to move away from outreach approaches that do not serve our goals.

Elizabeth C. Reetz

Textbox 13.1. A Journal Editor's Perspective

Ryan Wheeler

The *Journal of Archaeology and Education (JAE)* exists to foster the community of those engaged in teaching and learning in archaeology at all levels, including everything from pedagogy to practice. As an online, open access journal, *JAE* articles appear when they are ready and can be read by anyone with access to the internet. The *JAE* has a broad focus, and the editors welcome all original submissions. Since 2017, *JAE* has published on diverse topics, ranging from specific lessons and public programs, field school training, work with volunteers, accessibility, online teaching, student and instructor responses to COVID, the history of teaching and learning, collaborative archaeology, and more. The journal has published the proceedings of two conference symposia as well.

The work of teaching and learning has often been regarded as a secondary interest, rather than a major focus of study in archaeology, possibly explaining the lack of academic programs, conferences, or publication outlets. *JAE* founders recognized that many of those dedicated to archaeology and education did not know one another and often struggled to find a platform for their research and ideas. Often times, some did not know *how* to design and communicate their research. Thus, the *JAE* editorial board, comprised of archaeologists who are experts in teaching and learning, use their extensive networks to connect researchers with similar projects and ideas and coach or advise those who are new to this type of research.

Good research papers have two key elements. First, they tell the readers why their work is important. This is very centering, but often omitted in articles and book chapters, which tend to launch straight into the project. Second, and very importantly, they have explicit goals stated at the beginning of the piece.

As former *JAE* editor Jeanne Moe has observed, research and resulting publications that include assessment of archaeological teaching and learning are rare and highly prized. A major challenge, especially around submissions that involve assessment, is a lack of a human subjects review. In several cases, authors have sought to publish assessment data originally collected for internal use only, with lack of approval from an institutional review board. These review boards help scholars comply with federal legislation enacted to protect those participating in research. The *JAE* editors and editorial board revised the journal's policies to encourage those engaged in assessment research to have their work reviewed early.

Beyond an interest in increasing the literature around assessment in archaeology and education, the editors would love to see more submissions in areas like lifelong learning, accessibility, and community-based archaeology.

NOTES

1. Katharine Ellenberger and Lorna-Jane Richardson, "Reflecting on Evaluation in Public Archaeology," *AP: Online Journal in Public Archaeology* 8 (2018), 65–94, http://dx.doi.org/10.23914/ap.v8i1.141.
2. Eleanor M. King et al., "A Conversation on Heritage, Archaeology, and Education in the United States," *The Heritage Education Journal* 1, no. 1 (2022), https://theheritageeducationnetwork.org/the-heritage-education-journal.
3. Joshua R. de Leeus, Benjamin A. Motz, Emily R. Fyfe, Paulo F. Carvalho, and Robert L. Goldstone, "Generalizability, Transferability, and the Practice-to-Practice Gap," *Behavioral and Brain Sciences* 45, E11 (2022), https://doi.org/10.1017/s0140525x21000406.
4. "Social-Behavioral-Educational (SBE) Comprehensive," CITI Program, accessed August 3, 2023, https://about.citiprogram.org/course/human-subjects-research-2/.

RECOMMENDED RESOURCES

Colaninno, Carol E. "The Need for Discipline-Based Education Research in Archaeology." *Journal of Archaeology and Education* 3, no. 7 (2019). https://digitalcommons.library.umaine.edu/jae/vol3/iss7/1.

Ellenberger, Katharine, and Lorna-Jane Richardson. "Reflecting on Evaluation in Public Archaeology," *AP: Online Journal in Public Archaeology* 8 (2018): 65–94, http://dx.doi.org/10.23914/ap.v8i1.141.

Grad Coach. "Research Methodology & Design 101." YouTube playlist. https://youtube.com/playlist?list=PLvcb33xNTVUmfIpA5majoCXgLS5mFOcck&si=sCsTTIasmQQPGsVG.

Putting It All Together

14

Applying New Knowledge to Organize Public Archaeology Programs and Events

Elizabeth C. Reetz and Stephanie T. Sperling

Throughout this handbook, experts in public archaeology and outreach provide the building blocks to successfully prepare, plan, and implement effective archaeology outreach programs. We hope this content is accessible and enduring and that this resource becomes a useful reference that you access often. Sections I through III focus primarily on the *what* and *why* of various planning components and program formats. Here, we expand on *how* to apply what you have learned.

Use the tools presented in the appendices to craft a detailed work plan and maintain organized planning files. This will enable a process for efficient program review and revision and facilitate the creation of a library containing ready-to-go action plans. Moreover, sharing these program ideas with your network prevents colleagues from reinventing the wheel and fosters collaboration.

This book focuses on the "person-to-person" type outreach that archaeologists typically do, but public archaeology is not limited to the formats discussed here. Practitioners also produce K–12 curricula, museum exhibits, interpretive panels, and print and digital media, among other things. The elements in this book can also be used to create these types of projects. Your materials should be audience- and accessibility-focused and developed collaboratively with the communities they address or impact. No matter how small the project, your budget should reflect a realistic idea of the time and cost involved. And *all* public materials should be developed with established goals and outcomes and a plan to assess their effectiveness.

INTENTIONAL PREPARATION

Regardless of the format you choose, there are important questions to ask yourself during the planning process, whether it is your first or tenth time organizing the program. This will allow your choices to be deliberate but allow room for adaptations and modifications. Intentional preparation is about taking thoughtful and purposeful steps to set yourself up for success. It involves a conscious, proactive effort to ensure you are well-equipped for both the expected and the unexpected things that will happen during your program.

Revisit the following chapters to consider these questions in more depth:

Chapter 1:

- *What pedagogical and educational strategies should I consider?* Understanding how people learn and how to effectively teach them will provide a strong foundation for impactful public archaeology programming.

Chapter 2:

- *Who is my audience and how large is the group?* Consider age ranges, demographics, and experience to help craft jargon-free talking points that connect with a diverse array of people.

Chapter 3:

- *How can my program be more accessible?* This is not just a legal requirement but a fundamental aspect of creating an inclusive and equitable environment.

Chapter 4:

- *What strategies can I use to be intentional?* Craft solutions to potential problems that may arise from program conceptualization to actualization. Create clear goals and contingency plans to remain adaptable as circumstances change.
- *How will I define success?* Think in terms of the impacts, outcomes, and outputs that you hope to achieve.

Chapter 5:

- *Who are my partners?* Partners are vital to the success of your initiatives. Their local knowledge, resources, and relationships contribute to more effective, culturally sensitive, and sustainable programs.
- *Who has done this program previously?* Reach out to other organizations and ask for tips to avoid reinventing the wheel.

Chapter 6:

- *Are there legal or privacy concerns?* Establish contractor, landowner, and venue permissions (as applicable) and ensure you are permitted to share findings, artifacts, or remains.
- *What are my funding needs?* You may need to solicit grants and donations to complete the event.
- *How will I market the program?* Share widely on social media, on your website, during other programs, and through community partners.

Chapter 7:

- *What are my available strengths and resources?* Align the format of your all-ages program with your organizational capacity and goals, be that a virtual talk, a festival, a public dig day, or a guided tour.
- *What are my staffing needs?* Make sure to have enough experienced people in place for an appropriate professional-to-public ratio.

Elizabeth C. Reetz and Stephanie T. Sperling

Chapter 8:

- *What are the needs/wants/expectations of the classroom instructor or group leader?* Educators who enlist your services may want a fun activity or a hands-on lesson that aligns with standards. Communicate early and often to align your collaborative goals and outcomes.
- *How can I best connect with students?* Adjust the complexity of your content to suit the learning level of the children you are working with.

Chapter 9:

- *What does my community want?* Repeatedly ask this question on social media, on web-based surveys, and at community meetings. Engage in conversations with descendant communities.
- *How can I best promote the stewardship of cultural resources?* The success of these collaborative efforts hinges on integrating community priorities, meeting people where they are, and building interest.

Chapters 10 and 11:

- *What will I do if everything goes wrong?* Prepare a Plan B, stay flexible, document what happened, and learn from the experience. A sense of humor also goes a long way!

Chapter 12:

- *How will I evaluate the success of my program?* Collect assessment data and feedback, record cost-effectiveness, and document lessons learned.

Chapter 13:

- *How can I professionally research my program and publish my findings?* Start your research design in advance of program planning. You may need to draft data collection tools and apply for ethical approval for human subjects research before your program begins.

INTENTIONAL PLANNING

Much of this book has focused on "intentional planning," which will ensure that your efforts are purposeful and tailored to meet the needs and expectations of your audience. Something unexpected always comes up, but your program will be most effective with intentional prior planning. However, everyone has different ways of documenting information, organizing files, and delegating tasks. Whether you are solo-planning a program or working with a team, create a work plan with project management tools that align with your skills and budget. This may be a simple spreadsheet or an online platform (e.g., Trello, Asana). Regardless, ensure that you can download, save, and access the information for future use, because technology and software perpetually change.

Start by determining which planning components are integral. For example, you might not need a liability waiver for a one-hour indoor lecture, but it is vital to consider accessibility needs for this event. In all cases, outline an intentional strategy complete with goals and outcomes and be sure to assess or evaluate the program to the best of your ability. Table 14.1 describes the broad components of program preparation introduced throughout the book and examples of associated tasks.

Table 14.1. Common Program Planning Components and Examples of Associated Tasks

Program Planning Component	Associated Tasks
Audience Pre-assessment	Conduct demographics research, create and circulate a pre-registration questionnaire, solicit audience insights from program partners
Accessibility	Research facility or location infrastructure, book services, solicit requests from potential participants
Resource Procurement	Document what you have, what you need, and how/where to secure various resources (e.g., personnel, facilities, equipment/supplies, funding, etc.); hiring; booking; purchasing
Funding	Create a budget, write grant applications and fundraise as needed, generate contract proposals
Legal Considerations	Obtain or familiarize yourself with insurance policies, create and circulate liability waivers and photo/video permission forms
Marketing and Media	Develop a marketing plan; create and circulate ads, media kits, and press releases; plan a social media campaign
Program Design	Research applicable pedagogies, consider problems and solutions, create goals and objectives, compile a strategic plan
Assessment and Evaluation	Create a logic model and/or research design, develop assessment or data collection strategies, analyze and interpret data, publish results

For every program planning component, specify tasks that must be accomplished, assign responsible individuals, and set deadlines. Review this information repeatedly to ensure everything is completed in a timely manner and nothing important is forgotten. After the program, reflect on each of the components and document what worked, what did not, and why.

The following appendices include guides, models, and templates for your reference. These resources are meant to be copied or adapted for your projects, then archived and shared. Remember that certain protocols and legal forms vary among different countries, states, universities, and agencies. Always check with your workplace, sponsor, or affiliated institution to learn about their procedures and identify the proper forms, templates, or points of contact. If anything, the examples provided here serve to remind you that there are multiple considerations that you should investigate before launching a public program.

SUMMARY

With your new arsenal of tools and knowledge, you are better prepared to craft and deliver successful public archaeology programs. Remember, you are not alone in this journey. Your peers and colleagues are valuable allies who are ready to offer support and share insights. Draw inspiration from those who have done this work for years, and do not hesitate to seek assistance when needed. Remember to savor the process and ensure that joy and enthusiasm are woven into the fabric of your programs. Share your passion for archaeology with others! After all, the most memorable and impactful experiences often arise from a foundation of enjoyment. So, go forth, plan with intention, and have fun!

Elizabeth C. Reetz and Stephanie T. Sperling

Appendix A

AUDIENCES AND ACCESSIBILITY

Audience Characteristics

What do you need to know about your audience to best prepare for your program or event? As emphasized in chapter 2, you often won't know who your audience is until the program starts. Consider their expectations, prior knowledge, and points of confusion and anticipate necessary modifications or adaptations for inclusivity. Document what you learn about your audience and align this with your goals and outcomes.

Use these strategies to learn as much as you can, to the best of your ability:

- Research demographics
- Ask for insight from partners and co-organizers
- Convey notable information about the program location, accessibility accommodations, and potential physical demands on all promotional materials and communications and provide contact information for feedback
- Request specific information on registration forms or participant agreements when applicable

---

ESTIMATED AUDIENCE SIZE:
Note: How will the group size affect your set-up, instructional methods, or engagement? Maximum number of attendees? Instructor-to-participant ratio? Hands-on activities? Materials and supplies?

ANTICIPATED AGE GROUP(S) OR GRADE LEVEL(S):
Note: How can you adapt your content and delivery to reach varying age groups? What adjustments should be made?

KEY DEMOGRAPHICS:
Note: How might these demographics affect your program content and delivery and the audience's reception of that information?

SPECIAL NEEDS:
Prior to the program, encourage individuals to notify you of needs regarding mobility; visual or hearing impairments; learning or attention disabilities, language, health/diet. Note, what additional accommodations do you need to organize to optimize learning and access for all individuals?

OTHER INSIGHTS:

Figure A.1. A template for recording audience characteristics during program planning.
Courtesy of University of Iowa Office of the State Archaeologist

Accessibility Considerations

Whether your program or event will take place in your own facility, a partner facility or rented venue, or an outdoor location, there are multiple factors to organize during planning and additional factors to implement during set-up and operation. To begin with, budget for accessibility! Before you sign a contract or submit a grant proposal, budget for the best assistive services that are available to you and allow ample time to schedule these services. Many local and state governments in the United States advise booking services no later than seventy-two hours before a scheduled event, so it is encouraged to adhere to this courtesy.

Many universities have an accessibility statement or tagline that you can modify with your contact information. To comply with obligations under applicable federal and state laws, the statement must be included on publications (e.g., event listings, fliers, social media posts) that invite public participation. If your organization does not have a statement, consider drafting one and have it reviewed by an accessibility professional.

> "**[Insert your agency, department, organization name]** is committed to creating an inclusive and accessible event. To request a reasonable accommodation or discuss your needs, contact **[insert contact name and email/phone number]**. All requests must be made by **[insert date]**."

> "For questions or if you will need disability-related accommodations to participate in this event, contact **[insert contact name and email/phone number]**. Early requests are strongly encouraged to allow sufficient time to meet your access needs."

Figure A.2. Accessibility statement examples. *Courtesy of University of Iowa Office of the State Archaeologist*

Regardless of individual participant needs, there are some universal considerations applicable to every program or event.

- Integrate multiple learning styles (visual, auditory, tactile) when communicating content or demonstrating an activity to better reach learners with different abilities and strengths (see chapter 1).
- If you are creating presentation slides (see appendix B), handouts, or posters, be aware of font size, readability, and contrast.
- During presentations, provide a sign language interpreter (best), live human CART captioning (better), or automated live captions (okay). Recognize that AI captioning provides a subpar experience despite its growing use and improvements; however, this is an option for those on limited budgets.

Use the accessibility planning checklists prior to your program and during set-up. This basic guide provides a starting point; you may have other factors to consider based on your event format.

PRE-PROGRAM:

TASK	COMPLETE	DATE/INITIAL
Solicit requests for any needed accommodations		
If the facility lacks an accessible entrance, elevators, or lifts, inform the group beforehand		
Ask potential venues about accessible entrances, elevators/lifts, event rooms, public transport, parking or drop-off areas, and restrooms		
Book assistive services (translators, sign language interpreters, CART transcription services)		
Send presentation materials to sign language interpreters or other language interpreters so they can familiarize themselves with program topics.		
Produce and distribute screen-reader friendly electronic materials, programs, agendas, announcements, etc., including alt-text on social media images		
Notify presenters or tour guides of the need to verbally describe charts and visual elements in presentation slides or information booth displays and objects, features, activities, areas, etc. during tours and demonstrations		
Order catering, buy refreshments, or book restaurant reservations that accommodate a variety of dietary requirements		
Other:		

PROGRAM SET-UP:

TASK	COMPLETE
Provide ample space around tables, stations, seating, equipment, etc. to allow for easy movement for people using a wheelchair or mobility aids	
Use tables that have wheelchair-friendly and child-friendly heights	
Ensure that all stages or platforms are safely accessible and that podiums and microphones are adjustable for height and/or clearance	
Reduce background noise by closing doors and minimizing other distractions	
Use microphones to improve audio clarity. Provide a microphone to audience members who are asking questions	
Adjust lighting so that people can clearly see all screens, speakers, and interpreters. When presenting virtually, an LED light will provide clarity for those who are low vision or need to read lips	
Other:	

REMINDER: Verbally describe all charts and visual elements in presentation slides or information booth displays and objects, features, activities, areas, etc. during tours and demonstrations

Figure A.3. Pre-program and program set-up accessibility checklists. *Courtesy of University of Iowa Office of the State Archaeologist*

Outdoor Sites and Tours

With the exception of archaeological sites located at established facilities (e.g., parks, heritage areas), many sites are only accessed during active fieldwork or monitoring. These ephemeral projects are unlikely to have infrastructure in place, like accessible pathways, platforms, ramps, and rails. The costs of building or providing this infrastructure are probably beyond your (or the landowner's) scope or financial means. If you are hosting volunteers or site visitors or leading any sort of tour, notify all potential participants of the expected conditions so they can make an informed decision about their involvement. Communicate key information, including:

- Weather/temperature
- Insect or pest hazards
- Emergency or inclement weather plan
- Equipment or tools
- Expectations for hiking, standing, lifting, etc.
- Pathway/access conditions (width, distance, surface type, stairs/steps, slope)
- Presence/absence of platforms, ramps, hand/guard rails, and temporary barriers
- Potential obstacles to traverse or pass by (e.g., fences, livestock, ladders, streams/standing water)
- Proximity to and type of bathroom facility
- Rest or break amenities (seating type, presence/absence of shade, etc.)

Appendix B

PRESENTATION SLIDES

A poorly constructed presentation may drain your audience and lose their attention. But how do we know if our slides are bad?

Most presentation software bombards us with options for colorful templates, bullet points, and whirling animations. Many of us learned to construct slides using these options, and we put our faith in the software. We are scientists, but we don't typically consider the science behind our communication techniques. How much does slide structure impact learning, comprehension, and knowledge retention? Turns out, it's a lot.

Imagine strolling through a conference poster session. Which posters do you gravitate toward? Probably the ones that focus on high-quality imagery and make smart use of sparse text, because many of us feel overwhelmed by the information overload on text-heavy posters. Yet, we make the same mistake in our slides. Text-heavy slides will make your audience feel overwhelmed and fatigued, whether they realize it or not. This is backed up by cognitive psychology. Research shows that the standard layouts of most presentation software templates and some graphic choices are *not* conducive to comprehension or retention. Our minds have a limited capacity to process new information, so we need to be mindful of cognitive overload.

Here are some research-based facts and tips to help you improve your slides to optimize learning and retention:

- Audiences better understand the main points when presenters omit unnecessary information.[1] Presenters may hinder learners' comprehension by displaying extensive text (e.g., bullet lists) while speaking, even if simply explaining or repeating the on-screen text.[2]
- People have a limited amount of memory and attention. The longer and more complex your lecture is, the more details your audience will soon forget. When possible, integrate active learning techniques into your presentation to break up the lecture time. These could include discussions, hands-on activities, and problem-solving.
- Intentionally designing slides will force you to think about your content. If there is not an image or brief text that can explain a concept, it could be that the concept does not lend itself to the style of presentation slide—in that case, do not use a slide.[3] Crowded visuals also contribute to cognitive overload. Stick to one image per slide.
- The wrong font choice can tank your presentation. Sans-serif fonts are recommended because they have a slightly higher readability than serif fonts.[4]
- Visually, the most accessible slides have black font on a white background or vice versa. Good color contrast reduces cognitive strain and confusion and makes designs easier to understand. Appropriate color contrast helps everyone, and it especially supports people who have low vision, color blindness, visual stress, dyslexia, presbyopia (changes to vision that normally accompany aging), and other conditions.[5]

NOTES

1. Ricard E. Mayer and Logan Fiorella, "Principles for Reducing Extraneous Processing in Multimedia Learning: Coherence, Signaling, Redundancy, Spatial Contiguity, and Temporal Contiguity Principles," in *The Cambridge Handbook of Multimedia Learning*, 2nd ed., ed. Richard E. Mayer (New York: Cambridge University Press, 2014), 279–315.
2. Slava Kalyuga and John Sweller, "The Redundancy Principle in Multimedia Learning," in *The Cambridge Handbook of Multimedia Learning*, 2nd ed., ed. Richard E. Mayer (New York: Cambridge University Press, 2014), 247–62.
3. Rodney M. Schmaltz and Rickard Enström, "Death to Weak PowerPoint: Strategies to Create Effective Visual Presentations," *Frontiers in Psychology* 5, article 1138 (2014), https://doi.org/10.3389/fpsyg.2014.01138.
4. University of North Carolina Greensboro, "Making Design Elements Accessible," Accessibility Resources at UNCG, accessed July 7, 2023, https://accessibility.uncg.edu/getting-started-with-accessibility/accessible-design.
5. University of North Carolina Greensboro.

Appendix C

RESOURCE PROCUREMENT AND BUDGETING

Begin by creating a thorough checklist or spreadsheet of required programmatic resources to identify gaps and streamline fundraising. Subsequently, you can convert that file into your budget. Do not forget "hidden costs" or underestimate your needs! Table C.1 outlines components typical of a program resource list and budget; variability among project formats is expected.

Thoroughly research the parameters and limitations of each funding source. For example, some grants will not support personnel or indirect costs, others will not pay for travel, etc. Government agencies likely have use restrictions on purchasing cards, usually regarding companies that offer customer rewards (e.g., Costco, hotel chains). You may have to procure travel, food, or supplies through other means or budget them as a reimbursement rather than a direct purchase. Whatever the case, you will likely need to be creative to procure everything necessary to accomplish your program.

Typically, a budget is drafted as you write the proposal for a grant-funded program. Track any adjustments and modifications to the budget throughout the duration of your program and record all in-kind contributions, donations, and cost-sharing to document the actual effort and total costs necessary for implementation. Your end-of-program expenses might vary from your initial proposal, but you will have a better idea of how to plan for future iterations.

Cost-sharing is important. You can save money on certain resources with the right partners. For example, those affiliated with a university may have access to free or reduced-price venues, AV equipment, and webcasting services. A program partner might be interested in acting as a local guide for an out-of-town guest, saving on transit costs. Sometimes a local business will sponsor or donate refreshments. Explore options with all collaborators and keep a running list of the resources your own workplace can readily provide for yourself and partners.

The two budget examples here depict a single-day lecture supported by an outreach program's operating budget and a yearlong event series supported by an academic grant. Budgets vary greatly due to program duration and needs. Check with your funding source or workplace to learn if a specific budget template is required.

Table C.1. Common Components of Resource and Budget Planning

Category	Items	Considerations
Personnel	Hourly rates (actual or in-kind), honoraria or participant support, speaker fees, fringe benefits, stipends, consultant fees, support staff (tech, curation, archives, etc.)	Factor in hours required for all aspects of planning, implementation, and wrap-up/evaluation, including correspondence and meeting time; assess whether salary or rate increases will occur; if the funding source allows you to hire staff, you may need to pay for their employee benefits
Travel	Vehicle/bus/fleet rental, mileage, flights, local transit, accommodation, per diem, incidentals, motor pool maintenance	Universities and government agencies adjust rates annually for per diem, mileage, and allowable hotel rates
Facilities	Overhead or facilities and administrative (F&A) costs, venue rental or donation; janitorial, maintenance, or access fees; technological assistance	Some grants will not fund F&A or may cap it at a specific percentage of the budget; a venue might require fees to pay for in-house janitorial services, tech support, or security/after-hours staff
Food	Meals, snacks, catering, beverages	The venue (e.g., a university) might require in-house or approved catering services; accommodate a variety of dietary requirements
Accessibility	Assistive services (translators, sign language interpreters, CART transcription services), accommodations (e.g., extra legroom on flights)	In the United States, book services up to seventy-two hours before a scheduled event
Equipment	Electronics (laptop, camera, microscope, etc.), software and webcasting services, tools, items with a use-life in excess of one year	Grants often provide opportunities to purchase essential equipment that your organization might otherwise be unable to afford
Materials/ Supplies	Short-term, disposable, or consumable products	Keep excess items (non-perishable) for future programs that may not have a sufficient budget; some grants will not permit purchase of office supplies
Marketing	Advertising, printing, postage, graphic design, staff or participant apparel, online subscriptions for listserv or event management services	Assess your target audience to determine the most effective marketing approach
Other	Liability insurance, permits, registrations, memberships, publishing fees	

Speaker's Fee	Cost	Details
Honorarium	$300	
Travel		
Round-trip flight	$485	*direct flight on ABC Airlines*
Local transit (Lyft/Uber)	$150	*est. 6 rides over 2 days*
Hotel	$136	*1 night plus taxes, includes breakfast*
Meals in travel status	$40	*2 lunches*
Sub-total	**$811**	
Facilities & Food		
Small group dinner with speaker	$200	*5 attendees, $40 max per person*
Lecture venue	$0	*on campus, no cost*
A/V equipment	$0	*on campus, no cost*
Beverages for attendees	$0	*donated by society member*
After-hours security/lock-up	$40	
Sub-total	**$240**	
Accessibility		
ASL interpretation	$368	*2 interpreters for 2 hours*
Other		
Publicity	$0	*social media, listserv, events calendars*
Total Lecture Costs	**$1,719**	

Figure C.1. Sample budget for a guest lecture. *Courtesy of University of Iowa Office of the State Archaeologist*

Project Personnel			
Team Leaders			
State Archaeologist	*contributed effort/in-kind*		
Professor, Anthropology	*contributed effort/in-kind*		
President, Historical Society	*contributed effort/in-kind*		
Director, Tribal Historic Preservation	*contributed effort/in-kind*		
OSA Staff	**Cost**	**Fringe**	**Total**
Project manager (228 hrs)	$6,631	$2,560	$9,191
Research collections director (64 hrs)	$1,875	$735	$2,610
Site records manager (64 hrs)	$1,395	$546	$1,941
Lithics specialist (64 hrs)	$1,736	$681	$2,417
Faunal specialist (100 hrs)	$1,900	$232	$2,132
Assistant curation specialist (100 hrs)	$1,700	$207	$1,907
Students			
Anthro undergrads x 4 (576 hrs)	$8640	$588	$9,228
Honoraria			
Tribal partner, October	$500		$500
Tribal partner, April	$500		$500
Tribal artists x 5 ($500 each)	$2,500		$2,500
Historical society members x 5 ($500 each)	$2,500		$2,500
Sub-total	**$29,877**	**$5,549**	**$35,426**
Travel			
Staff/students, July community event	$794	*mileage, vehicle fees, accommodation*	
Staff/students, October community event	$366	*mileage, vehicle fees*	
Staff/students, April community event	$619	*mileage, vehicle fees, accommodation*	
Staff/students, training workshop	$344	*mileage, vehicle fees*	
Tribal partner, October community event	$153	*mileage*	
Tribal partner, April community event	$144	*mileage*	
Sub-total	**$2,420**		
Facilities & Food			
October venue rental & participant lunch	$438		
April venue rental	$743		
Indigenous catering company, April	$3,125		
Sub-total	**$4,306**		
Other			
Advertising	$600		
Tribal Media Services, livestream & photography	$4,000		
Native American dance performance	$3,000		
Sub-total	**$7,600**		
F&A waived			
Total Project Costs			**$49,752**

Figure C.2. Sample budget for a yearlong event series. *Courtesy of University of Iowa Office of the State Archaeologist*

Appendix D

Liability Waivers

Participant waivers vary among program formats. Align your form to comply with insurance and legal requirements. Identify the safety, compliance, or human resources point(s) of contact at your workplace or partner organization. They may have existing forms you can use or adapt, and they will want to review any new forms. When you circulate a liability waiver, communicate with your participants about any indoor or outdoor hazards relevant to your program.

The two styles of waivers shown here are for general informational purposes only; they do not constitute legal advice.

Liability Waiver for Volunteers: 13AB123 Public Days 2024

Name _____

Address _____

_____
City, State   Zip

_____
Email   Phone

A separate form is needed for each registrant.

BRING THIS SIGNED FORM WITH YOU YOUR FIRST DAY IN THE FIELD or SCAN AND EMAIL TO [insert contact name and email/phone number]

Please indicate by circling the dates you plan to be in the field.

SUN	MON	TUE	WED	THUR	FRI	SAT
					11/8	11/9
11/10	11/11					

Waiver of Liability: This is to certify that I have health and accident insurance to cover myself and/or my child (if applicable) while volunteering at the November 2024 13AB123 Public Days Project. I hereby release the landowner and the **[Insert your agency, department, organization name]** from liability for accidents or illness that might occur during this period.

_____
Signature   Date

OR: for participants under the age of 18:

_____
Signature of Parent/Guardian   Date

Figure D.1. Example liability waiver A. *Courtesy of University of Iowa Office of the State Archaeologist*

LIABILITY RELEASE & WAIVER

IN CONSIDERATION of the right to enter lands owned by John Doe's Farm Holdings, LLC, ("Property") for the purpose educational activities associated with the University of Iowa, ("Activity"), and in accordance with Iowa Code § 461C (Public Use of Private Lands and Waters), I agree:

1. **I FULLY UNDERSTAND** the Activity is potentially dangerous and participation involves risk of injury caused by my own actions or inactions, the actions or inactions of others or the Property or environment of the Activity.
2. **I FULLY UNDERSTAND** the Property may have hidden obstructions, dangerous flora (plants), fauna(wildlife), or other natural or man-made objects or hazards that may be dangerous to me or my property.
3. **I FULLY UNDERSTAND** I must look out for my own safety while on the Property and protect myself against all hazards that may exist on the Property.
4. **I FULLY UNDERSTAND** I am not authorized to excavate, dig, or otherwise alter the Property or remove anything from the Property.
5. **I PROMISE** I will not excavate, dig, or otherwise alter the Property or remove anything from the Property.
6. **I REPRESENT** I am physically and mentally fit for the Activity and I am solely responsible for determining my health and physical status and whether I can safely participate in the Activity.
7. **I REPRESENT** I assume all liability for all risks known and unknown associated with the Activity, and, I fully release John Doe's Farm Holdings, LLC, from all liability arising from my participation in the Activity. I will conduct myself in a safe and reasonable manner. I am not under the influence of drugs, alcohol or any other substance which may impair my ability to safely participate in the Activity.

I HAVE READ THIS FORM, UNDERSTAND THAT BY SIGNING IT I WAIVE RIGHTS I, MY HEIRS OR REPRESENTATIVES MAY HAVE, AND I FREELY SIGN THIS FORM AND VOLUNTARILY ELECT TO PARTICIPATE IN THE ACTIVITY.

_____

SIGNATURE OF PARTICIPANT   **PRINTED NAME**   **DATE SIGNED**

Figure D.2. Example liability waiver B. _Courtesy of University of Iowa Office of the State Archaeologist_

Photograph Permissions

Remember, permission to photograph someone is not the same as consent to circulate their identifiable image. Ensure that your permission forms clearly indicate whether you intend to use someone's likeness for commercial (such as promotional materials) or non-commercial (academic or research) purposes.

FLORIDA PUBLIC ARCHAEOLOGY NETWORK

A PROGRAM OF THE UNIVERSITY of WEST FLORIDA

Photo Release Form

In exchange for participation in the program, I grant the Florida Public Archaeology Network (acting for and on behalf of the University of West Florida Board of Trustees, a public body corporate) permission to use my likeness in a photograph or video in any and all publications, including website entries or social media posts, for whatever purpose, without payment or any other consideration in perpetuity. I understand and agree that these materials will become the property of the Florida Public Archaeology Network.

I am 18 years of age or older and am competent to contract in my own name. If I am younger than 18, my parent or guardian has provided consent below. I have read this release before signing below and I fully understand the contents, meaning, and impact of this release. I waive any right to privacy I may have in the photos or videos under the Family Educational Rights and Privacy Act, and the European Union General Data Protection Regulation.

_____
Signature/Date

_____
Printed Name/Date   Phone

_____
Address

_____
City   State   Zip Code

If the person signing is under age 18, there must be consent by a parent or guardian, as follows:

I hereby certify that I am the parent or guardian of_____, named above, and do hereby give my consent without reservation to the foregoing on behalf of this person.

_____
Parent or Guardian's Signature/Date

_____
Parent or Guardian's Printed Name/Date

FPAN Photo Release Form
OGC approved and revised 11/21/2023

Figure D.3. A sample photograph permission form. *Courtesy of Florida Public Archaeology Network*

Appendix E

MEDIA KITS

In addition to a standard press release that outlines your event details, it is helpful to create a media or press kit for your program or event, which can also be used by program partners. Reflect on prior communications regarding your organization. What are common mistakes made by the news media? Maybe partner organizations frequently refer to your workplace incorrectly (e.g., "State Archaeology Office" instead of "Office of the State Archaeologist"), or staff names or positions are often incorrect in news articles. Simple errors by the news media or partners won't make or break your event, but take the opportunity to prevent mistakes before they happen. Your events are a representation of your organization and brand, and you should always present yourself consistently.

Your media kit can be a static webpage or a document you modify for each event. The following information is beneficial to include:

- The official name and acronym for your organization
- Your organization's mission, role, or accomplishments
- Name/position or role for key organizers, personnel, and sponsors
- Definitions, terms, or acronyms to use or to avoid
- Social media tags for all program partners

Like a press release or marketing post, you can also include project or event specifics such as the title and description; partners and participants; date, time, location; schedules; and acknowledgment of the sponsor or funding source.

IOWA | Office of the State Archaeologist

PRESS KIT

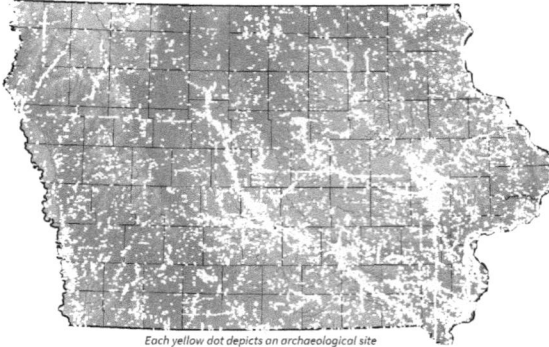

Each yellow dot depicts an archaeological site

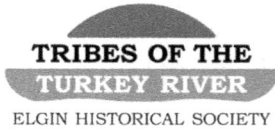

TRIBES OF THE TURKEY RIVER
ELGIN HISTORICAL SOCIETY

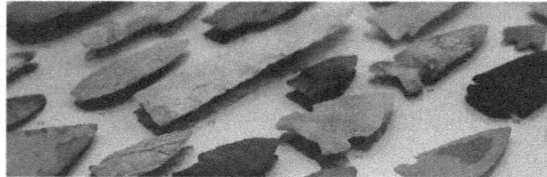

Who We Are

Founded in 1959, the **University of Iowa** (UI) **Office of the State Archaeologist** (OSA) is a nationally recognized research laboratory, repository, and public facility. Our staff members have special expertise in archaeology and history, architectural history, bioarchaeology, cultural resources management, curation, and public engagement. OSA works closely with federal, state, and local partners, and is a leader in promoting cooperative work between archaeologists and American Indians. The OSA is directed by **State Archaeologist, John Doershuk**, and is a unit of the **UI Office of the Vice President for Research**.

The OSA mission is:

to develop, disseminate, and preserve knowledge of Iowa's human past through Midwestern and Plains archaeological research, scientific discovery, public stewardship, service, and education.

What is Archaeology?

Archaeology is the study of the ancient and recent human past through material remains. It is the principal way to learn about humanity's ancient past. In Iowa, archaeologists discover and study the sites, artifacts, and physical remains that make up the past 13,000 years of human settlement.

31,700+	300+	5,200
ARCHAEOLOGICAL SITES RECORDED IN IOWA AS OF MARCH 2023	ARCHAEOLOGICAL AND ARCHITECTURAL INFRASTRUCTURE PROJECTS COMPLETED ANNUALLY	AVERAGE NUMBER OF IOWANS REACHED ANNUALLY THROUGH PUBLIC OUTREACH

Figure F.1. Media sheet side 1. *Courtesy of University of Iowa Office of the State Archaeologist*

About this Project

OSA is partnering with the Elgin Historical Society (EHS) to assist them in learning more about their area's Indigenous history and how to best document, interpret, and communicate the knowledge they already have based on family collections of artifacts and ethnographic objects and the locations of where these artifacts were found. To this end, the EHS has launched a multi-year effort, the Tribes of the Turkey River Project

As a community engagement effort, the partners are conducting an April 22 event to teach Elgin-area residents how to record and submit site information to the OSA and Meskwaki; identify, catalogue, and properly store artifacts. This event also celebrates Native American cultures through art, food, and dance.

Event Details

The University of Iowa Office of the State Archaeologist (OSA) is returning to Elgin in partnership with the Elgin Historical Society (EHS) to host the second Turkey River Archaeo-Blitz on April 22 at NFV Elementary/Middle School. Meskwaki Media will livestream the event at: **https://livestream.com/meskwakination**

When: April 22, 2023, 10:00 a.m. to 3:00 p.m.
Where: North Fayette Valley Elementary/Middle School, 23493 Canoe Rd, Elgin, IA 52141

Project Leads

- **Marilyn Schaer:** President, Elgin Historical Society
- **Elizabeth Reetz:** Director of Strategic Initiatives, UI Office of the State Archaeologist

Featured Presentation

This family-friendly event includes:

- A Native American dance performance by Larry Yazzie & The Native Pride Dancers.
- Craft demonstrations by Meskwaki and Ho-Chunk artists: Randall Blackdeer (lacrosse stick making; Ho-Chunk); Bill Quackenbush (flute making; Ho-Chunk); Daniel Young Bear-Brown (Meskwaki Beadwork); Hilda Young Bear (Meskwaki Applique); Nina Young Bear (plant fiber weaving; Meskwaki).
- A meal of traditional Indigenous foods catered by Kristina Young Bear (Meskwaki). This meal is available for a free-will donation. All donations support the future "Tribes of the Turkey River" interpretive project spearheaded by EHS.
- Archaeo-blitz activities: OSA uses the term "archeo-blitz" to describe the process of rapidly providing information to the public regarding artifact identification, artifact care,

and archaeological site recordation at a single outreach event. All archaeological sites documented at the event are added to the Iowa Site File maintained by OSA and their locations remain confidential. Seven OSA staff members and four University of Iowa Department of Anthropology undergraduate students are participating in the archaeo-blitz.
- Informational tables about the EHS and Tribes of the Turkey River project.

10:00 a.m. - 2:00 p.m.	Craft demonstrations, archaeo-blitz activities, information tables
11:30 a.m. - 1:30 p.m.	Lunch service
2:00 p.m. - 3:00 p.m.	Dance performance

Funding for this event was awarded through the University of Iowa Office of the Vice President for Research (OVPR) Community Engaged Scholars program.

Connect / Tag / Contact

www.fb.com/iowaarchaeology
www.fb.com/ElginHistoricalMuseum

@iowaarchaeology

@iowaarchaeology

archaeology.uiowa.edu
www.elginia.com/elgin-historical-museum

Official name and acronym:
University of Iowa Office of the State Archaeologist (OSA)

Address:
700 South Clinton Street Building
The University of Iowa
Iowa City, IA 52242

Phone: (319) 384-0732; **Email:** osa@uiowa.edu

Figure F.2. Media sheet side 2. *Courtesy of University of Iowa Office of the State Archaeologist*

Appendix F

GOALS AND OUTCOMES

Goals and outcomes are the foundation of every program. They should align with your potential audience, age level(s), situation (guided or defined parameters versus self-guided or self-paced), and the length of time you will spend with your participants.

GOALS

Remember, goals are the big takeaways that will help set priorities, support decision-making, and provide direction (see chapter 4). Verbs that are appropriate for general goals include: *apply*, *appreciate*, *comprehend*, *increase awareness*, *know*, *realize*, *understand*, *value*.

Questions to consider when creating a goal:

1. What are your hopes or values regarding the overall educational experience?
2. What kind of experience do you want to create for your participants?
3. What do you want your participants to remember one week from now? One year? Ten years?
4. What is the most important thing you want your participants to gain? Use the prompts in the figure below to help organize your thoughts about what you would like your participants to gain or achieve.

An awareness of _____

New knowledge about _____

An increased value for _____

Basic skills proficiency in _____

Action towards _____

A connection to _____

Figure F.1. Prompts to assist in goal development. *Courtesy of University of Iowa Office of the State Archaeologist*

OUTCOMES

Outcomes (also referred to as objectives) are what you want your participants to achieve by the end of the program or experience. If goals are where you want to be, outcomes are how you get there. They drive your choices on learning strategies, lesson or program material, and instructional activities. Refer to chapter 4 for an overview of SMARTE (Specific, Measurable, Attainable, Relevant, Time-Bound, and Equity-Minded) outcomes.

Standard convention is to have no more than three outcomes per lesson or activity because you want to ensure that you or your participants can achieve them within the parameters of the program. To write an outcome, it is helpful to break it down into three components: a conditional statement, a performance or action, and a qualifier or standards.

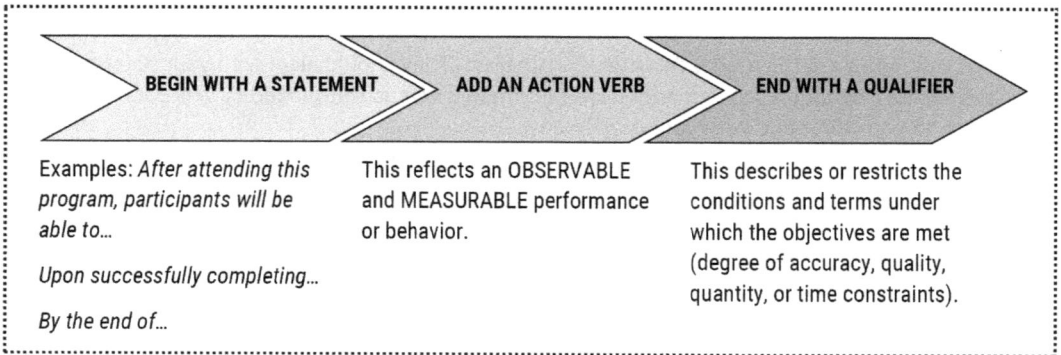

BEGIN WITH A STATEMENT	ADD AN ACTION VERB	END WITH A QUALIFIER
Examples: *After attending this program, participants will be able to...* *Upon successfully completing...* *By the end of...*	This reflects an OBSERVABLE and MEASURABLE performance or behavior.	This describes or restricts the conditions and terms under which the objectives are met (degree of accuracy, quality, quantity, or time constraints).

Figure F.2. The three components in writing an outcome. *Courtesy of University of Iowa Office of the State Archaeologist*

The following references provide a sample of public archaeology-oriented action verbs based on Bloom's Taxonomy (see chapter 1). The information is a synthesis of Bloom's Taxonomy Revised and Simpson's Taxonomy and adapted for public archaeology practitioners.[1] The action verbs are categorized into cognitive, affective, and psychomotor domains to align with knowledge, attitude, or skills-based goals. As a reminder, the levels of learning ascend in complexity, and you cannot expect people to meet a higher-level outcome until they master lower-level fundamentals.

Knowledge (cognitive domain): What should participants know?

Remembering: knowledge of facts, terms, classifications; recalling information

Understanding: comprehension of ideas, interpretations, and translations

Applying: use of knowledge in new or familiar settings to solve problems

Analyzing: examination of parts of information; making inferences and finding evidence to support generalizations

Evaluating: fusion of ideas to produce a unique plan, structure, or pattern; compiling data

Creating: forming judgments or arguments based on criteria and evidence; express and defend opinions

Lower Level ← → Higher Level

Knowing or Remembering	Comprehending or Understanding	Applying	Analyzing	Synthesizing or Evaluating	Creating
arrange	describe	calculate	analyze	critique	assemble
cite	discuss	demonstrate	categorize	determine	construct
define	distinguish	examine	classify	estimate	devise
label	explain	illustrate	compare/ contrast	interpret	generate
list	recognize	interpret	debate	predict	integrate
record	select	prepare	differentiate	revise	revise
relate	summarize	use	summarize	validate	write
Examples in Public Archaeology					
Labeling the parts of a pottery vessel	Recognizing point types based on characteristics	Illustrate a chronological timeline of projectile point types	Sorting and classifying artifact types	Interpreting subsistence activities based on tool types present at a site	Creating a chert ID chart based on color and grain size

Figure F.3. Knowledge learning outcomes. *Courtesy of University of Iowa Office of the State Archaeologist*

Attitude (affective domain): What should participants care about? This domain includes the manner in which we deal with things emotionally, such as feelings, values, appreciation, enthusiasms, motivations, attitudes, and self-efficacy.

Receiving: awareness, attentiveness, a willingness to hear, memory and recognition; the learner is a passive listener or observer

Responding: active participation or a reaction

Valuing: attaching significance or value to an idea, object, phenomenon, behavior

Organization: organizing values into priorities, building a value system based on what's been learned

Characterization: following internal values or beliefs that exert influence one's own behavior

Lower Level   Higher Level

Receiving	Responding	Valuing	Organization	Characterization
acknowledge	answer/reply	accept	collaborate	act
ask	assist	care (for)	consult	change
attend	cooperate	endorse	establish	commit (to)
follow	demonstrate	initiate	follow through	enhance
listen	discuss	preserve	investigate	motivate
observe	participate (in)	seek	qualify	serve
receive	try	value	recommend	volunteer (for)
Examples in Public Archaeology				
Attending an event or stopping by an information table	Participating in a discussion or questioning a concept in order to understand it better	Picking up litter at a cemetery	Accepting responsibility for ones behavior or accepting professional ethical standards	Showing a commitment to ethical practice

Figure F.4. Affective learning outcomes. *Courtesy of University of Iowa Office of the State Archaeologist*

Skills-based (psychomotor domain): What should participants be able to do? Includes physical movement, coordination, fine and gross motor skills.

Perception: Using sensory cues to guide motor activity

Set: readiness to take action; mindset

Guided response: early stages of learning a complex skill; includes imitation and trial and error

Mechanism: perform tasks in a habitual manner; intermediate stage of learning a skill; basic proficiency

Complex Overt Response: perform tasks efficiently and accurately, with coordination; expert

Adaptation: ability to modify the learned skills to meet new or special requirements

Origination: ability to create a new movement or develop an original skill from a learned skill

Lower Level → Higher Level

Perception	Set	Guided Response	Mechanism	Complex Overt Response	Adaptation	Origination
detect	adjust	copy	build	Same as mechanism, but using adverbs or adjectives that denote, quicker, better, etc.	adapt	build
differentiate	approach	duplicate	classify		alter	construct
distinguish	locate	follow	excavate		change	create
hear	place	imitate	illustrate		combine	design
see	position	repeat	measure		rearrange	invent
touch	prepare	trace	set up		revise	produce
Examples in Public Archaeology						
Feeling the textual difference between silt and clay	Knowing how to use a trowel	Using a hard hammer to knock off a flake after watching a demo	Correctly setting up a 1 x 1-meter unit	Consistently setting up and using a total station	Adjusting a troweling technique to avoid hand cramping	Designing a new precision tool to excavate a delicate object

Figure F.5. Skills-based learning outcomes. *Courtesy of University of Iowa Office of the State Archaeologist*

The table below includes examples of goals, outcomes, and assessment strategies for two different scenarios. In one scenario, archaeologists will facilitate consecutive sessions of a thirty-minute pottery activity for groups of students at a middle school STEM event. The activity involves examining photographs and authentic samples of precontact pottery and experimenting with various tools from nature to replicate and create decorations on air-dry clay. In another scenario, an archaeological firm will host an information booth for a family-friendly International Archaeology

Day fair at a local college. The employees intend to demonstrate flint knapping, address misconceptions about archaeology and collecting, and provide an overview of the state's archaeological chronology using an artifact timeline display. See chapter 12 for additional assessment strategies.

Table F.1. Examples of Goals, Outcomes, and Assessment Strategies

Scenario	Goal	Outcome	Assessment Strategy
Middle School STEM Event	Learners will gain an understanding that ancient potters were resourceful and technological innovators.	By the end of this program, participants will be able to list three different tools from nature that may have been used by ancient potters to decorate clay vessels.	*Exit ticket*: Before leaving, students will be provided with a Post-it Note and asked to list three tools used during this lesson.
	Learners will have an engaging and fun hands-on experience that introduces them to an archaeological artifact type.	During this program, students will create replica and original impressions on air dry clay with tools found in nature.	*Observation*: Quietly observe if all students are participating, on task, and/or using the materials correctly. Make adjustments in engagement as needed.
International Archaeology Day Event	The event will provide opportunities to discuss common misconceptions in archaeology with booth visitors.	Upon visiting our table, attendees who self-select to participate will answer three quiz questions on a tablet that test their existing knowledge about archaeology misconceptions.	*Quiz*: Participants who choose to do the quiz will answer three true or false or multiple-choice questions about archaeology misconceptions. Their answers will prompt discussions about their prior knowledge or incorrect assumptions.
	We will introduce attendees to flint knapping via a demonstration and archaeological time periods through our tabletop exhibit.	Upon visiting our table, attendees will observe an artifact timeline display and/or flint knapping demo.	*Count*: Track the number of visitors/observers with a clicker. Note: How many visitors stop to have a conversation with the flint knapper?

NOTE

1. Lorin W. Anderson and David R. Krathwohl, eds., *A Taxonomy for Learning, Teaching, and Assessing: A Revision of Bloom's Taxonomy of Educational Objectives* (New York: Longman, 2001); Benjamin S. Bloom, David R. Krathwohl, and Bertram B. Masia, *Taxonomy of Educational Objectives, the Classification of Educational Goals. Handbook II: Affective Domain* (London: Longman Group Limited, 1973); Elizabeth J. Simpson, *The Classification of Educational Objectives in the Psychomotor Domain* (Washington, DC: Gryphon House, 1972).

Appendix G

PROGRAM DESIGN

In formal classroom settings and informal settings like museums and parks, instructors design plans for activities, lessons, and educational programs. Comprehensive planning requires time and training, which archaeologists often lack. If such plans are created, we rarely share them with others or keep our files for reference, resulting in a constant spinning of wheels where practitioners repeat the work that they or others have already done. Front-end strategizing may feel like extra work that we don't have capacity for, but the reality of efficient planning is that it streamlines both current program development and future projects. Designing a plan doesn't have to be a time-consuming effort. The more you do it, the easier it gets!

PROBLEM AND SOLUTION TREES

Chapter 4 introduced the problem tree, a graphical strategy tool. It involves identifying and analyzing problems and their cause-and-effect relationships, leading to the development of solutions. This process helps you create a potential program strategy and enhances understanding of your project's *impact*.

Work through the following steps to create a problem tree. It is best to use this tool collaboratively with partners and stakeholders. Consider using index cards in place of the worksheets to provide more writing space.

- Step 1. Identify as many current problems as possible. Try to state these as negative situations (e.g., "Rock art is vandalized").
- Step 2. Build consensus to select a focal problem. This will become the trunk of the tree.
- Step 3. Identify the multilayered effects of the problem (the leaves). What are the consequences or symptoms? When you've identified these, dig deeper and ask, "Then what?" In other words, identify the consequences of consequences until you have branches of related effects. *Hint: you may be able to place some of the problems identified in step 1 as leaves.*
- Step 4. Identify the multilayered causes of the problem (the roots). What could have led to this? When you've identified a cause, dig deeper and ask, "But why?" In other words, identify related, deeper causes until you have a system of roots mapped. *Hint: you may be able to place some of the problems identified in step 1 as roots.*

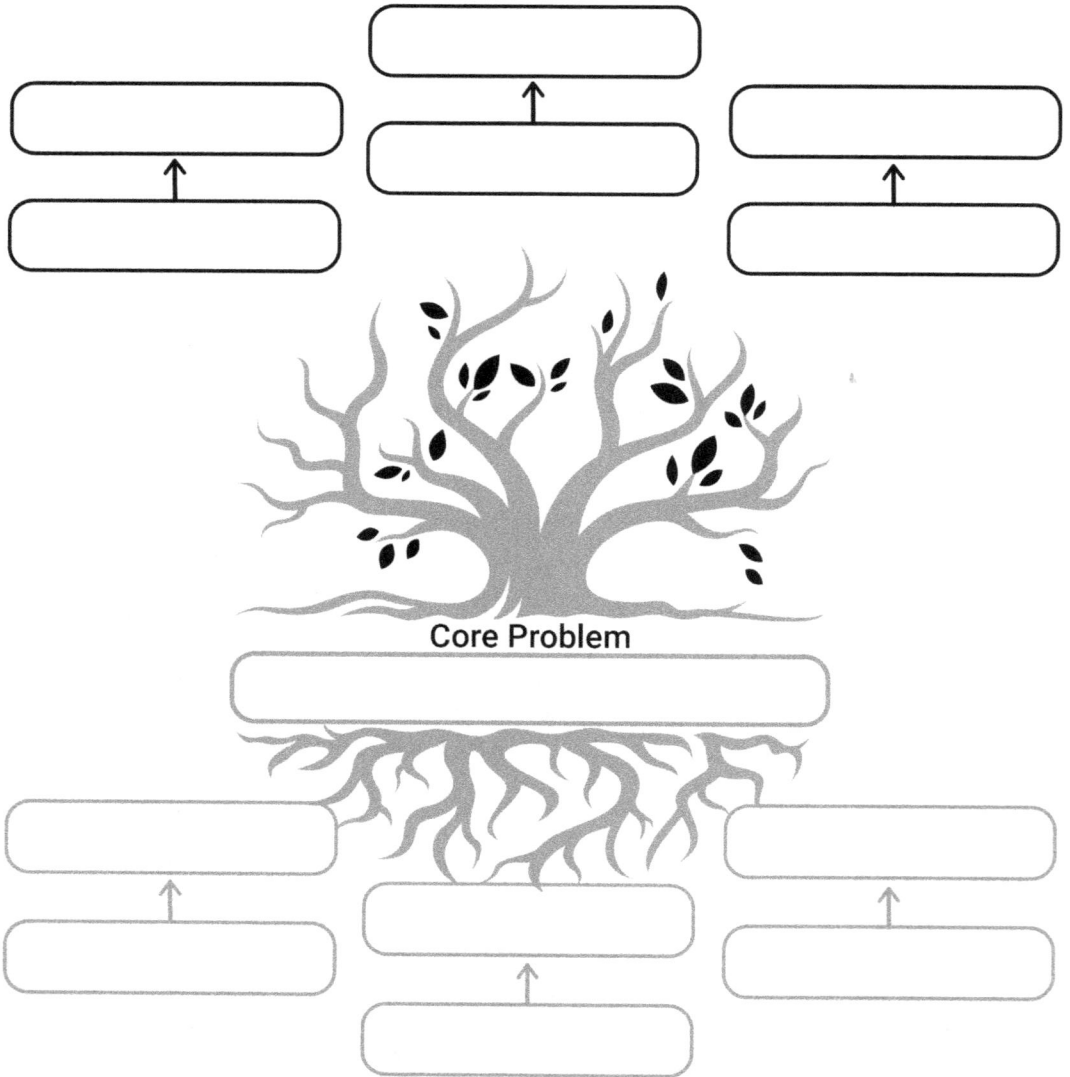

Figure G.1. A "problem tree" template. *Courtesy of Elizabeth Pruitt*

Core Problem

At this point, you should have a completed tree depicting the relationships between your focal problem's causes and effects. Now, it's time to transform the problem tree into a solution tree.

- Step 1. Imagine that your focal problem has been solved. Describe the future favorable situation by inverting the focal problem into your central goal (e.g., "Rock art is protected").
- Step 2. Similarly, reword every leaf as a positive achievement statement. Try to keep these desirable and realistic. Together with your inverted trunk, you have now identified potential project impacts.
- Step 3. Now, invert every root node. Typically, this will result in a statement that describes a necessary resource or activity.
- Step 4. Working from the bottom up, check to make sure that your previous cause/effect relationships are now means/ends relationships. Revise statements and add new impacts if necessary. Eliminate any that are unrealistic and identify any potential conflicts between stakeholders' interests and specific impacts.
- Step 5. Evaluate each pathway through your tree from the bottom up. These now represent alternative project options. Consider the likelihood of success, relevance, and costs and benefits. Build consensus to select the best strategies to pursue.

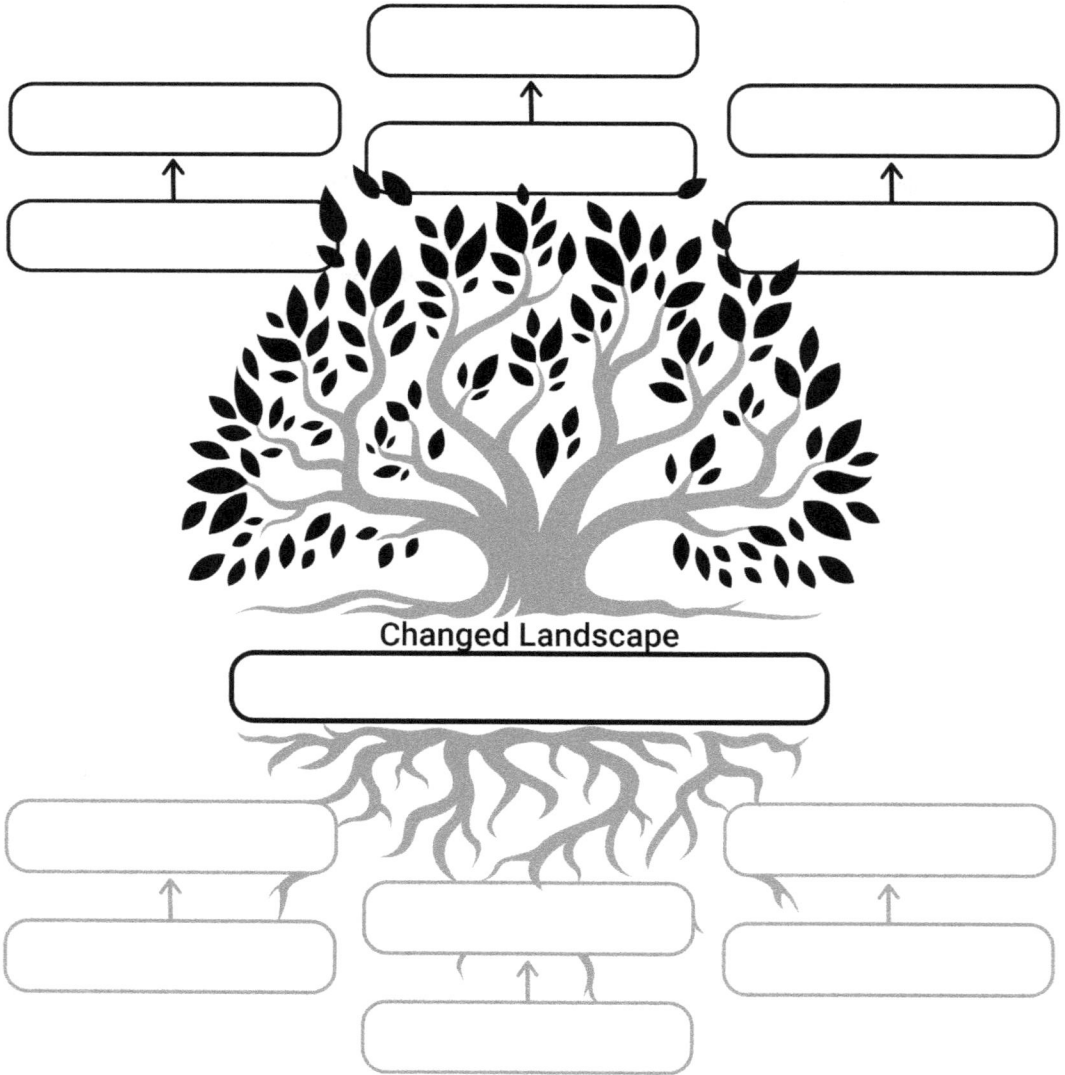

Changed Landscape

Figure G.2. A "solution tree" template. *Courtesy of Elizabeth Pruitt*

Congratulations! You should now have a completed solution tree that elucidates potential project impacts and the resources or activities your project needs to achieve those objectives. If you've completed this step collaboratively with your project team and stakeholders, you'll likely have a powerful and imaginative vision of a shared future.

DESIGNING A PROGRAM

Throughout this book, contributors reference Understanding by Design (UbD), or backward design, for planning and assessment. Again, we emphasize the importance of determining the *why* before the *what* and *how* when developing a public program. The following program planning template is inspired by UbD. It integrates the previous exercises used to understand your audience, create goals and outcomes, and determine assessment strategies into one comprehensive document. You can compile this format in word processing or design software and archive or share it with colleagues seeking to replicate or create a similar program.

[Title of program/activity/event]

Align these components with your goals & outcomes

AUDIENCE SIZE:	AGE GROUP(S):
AUDIENCE INSIGHTS: [note applicable demographics, needs, or relevant information]	
PROGRAM DURATION:	**LOCATION:**
SUBJECTS/STANDARDS/SKILLS: [if relevant]	

Step 1. Identify your desired results

GOAL: [insert goal or impact statement here]

OUTCOMES

1.
2.
3.

ENDURING UNDERSTANDINGS: [Optional. What do you want your audience to remember beyond the program, five years from now? Ten?]

Step 2. Determine evidence of success

ASSESSMENT: [Provide a specific plan for assessment. How do you know that you were successful? Were your outcomes met?]

Step 3. Plan your program content and activities

MATERIALS/SUPPLIES/EQUIPMENT

- [What is needed? List each specific item and quantity.]
-
-

VOCABULARY: [If applicable, list and define vocabulary that may be new to your audience or other practitioners following this plan. These are terms that will be emphasized during the program. Include acronyms.]

BACKGROUND: [Include information you want to impart to the audience and/or information designed to support other practitioners preparing to use this plan.]

PREPARATION: [List what needs to be accomplished/created/downloaded, etc. prior to the program.]

PROCEDURES: [Describe the methods you will use to present your information and work toward achievement of the outcomes. Provide specific directions to accomplish the planned lesson or activity. It is helpful to include an introduction.]

WRAP UP OR CLOSURE: [Include questions, a discussion plan, or an activity to summarize what was learned and/or that can encourage your audience to reflect on what they learned. This can also be integrated with your assessment strategy.]

Figure G.3. Program planning template using backward design. *Courtesy of University of Iowa Office of the State Archaeologist*

Appendix H

EVALUATION AND RESEARCH DESIGN

The examples here are adapted from a formative evaluation where an external evaluator and archaeology educators sought to better understand the knowledge and skills gained by students who were taught an inquiry-based archaeology and mapping unit at a summer camp.

Situation

Since 2018, the education and outreach program of a state archaeology office has partnered with a university summer honors program to teach a week-long archaeology camp unit for high school students. The archaeology unit focuses on reading and making maps as important skills that archaeologists use to understand and document evidence about the past. Students are introduced to ArcGIS online and ESRI StoryMaps and use authentic archaeological data to visually communicate information. Through a partnership with the university's College of Education, the archaeology office is seeking to understand the impact and effectiveness of their current camp curriculum, identify areas for improvement, and strategize future curricula revisions.

Inputs	Outputs		Outcomes		
	Activities	**Participation**	**Short-term**	**Medium-term**	**Impacts**

Human Resources
• External evaluator: A. Abbott
• Archaeology camp instructor: B. Brown
• Summer honors program director: C. Carson
 	
Teaching Resources
• Current archaeology camp curriculum
• ESRI GIS and StoryMaps collections
• Video tutorials
 	
Financial Resources
Evaluation budget ($3200)
 	
Partnerships:
• University summer honors program
• College of Education
• State archaeology office
	Student pre- and post-test questionnaires before and after the week-long archaeology unit is taught
	
	Direct observation of camp activities by external evaluator
	
	Analysis of evaluation data
	
	Evaluation report
	
	Archaeology camp unit revision
		State archaeology office education staff
		
		Summer camp evaluation team
		
		Camp students
		
		Peers and colleagues at professional conferences and in publications
			Summer camp students will:
			• Gain a basic understanding of
			  ○ Archaeological inquiry
			  ○ Stewardship and modern-day issues facing archaeological preservation
			• Improve skills by
			  ○ Reading maps with confidence and competence
			  ○ Learning to use GIS and StoryMaps technologies
				Pilot students will:
				• Complete the unit with a comprehensive understanding of the archaeology unit content and technology
				• Improve their understanding of human interaction with the landscape through GIS and StoryMaps
				
				Archaeology camp instructor & review team will:
				• Utilize student evaluation data to revise and improve the archaeology summer camp program
				• Improve future curricula developed by the archaeology education and outreach program
					Increased archaeology, science and STEM literacy among students
					
					Increased cultural understanding among students

Underlying Assumptions

1. Archaeology is an engaging and interdisciplinary STEM topic that children enjoy. 2. Archaeology is a topic that can help children better understand different cultures. 3. GIS supports STEM learning with integrative, project-based experiences, providing context to education; spatial analysis and critical-thinking skills prepare young minds to succeed in course work, further education, and life.

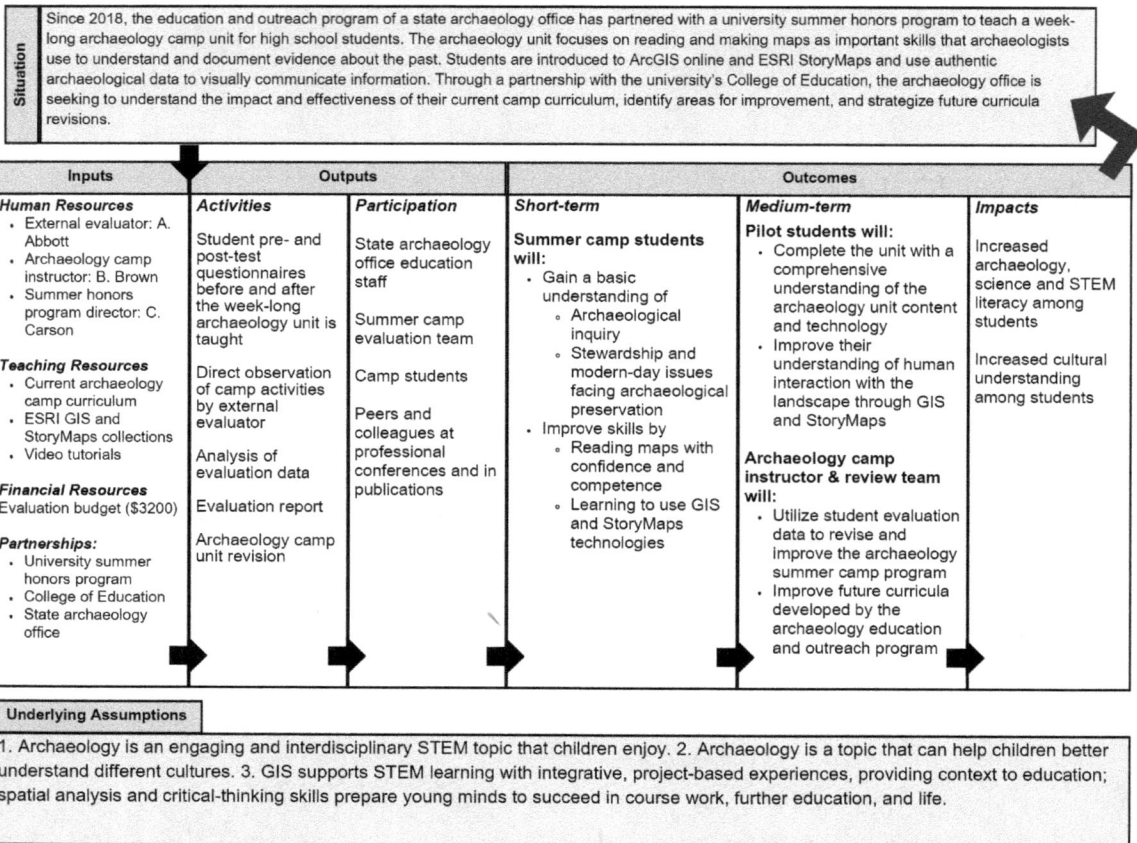

Figure H.1. The logic model documented desired learning outcomes and guided the evaluation process. *Courtesy of University of Iowa Office of the State Archaeologist*

Short-term Outcomes	Evaluation Research Questions	Indicators	Data Source	Data Collection
Gain a basic understanding of archaeology	Has students' understanding of archaeology and the archaeological profession increased? What was their understanding before and after summer camp?	An improvement in rubric scores for open-ended questions on the questionnaire. Direct observation notes that reflect gains in awareness or understanding, knowledge learned, and improved skills.	Direct observation by evaluation assistant (DO) Pretest/posttest questionnaire (Q)	DO: Single group observation of students in the summer camp. No sampling. Q: Single group pretest and posttest of all enrolled summer camp students. No sampling.
Gain a basic understanding of stewardship and modern-day issues facing archaeological preservation	Has students' understanding of stewardship and modern-day issues facing archaeological preservation increased? What was their understanding before and after summer camp?			
Improve skills by reading maps with confidence and competence	Have students demonstrated skills in reading maps with confidence and competence? To what extent did summer camp activities help improve these skills?			
Improve skills by learning to use GIS and Story Maps technologies	Have students demonstrated skills in using GIS and StoryMaps to complete summer camp activities?			

Figure H.2. The research design table outlined the chosen data collection methods used to answer the evaluation research questions. *Courtesy of University of Iowa Office of the State Archaeologist*

Dear camper, we need your help!

You are about to begin a week-long summer camp course called *Exploring Archaeology and Map Skills*. Please help us make this a better learning experience for future students by answering the questions below.

If you do not know the answer to a question, you can guess the answer or just leave it blank. You are not expected to know the answers to all the questions.

This questionnaire is anonymous! The first section will help to create a unique code instead of using your name.

Section 1: Your questionnaire code generator **(do not write your name on this paper)**

1. Your birthday is in which date range? Circle one

1. Mar 21-Apr 19	5. July 23-Aug 22	9. Nov 22-Dec 21
2. Apr 20-May 20	6. Aug 23-Sept 22	10. Dec 22-Jan 19
3. May 21-June 21	7. Sept 23-Oct 23	11. Jan 20-Feb 19
4. June 22-July 22	8. Oct 24-Nov 21	12. Feb 20-March 20

2. What is your middle initial? _____

3. What is the first letter of your mother's name? _____

Section 2: Student Questionnaire

1. Rate yourself on a scale of 1 to 5: Do you feel confident with reading and using maps? **Circle one:**

    1   2   3   4   5

No, not at all ← ————————————————— → Yes, very confident

2. List three types of information a map could provide:

3. Have you ever created your own map using a digital resource (website, software, GIS, mobile app):

    Circle one: YES   NO

3a. If YES, rate yourself on this scale of 1 to 5: How confident are you with your digital map making skills?

    1   2   3   4   5

No, not at all ← ————————————————— → Yes, very confident

4. How can a map tell a story or help to solve a problem?

5. What is the main job of archaeologists and why is this job important?

8. Name 2 things you think people should do if they find or visit an archaeological site. Explain your answers. Why should people do these things?

7. Name 2 things you think people should not do if they find or visit an archaeological site. Explain your answers. Why should people not do these things?

8. How does learning about past people and cultures benefit us today or in the future?

Figure H.3. A pretest-posttest questionnaire was administered to students to document potential changes in knowledge and confidence before and after participating in the archaeology summer camp. *Courtesy of University of Iowa Office of the State Archaeologist*

	Non-existent (0)	Under-developed (1)	Minimally-developed (2)	Well-developed (3)	Highly-developed/ Outstanding (4)
Indicators	Answer left blank or "I don't know"	Student only answered part of the question (if applicable) **AND**	Student only answered part of the question (if applicable) **BUT**	Student addressed all question components (if applicable) with accurate answers **AND**	Student addressed all question components (if applicable) with complete thoughts and accurate answers **AND**
	If there is any answer other than "I don't know", no matter how incorrect, the score is a 1	The answer is blatantly inaccurate or shows no real demonstration of understanding **OR**	The partial answer demonstrates an accurate understanding of concept **OR**	There are NO inaccuracies, the answer is technically correct. The student is not wrong, but...	The answer demonstrates an understanding of concepts taught in the camp lessons **OR**
		It is not evident to the coder that the student demonstrates an accurate understanding of the concept; their answer is confusing or overly vague	Student addressed all question components (if applicable) **BUT**		The answer is correctly applied to a concept outside of the camp lessons, demonstrating higher level thinking
			They're not blatantly wrong, but we don't exactly know what they mean by their answer. It would require asking, "What do you mean by that?" or "Could you please expand on that?"	Use of applicable vocabulary or keywords, but not a clear mastery of the words	Appropriate use of applicable vocabulary or keywords
In short...	*There is no answer.*	*This is without a doubt a wrong answer.*	*The answer is only partially correct and/or they did not answer all question components and/or we don't know exactly what they mean.*	*The answer is correct and they answered all question components.*	*The answer makes you clap or chair dance.*

Figure H.4. Four independent researchers used a rubric as an assessment strategy to rate student responses to open-ended questions on the pretest-posttest questionnaire. During its development, the rubric was piloted and revised until a 75 percent consensus agreement was reached among the four raters (i.e. validating that the researchers were consistent with their interpretation of the rubric conditions). *Courtesy of University of Iowa Office of the State Archaeologist*

Index

Page references for figures are italicized.

About the Editors

Elizabeth C. Reetz received an MA in landscape archaeology from the University of Galway in 2003 and worked in the private and public sectors of Cultural Resources Management in Wisconsin, Minnesota, and Washington. She earned an MEd in environmental education from the University of Minnesota Duluth in 2013 to gain experience in curriculum development, outdoor education, and evaluation and assessment. As director of strategic initiatives for the University of Iowa Office of the State Archaeologist (OSA), Reetz supervises statewide outreach, engagement, and education initiatives, often in collaboration with Midwest descendant communities and Tribal Nations. She served on the Project Archaeology Leadership Team and as chairperson for the Society for American Archaeology (SAA) Public Education Committee. Her OSA Education and Outreach Program received the 2023 SAA Excellence in Public Programming Award.

Stephanie T. Sperling earned a BA in anthropology from Pennsylvania State University in 1999 and a master's degree in applied anthropology from the University of Maryland in 2009. Her career has been spent in the Middle Atlantic region, with roles in cultural resource management, nonprofits (including the position of director of archaeological research for the Lost Towns Project of Anne Arundel County, Maryland), and local governments, where she served as the Senior Archaeologist for the Department of Parks and Recreation, Prince George's County, Maryland. Throughout her career, Sperling led community excavations and tours of diverse sites, from ancient Indigenous camps to colonial plantations and twentieth-century beach resorts. She has designed countless innovative and collaborative archaeological outreach programs aimed at promoting preservation, stewardship, and civic engagement.

About the Contributors

Meredith Anderson Langlitz is director of programs at the Archaeological Institute of America (AIA), where she has worked since 2009. She oversees the AIA's public, professional, site preservation, and membership programs, which include AIA outreach and education initiatives such as International Archaeology Day, a National Lecture Program, ArchaeoCon, web resources, online contests, and more. Langlitz holds an MA in archaeological heritage management and a BA in archaeology and history from Boston University.

Constance Arzigian earned her MA and PhD in anthropology from the University of Wisconsin–Madison. She worked as a research archaeologist with the Mississippi Valley Archaeology Center (MVAC) at the University of Wisconsin–La Crosse for over two decades before becoming a teaching professor with the archaeology and anthropology department, specializing in precontact archaeology and subsistence strategies in the upper Midwest. She has run college and public field schools, taught archaeology to educators, and regularly works with the public on identifying and documenting their finds, including by preparing videos for MVAC that explain basic archaeological concepts.

Sara Ayers-Rigsby is director for the Florida Public Archaeology Network's southeast/southwest regions. She is responsible for designing educational outreach and programming for Florida's southernmost nine counties, which comprise half of the state's population. Prior to this role, she spent ten years working as an archaeologist throughout the United States, with a regional focus on the archaeology of the Southeast and Mid-Atlantic. She earned her MA in archaeology for screen media from the University of Bristol, UK, and her BA in classical archaeology from Trinity College Dublin, Ireland. She currently serves as president elect of the Register of Professional Archaeologists (RPA). Her research interests include public outreach and archaeology, resiliency, archaeological compliance legislation, and industrial archaeology in Florida.

Dr. David A. Brown earned his master's degree in history/historical archaeology from the University of Massachusetts Boston in 2001 and his PhD in American history from the College of William & Mary in 2014. He is co-founder and current co-director of The Fairfield Foundation, a not-for-profit public archaeology and historic preservation organization based in Gloucester County on Virginia's Middle Peninsula. He is also the co-owner of DATA Investigations LLC, a cultural resource management firm that assists not-for-profits, localities, and private individuals and businesses. Brown won the Archeological Society of Virginia's Professional Archeologist of the Year award in 2010 and has been an adjunct professor of history at the College of William & Mary since 2007, teaching historic preservation, public history, and the history of museums. Brown is also a founding member of the Werowocomoco Research Group.

Nicole Bucchino Grinnan is a faculty research associate and public archaeologist with the Florida Public Archaeology Network, a program of the University of West Florida. She earned her master's degree in historical archaeology from the University of West Florida in 2014 and received a bachelor's degree in anthropology and a bachelor's degree in history from the University of Central Florida in 2010. Nicole is currently working on a doctoral degree at the University of St Andrews that focuses on engaging communities with professional efforts to manage cultural resources at risk from climate impact. Nicole is a registered professional archaeologist (RPA), a certified interpretive guide through the National Association for Interpretation (NAI), and a scuba instructor with Scuba Diving International (SDI). She also currently serves on the board of directors as membership chair for the American Academy of Underwater Sciences (AAUS). Grinnan's research interests include maritime archaeology and history, public interpretation of maritime cultural resources, and social history.

Dawn Suzanne (Wanatee) Buffalo is a member of Meskwaki Nation (Sac & Fox Tribe of the Mississippi in Iowa) and has worked in the clerk of court's office for Meskwaki Tribal Court since 2007. Suzanne has served on her tribe's NAGPRA Repatriation Committee since 1995. She presently serves on the Iowa Office of the State Archaeologist Indian Advisory Council and is a member of the Field Museum Native Advisory Committee. Buffalo co-authored a Meskwaki history CD along with her husband, Johnathan L. Buffalo, and Mary Bennett, special collections coordinator at the State Historical Society of Iowa, that contained primary source materials on the history, culture, and art of the Tribe, and received an Award of Merit from the American Association for State and Local History.

Suzanne says of her home on the Meskwaki Settlement in Iowa, "When I'm in my garden, I can see where my grandmother's garden used to be, just across the road, and I think of all the wonderful days I had with her. My umbilical cord was buried there after I was born. Today when I cook the food from our garden, it makes me happy that my family tastes the same things I did when I was young, and what our ancestors tasted when they were young, going way back in time. Our traditional foods and ways made us strong and kept us together. In my garden are the umbilical cords of my grandchildren."

Virginia L. Butler is professor emerita at Portland State University (Portland, Oregon), where she has been on the faculty in the department of anthropology since 1995. She earned her BA at the University of Georgia and her MA and PhD at the University of Washington. Her primary scholarship has focused on zooarchaeology, focusing on the enduring relationships between people and fish, and working on projects in the Pacific Northwest, Oceania, and deserts of western North America. Since 2010, she has turned more of her attention to public archaeology and education. Her scholarship has been published in international journals, including *Antiquity*, *Journal of World Prehistory*, *American Antiquity*, *Journal of Archaeological Science*, *Quaternary Research*, and *Ecology and Society*.

Mia L. Carey is a historical archaeologist and an inclusion, equity, belonging, and mattering (IEB&M) facilitator and consultant. As an archaeologist, Carey's research interests include nineteenth-century African American life and culture; critical race theory; Washington DC, Maryland, and Virginia; Islam in the Black experience, and zooarchaeology. She founded Unearthing Our Past Consulting LLC in 2021, which sits at the intersection of archaeology and IEB&M, to serve as a resource for those looking to engage in difficult conversations about racism, white supremacy, ableism, etc. She graduated with her PhD in anthropology from the University of Florida in 2017. Prior to her current position with the Washington, DC government, she was a Mellon Humanities postdoctoral fellow in the Legacy of the Civil Rights Movement with the National Park Service from 2018–2021.

Carol E. Colaninno is associate director for research and scholarship at the Center for Faculty Development and Excellence at Emory University. In this role, she develops and facilitates comprehensive programs, support, and resources for faculty in grant-seeking and broader impacts. Colaninno's research focuses on reimagining structures throughout the P-20 spectrum to support inclusive educational practices. Her most recent research centers on creating safe and inclusive field research environments for undergraduate students.

John L. Creese is an associate professor of anthropology at North Dakota State University. His research interests include archaeological theory, landscape and settlement archaeology, personhood and the body, and community and Indigenous archaeologies. His current fieldwork focuses on collaborative Indigenous archaeology in the Western Great Lakes of North America.

Amelia S. Dall (she/her/hers) is a deaf archaeologist currently working professionally for the federal government, Bureau of Reclamation, in Pueblo, Colorado. She earned her bachelor's degree in art history from Gallaudet University (2012), her master's degree in anthropology-archaeology from Texas State University (2017), and two certificates in geographic information systems from Front Range Community College (2022). Amelia earned one of the few Rising Stars 2023 awards from the Colorado Springs Business Journal and Sixty35 Media for her volunteer accomplishments with her online platform, Amelia the Archaeologist, and previous multiple board positions. In her personal time, she researches documented archaeological resources regarding Deaf people in antiquity.

Rebecca Dean received her BA in anthropology from the University of Michigan in 1995 and her PhD from the University of Arizona in 2003. She ran public archaeology programs as a professor of anthropology at the University of Minnesota Morris before transitioning her current role as director of assessment for undergraduate education at Michigan State University. Her work focuses on historic ecology, effective pedagogy, and the alignment of programs to strategic initiatives.

Marvin DeFoe is a member of the Red Cliff Band of Lake Superior Chippewa, an Elder, and expert crafter of birchbark canoes. Regarding his biography, DeFoe shares, "My Anishinabe name is Shingway Benase, which means 'sounds coming from Thunderbirds wings,' and my Clan is Namay (Sturgeon). My current work is Tribal Historic Preservation Officer (THPO) for the Red Cliff community, for which we protect sacred, archaeological, and burial sites past, present, and future. Our community in which I live is located on the south shore of Lake Superior, which we call Red Cliff. I am one of 1,500 Tribal members that reside here. My education is primarily attending Anishinabe school, lifelong learning of our traditions, stories, and knowledge. I have been taught by private professors that we call Elders. I am still going to school!"

Thane H. Harpole earned his bachelor's degree in anthropology and history from the College of William & Mary in 1996 and completed his coursework for a master's degree in history/historical archaeology from the University of Massachusetts Boston. He is co-founder and current co-director of The Fairfield Foundation, a not-for-profit public archaeology and historic preservation organization based in Gloucester County on Virginia's Middle Peninsula. He is also the co-owner of DATA Investigations LLC, a cultural resource management firm that assists not-for-profits, localities, and private individuals and businesses. Harpole won the Archeological Society of Virginia's Professional Archeologist of the Year award in 2011 and is a founding member of the Werowocomoco Research Group.

A. Gwynn Henderson is education director at the Kentucky Archaeological Survey, a program of Western Kentucky University's Department of Folk Studies and Anthropology. She received her PhD in Anthropology from the University of Kentucky in 1998. As a public archaeologist, she works with others to make information about Kentucky's archaeological heritage accessible to a wide audience and researches the effectiveness of public archaeology projects in Kentucky. In 2023, she received the Society for American Archaeology's Distinguished Achievement in Public Archaeology award. As a research archaeologist, Henderson studies the ancient Native farming cultures of the middle Ohio Valley. She also writes for children, and several magazines have published her nonfiction articles.

Alexandra Jones is founder and CEO of Archaeology in the Community. She completed her PhD in historical archaeology at the University of California, Berkeley in 2010. Her work focuses on African

Diaspora archaeology, community archaeology, and archaeology outreach. Jones has been an archaeology educator for more than eighteen years, focused on making archaeological knowledge accessible to all. Jones serves as the president of the Society of Black Archaeologists, serves as chair of the United States Cultural Property Advisory Committee, is president of the St. Croix Archaeological Society, and is an academic trustee for the Archaeological Institute of America.

Dan Joyce has his BA from Southern Illinois University and his MA from Eastern New Mexico University. He is the director emeritus and curator of archaeology at the Kenosha Museum campus and a research archaeologist at the University of Wisconsin–Parkside. He has been a museum professional and archaeologist for forty-five years. He has completed archaeological fieldwork in New Mexico, Texas, Louisiana, Alaska, Yukon Territory, Illinois, and Wisconsin. He is co-discoverer with Dave Wasion and Ruth Blazina-Joyce of the Schaefer mammoth, a 14,300-year-old mammoth kill site. His major temporal interests are the First Americans as well as the early historic period. He is a geoarchaeologist, ground penetrating radar specialist, and a lithic analyst. He has been an active public archaeologist for over forty years.

Susan M. Kooiman is an assistant professor of anthropology at Southern Illinois University Edwardsville. She holds an MA and PhD from Michigan State University, where she was a fellow in the groundbreaking Campus Archaeology Program, which emphasizes public outreach, education, and collaboration. She uses culinary archaeological research to inform food-based outreach activities in both the classroom and local communities. In her public archaeology course, students learn about the various aspects and ways of interacting with communities and carry out independent outreach projects.

Randi Korn was founding Director of RK&A, a company that partnered with cultural organizations to plan and evaluate their work around achieving impact. Prior to starting RK&A in 1989, Korn held a variety of positions in museums, including executive director, exhibition designer, interpretive planner and writer, and audience researcher and evaluator. She blended together her BFA in design and MS with a concentration on educational research methodology to feed her passion for museums. She has authored numerous articles on intentional practice, evaluation, and interpretation (www.myintentionalpractice.com), and before retiring, she authored *Intentional Practice for Museums: A Guide for Maximizing Impact*.

Korn was a visiting scholar at the University of Michigan; named the Southeastern Museum Education Division's Museum Educator of the Year by the National Art Education Association (NAEA) where she was also appointed and served as a research commissioner; taught evaluation at The George Washington University for eighteen years; and has lectured at the University of Maryland, Johns Hopkins University, and University of Washington, among others. She continues to guest lecture in museum studies programs, currently serves on a nonprofit board, and remains active by helping organizations clarify their intentions and work toward achieving impact.

Angela M. Labrador is assistant program director and a senior lecturer for the MA in cultural heritage management and MA in museum studies programs at Johns Hopkins University. She has focused her research on the policies and ethics of safeguarding cultural heritage. A co-founding partner of Coherit Associates, Labrador has developed capacity-building projects in the United States and the Caribbean and has worked as a consultant on UNESCO's online Clearinghouse on Living Heritage and Education. She recently co-directed an NEH Landmarks of American History and Culture grant to train K–12 teachers in place-based education using local heritage sites during COVID-19. She serves on the Project Archaeology Leadership Team, is co-chair of the Society for American Archaeology's Public Education Committee, is an expert member of the ICOMOS International Committee on Intangible Cultural Heritage, and is past president of the Vermont Archaeological Society. She co-edited *The Oxford Handbook of Public Heritage Method and Theory* (2018) and holds a PhD in anthropology from the University of Massachusetts Amherst.

Dr. Linda S. Levstik is professor emerita at the University of Kentucky. She received her PhD in humanities education from Ohio State University. She received the Jean Dresden Grambs Distinguished Career Research Award (2007) from the National Council for the Social Studies for her work on historical thinking. More recently, she has collaborated with A. Gwynn Henderson on research related to archaeology education's impact on students' historical thinking and developing related curricula. Among other publications, she is co-author with Keith C. Barton of *Doing History* (2023), *Teaching History for the Common Good* (2004), and *Researching Historical Thinking* (2008), and with A. Gwynn Henderson of *Reading Objects: Children Reading Material Culture* (2016), and *A Human Dependence on Things* (2016).

Stephen Mandal is the co-founder of award-winning educational organizations: the Irish Heritage School, the Irish Archaeology Field School, Cultural Tourism Ireland, and Dig it Kids. He co-founded four major research projects: the Blackfriary Community Archaeology Project, Digging the Lost Town of Carrig, Discovering St Aidan's Monastery, and most recently, the Monastic Midlands Project. Mandal has co-authored three books, *The Irish Stone Axe Project: Monograph 1* (1998), *Carrick, County Wexford: Ireland's first Anglo-Norman Stronghold* (2019), and *Discovering Medieval Ferns, County Wexford* (2023) and contributed to more than a dozen others. He serves on the executive board of the Discovery Programme, the state center for archaeology and innovation in Ireland, and is a research associate of the Smithsonian Museum. He also served as vice-chairperson of the Royal Irish Academy Committee for archaeology, external examiner in applied archaeology at Sligo Institute of Technology, and international guest speaker for the Archaeological Institute of America. In 2013, Mandal was appointed to a European Commission DG Enterprise Project to review cultural heritage tourism across the European Union.

Rayette Martin is a co-founder and executive director of Nevadans for Cultural Preservation, a non-profit dedicated to the preservation of cultural resources through educational initiatives. She earned her MA in anthropology from the University of Nevada, Las Vegas, and has over eleven years of expertise in Nevada archaeology, having served as a contractor for the Nevada State Historic Preservation Office since 2012. Her specific skills encompass project management, public education/interpretation, and addressing graffiti-related issues at cultural sites.

Lyssia Merrifield is project manager for the Archaeology Roadshow, a public outreach event series based out of the Portland State University anthropology department. In her ten years working on the Archaeology Roadshow, she has helped it grow from a single campus-based event to four locations across Oregon. She received a BA from Linfield University in studio art and creative writing and a BA from Portland State University in anthropology.

Sarah E. Miller is regional director for the Northeast and East Central centers of the Florida Public Archaeology Network hosted by Flagler College in St. Augustine, Florida. She received her master's degree in anthropology from East Carolina University in 2001 where she developed archaeology education programs at Tryon Palace in New Bern, North Carolina. Upon graduation from ECU, Miller supervised field and lab projects with public involvement for the Kentucky Archaeological Survey, as well as reviewed compliance projects for the Kentucky Heritage Council. She currently serves on the board of directors (secretary) for the Society for Historical Archaeology, chair of the Society for Historical Archaeology's Heritage at Risk Committee, and serves on the editorial board for the *Journal of Archaeology and Education*. Her specialties include historical archaeology, archaeology education, site stewardship, heritage at risk, advocacy, and historic cemeteries.

Jeanne M. Moe, EdD has more than forty years of experience in archaeological fieldwork and analysis, heritage and archaeology education, and project management. She holds master's degrees in both archaeology and education and a doctoral degree in curriculum and instruction. Moe worked for BLM for thirty-two years, including directing the National Project Archaeology Program for twenty-four years, where she developed national cultural resources stewardship curricula and professional development instruction methods. She is one of the founding board members of the Institute for Heritage Education and currently serves as chair of the board. She served as the editor of Journal of Archaeology and Education from 2020 to 2023.

Rico Newman is a member of the Elders Council of the Choptico Band of Piscataway-Conoy Indians. He retired as a cultural information specialist at the Smithsonian Institution's National Museum of the American Indian, then spent six years serving on the Maryland Commission on Indian Affairs. A member of the Archaeological Society of Maryland, he engages in fieldwork and study of Native American history and material culture. He is the founder of the Maryland Indian Tourism Association, Inc., and currently devotes time to the Accokeek Foundation as a board member.

Adam Novey holds an MA in history from by Liberty University (Virginia). He additionally is recognized as a certified nonprofit professional by the Nonprofit Leadership Alliance and holds a certificate in museum studies from Northwestern University (Chicago). Novey has served as executive director and curator of the Historic Indian Agency House in Portage, Wisconsin, since 2019.

Bonnie Pitblado is the Robert E. and Virginia Bell Endowed Professor of Anthropology at the University of Oklahoma. She also founded and directs the Oklahoma Public Archaeology Network (OKPAN). She has traditional archaeological expertise in the earliest archaeology of the Western Hemisphere and does her fieldwork in the Southern Rocky Mountains. Currently, however, Pitblado spends most of her time working on projects designed to improve the practice of archaeology in ways that make it more inclusive of all the people who share archaeologists' passion for the past.

Elizabeth (Beth) Pruitt is director of education at Archaeology in the Community, a Washington, DC–based archaeology education nonprofit. She has an enthusiasm for communicating about local history and cultivating scientific curiosity. For over ten years, Pruitt has engaged with the public by working with students, educators, descendant communities, museums, libraries, and other nonprofits and institutions. She received a BA in anthropology from Michigan State University and a master's of applied anthropology and PhD from the University of Maryland. From 2017 to 2023, she worked as the education and outreach manager at the Society for American Archaeology and has experience contracting with the National Park Service.

Samantha R. Rubinson is a scientifically trained historical archaeologist who runs the Nevada Site Stewardship Program for the Nevada State Historic Preservation Office (SHPO). She has a PhD in archaeometallurgy from the University of Bradford in Bradford, United Kingdom. She has worked as a professional archaeologist in both Europe and the United States. Since moving to Nevada in 2011, she has worked as a contract archaeologist and for SHPO. In addition to her day job, she is a founding member of Nevadans for Cultural Preservation, a 501(c)(3) nonprofit organization that focuses on "Preservation through Education," and she has helped build the National Site Stewardship Network, an organization focused on supporting site stewardship programs throughout the United States.

Dr. Denis Shine is co-founder of the Irish Heritage School, based in County Offaly, Ireland. He co-founded three major research projects: Digging the Lost Town of Carrig, Discovering St Aidan's Monastery, and, most recently, the Monastic Midlands Project. Shine co-authored two resulting books, *Carrick, County Wexford: Ireland's First Anglo-Norman Stronghold* (2019) and *Discovering Medieval Ferns, County Wexford* (2023). His PhD (2014) from Monash University–Melbourne, "Changing Places: An

Archaeological Study of Manilikarr Country in Western Arnhem Land," focused on community-led ethnoarchaeological research, which ignited a continuing passion for community archaeology. Shine also worked as a professional archaeologist for nearly ten years. He was granted full Irish archaeological license eligibility in 2006 and has acted as senior archaeologist on a range of projects. Shine's current research interests lie in the subdisciplines of community archaeology, medieval Irish, Indigenous Australian archaeology, and the historical emergence of identity. He has published locally, nationally, and internationally and continues active research collaborations in Australia. He also served as an adjunct researcher at Australia National University.

Rebecca (Becca) L. Simon is the staff archaeologist at the Colorado Department of Transportation. Simon's experience includes being Colorado's Assistant State Archaeologist, an archaeologist and educator at Crow Canyon Archaeological Center, and positions with several private cultural resource management firms. She has bachelor's degrees from Pennsylvania State University and a master's degree in anthropology from Colorado State University. Simon's interests include public outreach and education, Southwest archaeology, the protohistoric era, preservation, and most importantly, her dog, Minnie.

Julie Spotted Eagle Horse Martineau is a museum curator and archivist. She is a member of the Oglala Sioux Tribe of South Dakota and lives in southeast Iowa with her husband and her father. Martineau is currently a member of the Iowa Office of the State Archaeologist Indian Advisory Council, and she has worked to repatriate artifacts and remains back to their people through NAGPRA and her work in the museum field. She is also a volunteer archaeologist and anthropologist with the Illiniwek Archeological Society. Martineau is also a champion Women's Northern Plains Powwow Dancer and past Powwow Princess.

Nichole A. Tramel earned her museum studies graduate certificate in 2011 and her master's degree in anthropology in 2013. She has continued to academically and professionally explore the intersection(s) of anthropology, historic collections, and education ever since. Tramel has coordinated public anthropology and educational outreach experiences for Western Michigan University, Crow Canyon Archaeological Center, Montana State University, Project Archaeology, the National Park Service, Riversdale House Museum, and the University of Maryland.

Heather Walder is an assistant teaching professor at the University of Wisconsin–La Crosse and a Research Associate at the Field Museum, Chicago, Illinois. Community-based, collaborative research and outreach in Wisconsin is her primary focus for archaeological fieldwork. Her methodological area of expertise is archaeological chemistry, and she co-edited a 2022 open-access volume: *The Elemental Analysis of Glass Beads: Technology, Chronology and Exchange*. She is the lead author of recent publications in *Archaeometry* and the *Canadian Journal of Archaeology*.

Ryan Wheeler is the eighth director of the Robert S. Peabody Institute of Archaeology, situated on the unceded lands of the Abenaki, Massachusett, Wampanoag, Wabanaki, Pokanoket, and Nipmuc Nations. Since joining the Peabody team in 2012 he has worked to refine and advance the strategic vision of the institution with a focus on collections care, education, and repatriation. In 2018 he helped unite the diverse voices of archaeologists, alumni, faculty, and staff in telling the incredible story of the Peabody in *Glory, Trouble, and Renaissance at the Robert S. Peabody Museum of Archaeology* (2018). Prior to his move to the Boston area in 2011, Wheeler worked as Florida's State Archaeologist, where he led education and preservation efforts, including the Miami Circle sacred site and the Lake Pithlachocco canoes. At the Peabody, Wheeler has continued his editing and writing interests by co-founding the *Journal of Archaeology & Education*, the only academic journal devoted to the intersection of these two fields. Wheeler lives in Medford, Massachusetts, with his family.